T5-BCA-498

JOURNAL FOR THE STUDY OF THE OLD TESTAMENT
SUPPLEMENT SERIES
22

Department of Biblical Studies
The University of Sheffield
Sheffield S10 2TN
England

AT THE MOUNTAIN OF GOD

Story and Theology in Exodus 32-34

R.W.L. MOBERLY

Journal for the Study of the Old Testament
Supplement Series, 22

ISSN 0309-0787
ISBN 0 905774 44 2 (hardback)
ISBN 0 905774 45 0 (paperback)

Published by
JSOT Press
Department of Biblical Studies
The University of Sheffield
Sheffield S10 2TN
England

Printed in Great Britain by Redwood Burn Ltd
Trowbridge, Wiltshire
1983

British Library Cataloguing in Publication Data

Moberley, Walter
At the mountain of God --(Journal for the study of the Old Testament, supplement series
ISSN 0309-0787: 22)
1. Bible-O.T. Exodus XXXII - XXXIV --
Criticism, interpretation, etc
I. Title II. Series
222'.12 BS1245.2

ISBN 0-905774-44-2

TABLE OF CONTENTS

TO MY FRIENDS IN KNOWLE

בְּכָל־עֵ֭ת אֹהֵ֣ב הָרֵ֑עַ

(Prov. 17:17a)

PREFACE

This book is based upon a doctoral dissertation entitled _Principle and Practice in the Study of Biblical Narrative: A Fresh Approach to Exodus 32-34_ which was submitted to the University of Cambridge in 1981. Substantial revisions have been made to prepare the work for publication.

Throughout the work I have tried to keep the footnotes uncumbersome. Consequently references to scholarly works have usually been made in an abbreviated form, and the footnotes should be used in conjunction with the bibliography where full details are given of all works cited. The bibliography also contains certain works which have not been cited (_brevitatis causa_) but which are relevant to the discussion and whose arguments have been taken into consideration.

The study has been based upon the Hebrew text in _Biblia Hebraica Stuttgartensia_ (Stuttgart, 1966/77).

Many friends and scholars have helped, encouraged and advised me along the way. Among these, Dr G.J. Wenham, Rev. J. Goldingay and Professor E.W. Nicholson all read certain sections at an early stage and offered constructive suggestions. And I would like to express particular gratitude to Dr G.I. Davies who supervised me for the greater part of my research. Finally, I am grateful to the successive wardens and librarians of Tyndale House Library, who provide the ideal facilities and surroundings for biblical research.

R.W.L. Moberly
St. Anne's Cottage
Knowle
West Midlands

January 1982

INTRODUCTION

In a recent review of R. Rendtorff's important work *Das überlieferungsgeschichtliche Problem des Pentateuch* W. McKane writes,

> The attitude of restless interrogation which marks the book is a hopeful sign, for Old Testament scholarship suffers from the burden of too many received critical assumptions hung about the necks of its practitioners like Coleridge's albatross. It needs the transfusion of a kind of scholarship which is not a further development of critical positions accepted as premises but is rather an *ab initio* investigation, unburdened by too many bibliographical cares, and concentrating a fresh eye on the Hebrew Bible.[1]

The precise form that such a fresh investigation might most profitably take is not specified. Clearly it is neither possible nor desirable to produce any serious study of the OT that will not be heavily indebted to modern critical work. The point is that, whatever one's indebtedness to past work, it is important not to be trammelled by it but to remain open to new and fresh possibilities. It is in the belief that a fresh approach, combining old and new, is indeed necessary in many areas of OT study, and in particular the Pentateuch, that this present essay is offered as a contribution to the debate.

The subject of the present study is Ex. 32-34. The Sinai narrative in the book of Exodus has been the subject of intensive investigation in recent years, and a vast literature exists. Yet, curiously, there is a sense in which one of its major sections, that is Ex. 32-34, has been comparatively neglected. A look at the six major works on the early history of Israel to be written in recent years, those of Noth, Bright, de Vaux, Herrmann, Hayes and Miller, and Gottwald,[2] reveals little reference to these chapters. At best, one or two aspects of the chapters are taken individually and in isolation from each other. There is a similar situation if one consults OT theologies, such as those of Eichrodt, von Rad, Zimmerli, and Clements.[3] Only certain verses within Ex. 32-34 are treated in any one work, and then only as a part of a larger topical discussion.

That Ex. 32-34 as a coherent narrative might be significant either historically or theologically is not raised as a possible option in any of these works.

The reason is not difficult to discover. It is the belief, based upon intensive analysis, that Ex. 32-34 is a complex of fragmentary and conflicting traditions whose present combination makes little attempt to conceal their diversity. As such it is only the individual units of tradition which can be meaningfully interpreted, and only some of the units are of historical or theological significance. The following statements, which could be multiplied without difficulty, may be taken as typical:

> M. Buber: "... this passage [Ex. 32] ... is apparently the most difficult in the Pentateuch when regarded from the textual and literary viewpoint."[4]
>
> M. Noth: "The state of the sources is certainly extremely confused in this complex."[5] "In view of the gravity of what is narrated here it is quite conceivable that the narrative of the Sinai event (Ex. 19-24, 32-34), through expansions and insertions, had already become such a complicated compilation within the old Pentateuchal tradition that today an intelligible analysis can no longer be successfully undertaken."[6]
>
> J. Muilenburg: "Whereas the first [Ex. 19-24] is a recognizable unity, the second [Ex. 32-34] has every appearance of being a catena of originally separate pieces which originally had little or nothing to do with each other. They are more perhaps than a <u>disiecta membra</u> [sic], but the several parts do not cohere well with each other."[7]
>
> R. de Vaux: "These [Ex. 19-24, 32-34 together] are difficult passages especially with regard to literary criticism and most scholars are in a state of despair, so great is the uncertainty concerning them."[8]
>
> S. Terrien: "... the chaotic cluster of material dealing with the breaking of the first set of stones and the granting of the second set."[9]
>
> N. Gottwald: "The two periodized sets of historicized cultic action [Ex. 19-24, 32-34] are not internally coherent. The resultant hodgepodge strikes the reader as an ill-digested compendium of very imperfectly historicized liturgical speeches and rubrics .... Supremely within the body of the early Israelite traditions, the shape of the Revelation at Sinai traditions strikes us as a compromise formation."[10]

The most significant dissentient voice is that of Brevard Childs, who argues that "these chapters [Ex. 32-34] are held together by a series of motifs which are skillfully woven into a unifying pattern".[11] But the disagreement, while striking, is only partial in that Childs here is concentrating upon the redactional shaping of the chapters into their final form: he does not dispute the analysis of the material as being originally diverse and composite.

The consensus of so many scholars is impressive. Nonetheless, this study has a twofold aim: first, to see whether there is not in the text as it now stands a greater degree of unity, both literary and theological, than is usually allowed; and secondly, to ask whether an account of this unity as redactional is sufficient to do justice to it, and whether it may be possible, or even necessary, to maintain that the unity was substantially inherent in the tradition at the early stages of its history.

The suggestion of such a divergence from accepted views will not be put forward lightly. It has arisen out of a prolonged study of the text, a study in which accepted scholarly positions have been adopted as working hypotheses but have had to be abandoned as being unable to explain the text satisfactorily. It has been out of a deepening grasp of the meaning of the text and the nature of the tradition that the realization of the need for a fresh approach to the exegetical task has also become clear.

The questions one puts to the text determine to a considerable extent the sort of answer that will be received. It is important, therefore, that the practice of exegesis should be combined with reflection upon the assumptions implicit in that exegesis. Thus the study begins with a theoretical discussion of how to approach a literary narrative such as Ex. 32-34, and then seeks to show the practical fruitfulness of the particular approach advocated. It is essential that principle and practice be held together, for it is through the reciprocal influence of the one upon the other that understanding is refined and advanced.

One regrettable limitation of the present work must be specified at the outset. Considerations of space have meant that it has not been possible to extend analysis beyond Ex. 32-34. In particular, it has not been possible to offer any thorough treatment of Ex. 19-24, even though any comprehensive reassessment of the Sinai material must include this section which is so closely related to chs. 32-34. This remains as a task for further research.

Several recent monographs on the Sinai material, especially those of F.-E. Wilms, J. Halbe and E. Zenger,[12] offer useful surveys of modern research on Ex. 32-34, and obviate the need to cover the same ground again. Indeed, as the present argument develops, comparatively little reference will be made to the different advocates of the various exegetical options. This is not because their positions have not been taken into account but because the greater bulk of footnotes arising from comprehensive documentation would be cumbersome and would not significantly further the main discussion.

To conclude this introduction, the provisional and exploratory nature of this work must be stressed. Although it is hoped that the most important part of the study, the exegesis proper, will not prove unduly controversial, it is not expected that the suggestions for re-appraising the nature and origins of the material will meet with universal approbation. The purpose of the study is to suggest new ways of letting the light shine on old issues and it is hoped that a fruitful debate will ensue. Numerous problems even within Ex. 32-34 have not been discussed. As such, this study does not purport to be my, let alone the, final word on the subject, but is intended to contribute to a fresh understanding of the biblical text. The extent to which such a fresh understanding has been achieved will constitute the justification for the approach adopted and will provide the incentive for yet further study.

Chapter 1

SOME CONSIDERATIONS OF METHOD IN NARRATIVE INTERPRETATION

Introduction

The observation that there is something of a ferment and upheaval in contemporary pentateuchal studies can hardly lay claim to originality. Many fundamental questions about the understanding of these texts are being re-opened. The source-critical foundations of modern pentateuchal interpretation;[1] the correct use of traditio-historical analysis;[2] the extent to which an historical basis can be said to underlie pentateuchal traditions;[3] all these questions, and others, are now being keenly debated again.[4] There is a sense in which all these questions are variations on the theme of what constitutes the correct approach to the biblical text. What are the correct methods to use to understand the material? In particular, are the critical tools in general use really sharp enough to produce a correct analysis, or do the arguments tend to be circular, being determined largely by the presuppositions inherent in the particular critical approach? And are the different scholarly tools, which are usually treated as complementary, in fact to some extent incompatible?[5]

These questions are being debated for the most part among scholars who accept the priority for exegesis of the historical-critical method[6] as developed over the last two centuries or so. There is therefore no disagreement among them over the basic assumptions implicit in their approach to the text. There is, however, a growing debate over precisely these assumptions. Despite many variations of emphasis, the debate essentially revolves around the appreciation of the text in its final, received form. Whereas historical-critical studies have been predominantly concerned with penetrating behind the present text and have assumed that questions of sources, history, tradition-history and redaction are of primary importance for understanding the text, the newer approach stresses the primacy of analyzing the text as it stands, an analysis in which the role of the traditional critical approaches is of doubtful, and certainly as yet ill-defined, relevance.

Perhaps the most formidable recent exponent of the 'critical orthodoxy' against which voices are now increasingly raised has been Martin Noth. His magisterial History of Pentateuchal Traditions has dominated recent study of pentateuchal narratives. Noth's work is entirely directed towards penetrating behind the final text so as to reconstruct its origins and development - a kind of literary archaeology. One looks in vain for any discussion of the canonical text as itself meaningful and of interest. Even scholars such as Gunkel and von Rad, who gave more thought than Noth to the literary and aesthetic qualities of the text, tended to direct their literary appreciation towards reconstructed sources or isolated units and so focussed on something other than the text as we now have it. In reaction against this discounting of the final text there has been a growing swell of voices insisting that it is the final text[7] rather than its prehistory that is of primary significance.

The difference of approach is most marked in the work of structuralists, some of whom speak of a paradigm shift[8] in understanding, the change being from a historical to a literary approach to the text[9]. It is not, however, limited to structuralists but is evident in the work of OT scholars who are also practitioners of the historical-critical method and show no sign of being attracted to structuralism as such. Amidst the growing swell of studies in this area, notable recent contributions have been from B.S. Childs,[10] D.J.A. Clines,[11] J.F.A. Sawyer,[12] G.A.F. Knight,[13] D.J. McCarthy[14] and B.W. Anderson,[15] who all, in one way or another, stress the priority of interpreting the received biblical text over investigations into its prehistory.

One way of posing the issue would be to say that the present debate is a debate about the continuing value and role of the historical-critical method. The term "historical-critical method" is meant not to designate any particular exegetical tool, but rather to indicate a type of approach to biblical study in which the posing of historical questions of various kinds to the biblical text has been the predominant concern of exegetes. The well-nigh universal acceptance of this method of study has been the hallmark of the rise of modern biblical criticism. The irony is that the very "objectivity" which made historical-critical study initially so welcome is that characteristic which now seems to cast doubts upon its continuing value. For this historical objectivity has had little to offer in either explaining or furthering the profound religious impact that the biblical writings have made upon countless readers down the centuries. W. Wink, in his provocative little work, The Bible in Human Transformation, has declared the historical-critical method to be bankrupt.[16] While most scholars would not express themselves quite so forcefully, there is nonetheless an unease that an historical-critical approach may be insensitive to, and unable to deal with, those dimensions of the biblical text which may be of most importance and value to its readers. The problem is as real for the NT scholar as for the OT scholar. G.N. Stanton, for example, says, "I take one of the most important tasks facing Biblical and theological scholarship today to be to clarify the role of the historical critical method".[17] Although the present discussion will be within the confines of one section of OT study, it is appreciated both that the issues at stake extend beyond the OT and that many important contributions to the debate are being made within other fields.

Despite the far-ranging implications of the debate, the necessarily limited scope of this present work must be clarified at the outset. In the first place, no attempt is being made to discuss any overarching framework for the practice of biblical exegesis. Except in so far as the detailed argument requires it, it is wished neither to affirm nor deny approaches like that of Childs, who argues for the significance of canon as providing the perspective within which exegesis should be undertaken, or that of Ricoeur, who proposes a philosophical perspective which overcomes the limitations of the historical-critical method.[18]

Secondly, the reflections which follow are to be taken specifically in the context of the current debate about biblical narrative. The recital of historical, or history-like,[19] narrative, is central to the Bible. It is narrative that contains the biblical paradigms of salvation, the Exodus and Sinai covenant in the OT, and the life, death and resurrection of Jesus in the NT. Narrative is also, or perhaps therefore, the area that has given rise to most controversy and is much in need of a fresh approach.

Even within the restricted field of biblical narrative it is not possible at present to offer any comprehensive methodological programme. Given the enormous diversity of types of narrative within the OT, any comprehensive statement of method would need to be long, complex and full of qualifications. The present undertaking is more modest in scope. It aims to concentrate upon one important and problematic section of biblical narrative, Ex. 32-34, and to justify analyzing it in hitherto largely unprecedented fashion. No claim is being made that other narratives would yield equally fruitful results if approached in the same way. They may do. But that can only be decided in the light of a thorough study of the characteristics of the respective narrative in question. For the passage being studied here is not necessarily typical of OT narrative. Indeed, the peculiarity and distinctiveness in many ways of Ex. 32-34 even within the Moses traditions, let alone the larger area of early OT traditions, has been one of the conclusions to result from this work.

The following methodological reflections, however, while primarily an introduction to the exegesis of Ex. 32-34, are not solely an introduction, a justification for doing it "my way". Because they are taking place within the context of a larger debate, one cannot help but reflect on the issues in more general terms and try to suggest ways in which those considerations which have been found helpful in interpreting Ex. 32-34 may have broader application and relevance. It is hoped, therefore, that this work will, in some small way, contribute towards providing fresh perspectives for the study of OT literature more generally.

RECENT ARGUMENTS FOR THE IMPORTANCE OF INTERPRETING THE FINAL FORM OF THE TEXT

It will be helpful to survey briefly the arguments that have been raised for giving primary attention to the final form of the text, since this present study will seek to build upon them.

Literary Arguments

First, one may note certain scholars of modern literature who, while not concerned with OT literature as such, set out general principles of literary criticism which are not infrequently appealed to by biblical scholars. Dame Helen Gardner, for example, discusses a shift away from examining the origins and sources of literary works towards an appreciation of a work in its own right and comments,

> Trends in literary scholarship thus give support to critics who regard it as their duty to see works as integrated wholes, and the body of an author's work as a totality proceeding from a single mind.[20]

And again,

> The assumption today is more and more in favour of single authorship, unless there is clear external evidence to the contrary, and of taking works as they stand and not postulating earlier versions to account for inconsistencies.[21]

In a similar vein, N. Frye writes,

> The primary understanding of any work of literature has to be based on an assumption of its unity. However mistaken such an assumption may eventually prove to be, nothing can be done unless we start with it as a heuristic principle. Further, every effort should be directed toward understanding the whole of what we read.[22]

And R. Wellek and A. Warren say,

> Nobody can deny that much light has been thrown on literature by a proper knowledge of the conditions under which it has been produced; the exegetical value of such a study seems indubitable. Yet it is clear that causal study can never dispose of problems of description, analysis, and evaluation of an object such as a work of literary art. Cause and effect are incommensurate: the concrete result of these extrinsic causes - the work of art - is always unpredictable.[23]

From among those biblical scholars who have advocated a more truly literary approach to the text, it must suffice to cite three examples. J.F.A. Sawyer, in From Moses to Patmos, vigorously affirms his intention "to liberate OT study from the grip of archaeologists, philologists, and latter-day Marcionites".[24] Although one must maintain a balance between the study of the present text and historical investigation, nonetheless "it is the meaning of the text that is important, whether or not it is historically true".[25]

Secondly B.W. Anderson, appealing to the work of H. Frei, argues that "The beginning and end of exegesis is the text itself - not something beyond it".[26] Furthermore,

> since efforts to recover preliterary stages lead us away from the givenness of the text itself into the realm of hypothesis, it is not valid to regard the reconstructed Urform as normative for interpretation or as having some

> superiority to scripture itself. Whatever excursions into the prehistory of the text are possible or necessary, the beginning and end of interpretation is 'a free encounter with a writing in its final form' (Wilder).[27]

Thirdly, D.J. McCarthy, in a discussion of Ex. 3:14, argues for the independence of the meaning of a text from an historical-critical analysis.

> Contrary to what I have heard said, it is perfectly possible to understand a text without knowing whether it is E or whatever. If I insist on a documentary setting, or an historical setting in which the text was composed, I am often, even usually, tied to pure hypothesis: the connection with a source is dubious, the existence of the source (E) is in question. In any case the historical setting of the passage's composition is largely a guess. And still the text itself in its most important setting, its actual place in scripture, lies before me to study as a grammatical and literary structure that I can analyze with some confidence without beginning with a chancy guess about origins.[28]

Literature has its own truth that makes demands upon the reader. As any literary classic makes an impact upon the reader regardless of knowledge of its historical origins or referent, so too does the Bible.[29]

All these literary arguments for the importance of the final text are clear and, in my opinion, both uncontroversial and irrefutable. The slightly polemical tone in which they are couched is occasioned by the need to gain a hearing for a position long neglected. But the point once made is self-evident.[30]

Theological Arguments

In addition to the literary arguments for directing attention to the text in its final form, theological arguments have also been raised, most notably by Childs.[31] Theological treatments, whether synchronic or diachronic, have usually been applied not to the final text but either to its reconstructed sources or to the units of material considered most historically accurate. This has presumably been connected to a considerable extent with a desire to base theology upon history in classic fashion. If, however, it is accepted that history is not the sole factor of importance in the determination of theological veracity, the theological significance of sources needs to be re-assessed. The attempt to loosen, though not deny, the connection between theology and historicity, and so to be free to find theological significance in the final text, is a major concern in Childs' work. The detachment, to a greater or lesser extent, of theology from history (or historicity) is reminiscent of von Rad's approach. But Childs' use of it is distinctive.

Childs appeals to the profoundly theological shaping of the biblical material which he sees as characteristic of the canonical process. The biblical literature was deliberately so moulded that its final form would function as a permanently valid theological witness. This means that it must be the final form of the text which is the locus of theological meaning and authority. Whatever sources and different levels of meaning may underlie a text, and Childs has no argument with the validity of customary historical-critical reconstructions, they should be allowed no priority over the meaning of the text as it now is. On the contrary, the final text provides the norm for critical assessment of earlier levels of meaning. Whatever the difficulties for the overall significance of canon as argued by Childs, his point about the theological moulding and significance of the final text is a valuable insight.

As a corollary of the significance of the final text, Childs also points out that the focussing of theological study upon reconstructed sources makes one's theologizing inevitably hypothetical.[32] The final text, as an objective reality with definite parameters, provides a firm foundation for theological study. D.J. McCarthy likewise advances a similar argument:

> Historical criticism is a constant search for hypothetic historical referents or for sources where the material at hand is simply insufficient to allow anything but highly speculative results. As a basis for theological (or other) developments it has become a foundation of sand.[33]

It can be seen, then, that for both literary and theological reasons many scholars are arguing for the importance of the study of the biblical text in its final form. And, as already stated, the point once grasped is self-evidently correct. That is why the major part of this study will be a literary and theological exegesis of Ex. 32-34, taken as meaningful in itself, and laying aside (temporarily) questions of the origins and composition of the material.

THE RELATIONSHIP BETWEEN THE STUDY OF THE FINAL TEXT AND THE STUDY OF ITS PREHISTORY

To establish the importance of studying the final form of the text in its own right is an important step. But it does not constitute the answer to the current questioning of how best to approach OT narrative. Rather it poses the issue more sharply. For none of the scholars cited would deny the propriety of a traditional historical-critical analysis of the text; they are seeking rather to relativize its significance. It is not that either a literary or an historical-critical approach to the text must be chosen as "the correct method". For they are both valid and legitimate approaches to the text. The problem is rather how to combine and hold together these two approaches with their markedly different ways of handling a text. This, I suggest, is the crucial issue in the current debate.

Having first established the independence of a literary and theological approach from an historical-critical investigation, it is of crucial importance to take the further step of re-integrating the two tasks if one is to have a coherent understanding of any text. One must not allow a kind of schizophrenia within the biblical exegete whereby he does his historical-critical research on the one hand and his literary and theological exegesis on the other, and either does not see how, or feels himself under no obligation, to bring together these two approaches to form a coherent understanding of the text. The phoenix of a conservatism which simply studies the final text and eschews any kind of historical criticism might swiftly arise from the ashes.[34] The responsible interpreter must deal with every aspect and dimension of the text he is seeking to interpret.

It is possible to deny that there is any problem. For one can point out that the literary and theological study of the final text and the historical-critical study of its antecedents are different kinds of study. They can be seen as essentially complementary rather than in conflict with each other. To argue, for example, that a text displays unity and pattern in its present shape is perfectly compatible with arguing for disunity and fragmentation in its prehistory. No contradiction is involved since in each case different questions are being asked and answered. The distinction between what a text is and what it once was must be clearly preserved. They are separate issues.

This distinction is indeed correct, and it is important not to lose sight of it. Nonetheless the recognition that we are dealing with different kinds of study does not answer the question of how the one bears upon the other. And that is the point at issue.

The holding together of these different approaches is a complex matter requiring extended discussion. One point, however, seems clear. This is that there will be no single or invariable way of holding them together. A diversity of texts will necessarily require a flexibility of treatment. One procrustean approach would necessarily mutilate numerous "inconvenient" texts.

Given this basic need for flexibility, it is still appropriate to focus on one particular way of holding the two approaches together - a way which has been found fruitful in analyzing Ex. 32-34 and which should in principle be applicable to a good number of other texts. It may be stated in general terms as follows.

It has already been seen that a literary and theological interpretation of the text in its final form and an historical-critical investigation of its prehistory are different kinds of explanation of a text and not, in themselves, in conflict with one another. The present unity of a text is not incompatible with complexity and disunity in its prehistory. What a text may have meant once does not determine what it means now. The question that arises, however, is how one can reconstruct, however hypothetically, the prehistory of a text; by what means can one penetrate behind a text to its earlier stages and ultimately, where appropriate, to the historical events that underlie it? When the sources that a writer used still exist independently of his work, then this task is greatly facilitated. The greater the extent of surviving source material, the easier the task of reconstructing the history of the development of the literary work - though there will always be problems! Unfortunately, for the majority of the narrative portions of the OT, and certainly for all the pentateuchal narratives, no such independent sources survive. All sources have to be reconstructed from the work into which they have been incorporated.[35] Such reconstruction of sources is therefore entirely dependent upon unevennesses and difficulties in the present text - doublets, contradictions, anachronisms, variant linguistic usages, divergent theological emphases, etc. The problem obviously is to determine what constitutes a genuine unevenness. This brings the proposed solution into focus. It is only a rigorous examination of the final text, treated in its own right as a literary and theological composition, that will enable one to pronounce with any certainty upon what are genuine difficulties in the text such as suggest a complex prehistory. This literary and theological analysis, while not contributing as such to the task of source-critical, redactional, traditio-historical or historical analysis, nonetheless forms an important preliminary in that only thus can one accurately perceive the contours of the material behind which one aims to penetrate. This means that an historical-critical analysis, while a different kind of approach from the literary and theological, may often be dependent upon the results of a literary and theological exegesis. Methodological priority should often be accorded to the exegesis of the text in its final form.

The point is self-evident, and most scholars would doubtless concur with it. Why then focus upon it? The reasons are twofold. First, the concern to discover a text's prehistory has meant that often in practice little more than lip-service has been paid to the preliminary step of exegesis of the final text. Among, for example, recent monographs on the Sinai pericope,[36] one looks in vain for any literary and theological exegesis or appreciation of the text as a whole. The assumption is that one starts directly with the analysis of individual units or verses and moves immediately into the tracing of their prehistory. If the point which I presume to label as self-evident is indeed correct, then a practical approach which ignores it must surely be methodologically doubtful;[37] and the wide diversity and disagreement between analyses so obtained surely supports this contention.

Secondly, the practical implications of the principle need to be spelt out more fully than hitherto. For the practical holding together of two such different approaches to the text raises delicate problems. For while the literary and theological exegete will be looking for unity and pattern, for that which makes a narrative cohere, the historically-orientated critic will tend to look for tensions and dislocations, for that which may indicate the sources and traditions which underlie the narrative.[38] Now these approaches need not necessarily be opposed to one another. In Gen. 1-11, for example, it is not difficult simultaneously to appreciate the literary and theological patterning that binds the material into a coherent whole, and also to perceive the disparate nature of the various traditions which is eloquent of their diverse origins. But what is clear to see in Gen. 1-11 may be far less clear elsewhere. And in Ex. 32-34 in particular, despite the generally-held consensus about the evident disparity of its sources and traditions, it becomes extremely difficult, if the exegesis here offered is correct, to distinguish paradoxes and tensions that are deliberate stylistic devices from those that may indicate underlying fragmentation.

The problems involved in penetrating behind a narrative text have often been insufficiently appreciated both by "critically orthodox" scholars and by their "fundamentalist" detractors. Before the advent of historical criticism, it was customary to explain doublets, discrepancies and other difficulties purely in terms of the text as it stood. The right approach was assumed to be harmonizing. There was no allowance for historical "depth" in a text. Since the acceptance of historical-critical study it has been customary to explain the same difficulties in terms of the use of different sources. The right approach has been assumed to be fragmentary. Until recent years any attempt to explain the text as it stands tended to labour under opprobrious epithets - precritical, midrashic, harmonistic, etc. Insofar as the practitioners of the approach tended to be conservative scholars with doubts about the propriety of historically-aware criticism and an insufficient appreciation of the issues at stake, the epithets were not altogether undeserved. Nonetheless it must be said that their instinctive awareness of the importance of the final text and the priority of exegesis of it was a sound instinct.

A good example of the recognition of the problem with only a partial exploration of its ramifications is provided by the recent work of J. Licht, *Storytelling in the Bible*. After producing many valuable examples of a literary and aesthetic appreciation of the biblical text Licht adverts briefly, in an epilogue,[39] to the question of integrity versus fragmentation in literary narratives. Licht is not concerned to deny a possibly complex prehistory to any given text. He concludes that,

> one should never use one's aesthetic observations to evaluate the textual [in context this means source-critical] integrity of a passage. The danger that one's preconceptions and expectations in one field will distort one's judgment in another is greater than the actual profit to be gained from the method. Or, to put it more bluntly, it is far too easy to find some aesthetic perfection when one looks for it *because* one needs it as an argument to

establish the integrity of a given story.[40]

Undoubtedly so. But that is only half the problem. It is indeed easy to find some aesthetic perfection because one wants to argue for integrity. But it is equally easy to overlook or dismiss aesthetic qualities and to produce discrepancies because one wants to demonstrate underlying sources. The tu quoque is inescapable.

How then is one to proceed? How can the historical penetration behind a text be combined with the literary and theological search for the text's pattern and coherence, especially when the former is to a considerable extent dependent upon the results of the latter? Clearly there can be no simple rule-of-thumb. The role of the literary critic is perhaps analogous to that of the historian. The situation of the historian is described by G.R. Elton thus:

> However wise it may be to question motive at all times, and however capable of deliberate perversion all men may be, it remains a fact of experience that simplicity, straightforwardness and transparency also exist. The historian cannot therefore proceed on any single line of judgment; his mind must be forever open to the two possibilities that the evidence means what it says and that it does not mean what it says. To achieve as secure a judgment as possible, the historian here requires his most rare and almost most dangerous gift: an all-embracing sympathy which enables him, chameleon-like, to stand with each man in turn to look upon the situation. The gift is dangerous because it may in the end bring him to a total inability to judge or even to make up his mind; it need not do so but it often does.[41]

This is a salutary statement of the critical task. In literary terms it means that the critic inclined to source analysis must be open to a literary solution which may exclude sources, while the critic who is looking for literary unity must be open to recognize the possible presence of diverse sources. A fine judgment is called for. This is perhaps made all the more difficult by the fact that, since literary unity rather than disunity must be one's initial heuristic assumption, the scales are naturally somewhat weighted in favour of arguments for the former. Although these arguments about method are suggesting that historical-critical analysis should occupy a more modest position than is customary in the interpretation of a text, and that it should often be practised after, rather than before, a reading of the text in its own right, there is no intention to banish it altogether; on the contrary, the hope is to set it upon a firmer foundation so that there should be less arbitrariness and variation in its results. The practical outworking of this, combining historically-alert criticism with sensitive literary and theological exegesis, will be a demanding task.

A CONSIDERATION OF SOME IMPLICATIONS OF THE PROPOSED APPROACH TO THE TEXT

What will be the practical results of prefacing historical penetration of a text with literary and theological exegesis? Here are offered a few preliminary observations on principles to be observed and problems that may arise.

It is likely that the study of the text in its own right will sometimes simply invalidate and sometimes to a greater or lesser extent modify already-existing analyses of its prehistory. The extent to which this will happen cannot be predicted in advance when as yet comparatively little work has been done with this perspective. The nature of the shift may perhaps be suggested by the two recent articles on the flood narrative by B.W. Anderson[42] and G.J. Wenham.[43] Each writer argues for the dynamic coherence of the narrative in its present form and on the basis of this each suggests a modification in the generally accepted source-critical analysis of the chapters; instead of independent J and P narratives later combined by a redactor, each suggests that to posit a separate P narrative becomes unnecessary and that P and the redactor should be identified; instead of two sources combined they suggest one source reworked, a priestly recasting of traditional epic material. It is not the present purpose to argue the correctness of their analysis. It is the tenor of their arguments that is of significance.

The way in which exegesis of the final text may bear upon historical-critical enquiries will of course vary considerably, depending upon which sort of critical analysis is under consideration. It will bear most strongly upon source criticism and redaction criticism where one is most dependent upon finding unevennesses and seams in the present text. Its relation to traditio-historical and historical criticism will be more nebulous since the scholar in these areas necessarily works with larger and less tangible considerations such as coherence and likelihood, and his overall historical understanding may lead him to hypothesize an origin and development of a text for which there is little direct evidence in the text itself. But while one must defend the historian's right to work in this way, it may also be appropriate to sound a cautionary note, especially with regard to traditio-historical analysis.

Traditio-historical study,[44] by its very nature, relates somewhat obliquely to the data of the text. In the Pentateuch it treats of a process no longer visible, whose end result is the only firm evidence we have.[45] When the development of tradition imagined is, as is generally the case, a process not only of agglomeration but also of transformation, it may legitimately be asked how one can know what the earlier stages of the tradition were.[46] Another way of posing the question is to ask what textual data would count as falsifying a traditio-historical theory; or are many traditio-historical reconstructions in fact impervious to such criticisms? In some recent work that is left ambiguous, and such ambiguity affects the status of the claim of tradition-history to constitute, in some sense, an empirical and inductive, rather than an a priori, explanation of the text.[47] To say this is not to deny the legitimacy of tradition history in the Pentateuch. But it is to urge caution in its practice; the more so since tradition history should, ideally, take over where source analysis ends, and any greater uncertainty concerning the literary sources must necessarily entail greater uncertainty concerning the pre-literary stages. A fresh perception of literary and theological coherence in the final text may therefore have a certain bearing upon traditio-historical reconstructions.

Given this variability of possible effect when prefacing historical-critical analysis with literary and theological exegesis, it is not possible to predict the sort of results that may ensue. But it is worth briefly considering three areas where interesting problems may arise.

Characteristics of Hebrew Narrative Style

In the first place, it is important to analyze the characteristics of Hebrew narrative. There has been an increasing volume of writing in this area recently, but much work remains to be done.[48] There is a particular danger of imposing anachronistic criteria by which to assess a narrative. This is the complaint of R.N. Whybray in his discussion of the

Joseph story in which he sees an irreconcilable tension between the standard source-critical analysis of the material and the newer appreciation of the story as a wisdom novel of genius. Inclining to the latter assessment he comments that there is an

> insufficient understanding of the gap which exists between our modern standards of consistency of narration and those of the ancient world.[49]

The observation is not new. It constituted an important part of the criticism of I. Engnell and the Scandinavians against the documentary hypothesis.[50] But in the absence of a thorough demonstration of what standards of consistency can reasonably be expected of Hebrew narrative, this point lacks cutting edge.

Three examples of this problem may be given. The first is of historical interest as it is from the work of Richard Simon, the founding father of modern biblical study. In his *Histoire critique du Vieux Testament*, Simon sought to show that Moses could not have been the sole author of the Pentateuch. Among other arguments for composite authorship he cited the repetitious character of certain narratives:

> Take for example the account of the flood in the seventh chapter of Genesis; in verse 17 we read, "The waters increased, and bare up the ark, and it was lift up above the earth". In verse 18, "And the waters prevailed and were increased greatly upon the earth: and the ark went upon the face of the waters". In verse 19 we have, "And the waters prevailed exceedingly upon the earth, and all the high hills that were under the whole heaven were covered", which is again repeated in verse 20, which reads, "Fifteen cubits upward did the waters prevail, and the mountains were covered". Is it not reasonable to suppose that if one and the same writer had been describing that event, he would have done so in far fewer words, especially in a history?[51]

(Some disunity in this same passage has generally been felt by modern scholars also. It is customary to ascribe vv. 17a, 18-20 to P and v. 17b to J. This decision however has been almost entirely dictated by the larger source division of the flood narrative as a whole, rather than by the characteristics of these four verses as such. The modern division is therefore not relevant to the present point. Even the reconstructed P version would doubtless have seemed prolix to Simon!)

Adopting a more literary perspective, B.W. Anderson comments that "the swelling of the waters is vividly portrayed by the repeated use of the key words "the waters prevailed" to create an ascending effect.

"wayyigberû hammāyim (v. 18)
wehammāyîm gāberû (v. 19)
gāberû hammāyîm (v. 20)."[52]

One should also include v. 17 within this total effect so that one has four successive stages of the increase of the flood;[53] a forceful and aesthetically satisfying depiction.

If this literary perception is correct, two further observations may be made. First, although the present literary unity is not incompatible with composite authorship, one cannot take this one factor in the text, that is the fourfold repetition, and argue that it shows both unity and disunity. If the literary assessment of the repetition as a unity is sound, then the fact of repetition in itself provides no evidence of composite authorship; that could only be argued on the basis of other criteria in the larger context. Secondly, the weakness in Simon's approach is not simply that of literary insensitivity, but the fact that his insensitivity seems to be based upon an anachronistic application of the notion of literary coherence and appropriate style. He begged a most important question, and as such set an unfortunate precedent.

A second issue in the assessment of Hebrew narrative style is the possible use of compositional techniques in a way not dissimilar to the effect achieved by modern punctuation devices. For example the occurrence of an introductory speech formula in the middle of a speech is frequently taken as evidence of diverse sources and/or redactional overworking. The comments of Noth and Childs on the threefold wy'mr in Ex. 33:19-21 are typical.[54] But since each formula introduces some different aspect within Yahweh's speech, which yet forms a continuous whole,[55] may it not be that they are intended to function as, so to speak, paragraph markers? And if so, how is this to be weighed against the claim that the formulae reflect literary tension and disunity?[56]

A third, and far more problematic, issue in Hebrew style is the phenomenon of the so-called "doublet". As O. Kaiser puts it,

> The one most basic criterion for a division into sources is the repeated occurrence of the same material in different versions, that is, doublets.[57]

A similar view is also expressed by Noth[58] and by Richter, who calls the presence of doublets "das wichtigste Kriterium" for discerning different sources.[59] That there may be difficulties with a doublet analysis is a point that has received insufficient attention. Although Richter, for example, does discuss the distinction between a repetition which is stylistic and one which reflects sources, the examples he gives of stylistic repetition, Gen. 1 and the redactional framework of Judges, are too easy and obvious to offer any help in more problematic contexts.[60]

The notion of a doublet, though seemingly clear, is in fact somewhat vague. It was developed primarily within the analysis of Genesis with reference to such obviously similar narratives as the expulsions of Hagar (Gen. 16; 21:8-21) or "the ancestress of Israel in danger" (Gen. 12:10-20; 20:1-18; 26:6-11). Its applicability elsewhere is far less clear.[61] For example, Ex. 34, with its theophany and law-giving, is generally considered the J version of the E theophany and law-giving in Ex. 19-20.[62] Does it therefore qualify as a doublet? In fact Ex. 34 is so different in certain significant respects from Ex. 19-20[63] that it is doubtful whether "doublet" is a useful category.

Another way of putting this point is to say that the doublet analysis necessarily focusses on the similarities between two narratives. Differences tend to be considered secondary and unimportant. The point at which the differences between two stories, similar in some respects, become as significant as the similarities cannot be generally prescribed or quantitatively assessed; it must be left to the judgment of the critic according to each situation. Nonetheless there remains in principle a genuine difficulty which is insufficiently recognized. What distinguishes one story told in two variant traditions from two different stories either somewhat similar in themselves or told in such a way as to bring out a similarity between them? It is argued below, for example, that Ex. 34 was most likely never an account of an initial covenant making but was always a covenant renewal. When it is objected that (inter alia) it looks so similar to an initial covenant making, one may respond by asking, How else _would_ a covenant renewal appear?[64]

A further difficulty in the doublet analysis has to do with the basic pattern of literary development which the scholar is to assume. The pattern assumed in a standard doublet analysis is that of one story being diversified in different literary traditions. What, however, of the implications of a storytelling technique such as Olrik's ninth epic law, the Law of Patterning, according to which different people and situations are depicted in such a way as to show similarity between them?[65] The development imagined here is that of diverse events being unified. One might perhaps describe it as a literary typology. The difficulty is that the two approaches presuppose different patterns of literary development; unity to diversity, diversity to unity. This is not to argue that one approach is right and the other wrong. Both are demonstrable literary phenomena. The point is simply to urge caution over the sort of source-critical or traditio-historical patterns which may be assumed to underlie a text.

The Role of Assumption and Allusion in Narrative

In addition to the need to be sensitive to specific narrative techniques, there is also a more general principle of narrative writing to be observed. A writer will frequently be allusive in style. He will not want or need to elaborate on matters of which the reader is presumed already to possess knowledge, either through general knowledge or through what the writer himself has previously said. The preoccupation of historical-critical analysis with penetrating behind the text makes difficult an appreciation of this aspect of literary style. Silence about, or only a brief reference to, some feature in the preceding narrative is customarily taken as showing either ignorance of this feature, thus constituting evidence for the discernment of sources, or else a secondary gloss or harmonization, thus providing evidence for redactional compilation. To interpret silences or allusions as assuming a knowledge of the preceding narrative may have far-reaching implications. In the exegesis of Ex. 32-34 it is proposed that frequently sense may best be made on the assumption of a knowledge of the preceding narrative in Ex. 19-24; (25-31); and more generally Ex. 1-18. This point is a corollary of the importance of context for exegesis. The more a writer assumes that the context makes his meaning clear, the less he need specify individual points. It is hardly surprising, therefore, that the less the context is taken into account, the wider the range of interpretations of any given unit that becomes available.

The difficulty, of course, is that while one must be open to a writer's use of hint, allusion and assumption which presupposes both background and context, one must equally be aware of the possibility of producing a falsely harmonizing exegesis which glosses over genuine difficulties. Again, there is no simple resolution of the problem. The justification of an appeal to the writer's tacit assumptions will be found in the persuasiveness of the resulting exegesis.

Implications of Theological Paradox

A further difficult issue concerns the way in which theological coherence in the final text bears upon the possible discernment of sources. Since theological disunity has frequently been cited as evidence for literary disunity, the converse can hardly be objected to. But how will this work in practice? We may briefly consider one potentially problematic issue. This is the fact that much theological writing may involve the use of paradox and antinomy. Such is the inherently mysterious nature of God and his ways with men that it is often difficult to make a statement in a theologically reflective way without wishing to qualify it, sometimes by the assertion of an apparently opposite truth. The fact that one writer may make two seemingly incompatible statements[66] in attempting to express a paradoxical theological truth raises two problems. The first is that one may simply fail to recognize that a paradox is being elaborated. Take, for example, the presence of Ex. 33:11 in the same narrative with 33:20 (33:14 also belongs theologically with these). In the exegesis it is argued that we have here a typical theological paradox straining to express the possibilities and limitations in man's approach to God. The one complements the other. To argue, therefore, that these reflect conflicting conceptions of man's approach to God and so belong to different sources[67] would be a misunderstanding, or at least a gross oversimplification.

The second problem is this. If one has recognized the complementarity of the two poles of the paradox, one should beware of assuming that their unity must be, or is even more likely than not to be, the work of a redactor; that the emphases were originally distinct and only secondarily conjoined. Here a scholar's general theological understanding is an important factor. Von Rad, for example, tends to dissolve theological tensions in the present text into diverse traditio-historical developments. A notable instance is his presentation of the difference between the tent and the ark.[68] The tent presents a theology of Yahweh's intermittent manifestation, while the ark represents Yahweh's abiding presence. The two theologies are "completely different".[69] These two heterogeneous streams of tradition were later coalesced (imperfectly) in the Priestly conception of the tabernacle. The details of von Rad's argument have met with various criticisms,[70] but that need not concern us here. What is of significance is that von Rad's argument is controlled by the assumption of the essential incompatibility of the notions of presence and visitation. This results in his treating a passage such as Ex. 29:42-45, where the two are juxtaposed without any sense of incongruity, as of no significance; the idea of presence in v. 45 is dismissed as an unintended hangover from a superseded tradition.[71] But might it not be that Ex. 29:42-45 should be taken at its face value as an attempt to express a paradoxical theological truth, an OT version of the paradox of immanence and transcendence? And if so, does it not undermine the assumption basic to von Rad's argument, as being based on too narrowly logical an understanding of the issue at stake?

The problem here is the theological counterpart of general literary considerations. Just as one must first determine what constitutes Hebrew literary consistency before pronouncing a text to be inconsistent, so too one must determine what constitutes theological consistency before pronouncing on the matter of inconsistency. A fine judgment is called for.

THE EXEGETICAL SIGNIFICANCE OF LITERARY GENRE AND THE VALUE OF THE CONCEPT OF STORY

One final issue to treat of in this brief sketch of methodological considerations is the significance of literary genre for understanding the text. The moment, relative to the exegesis of the text and the discussion of its prehistory, at which one should come to a decision concerning genre is difficult to prescribe. In practice there will inevitably be a certain oscillation between the two.

In general literary study the more one knows about the literary conventions within which an author was operating, the better one can appreciate the meaning and implications of his work. But for the early Hebrew writers in their Israelite and ancient Near Eastern context we know all too little about the literary conventions within which they wrote. Moreover such literary conventions as they had would have been qualified in significance by the givenness of the traditions of Israel which they had to handle.[72] This means that the modern reader has to accept yet another imponderable element in his assessment of the ancient Hebrew texts.

It may be suggested, however, that for many narrative portions of the OT, including Ex. 32-34, questions of literary genre are of comparatively little significance for arriving at the meaning of the story, and assume more importance in discussions of the story's origins or historicity. Obviously one must make some kind of genre assessment at the outset, but this is true of any literature and is no difficulty if one has been properly taught to read.

It is in this connection that the currently fashionable notion of "story" is of assistance. One of the advantages of the term "story" is that it is conveniently vague about the precise nature of the material to which it is applied but focusses rather on those elements which bring a narrative to life - plot, irony, suspense, climax, etc. - and which involve the reader imaginatively in the material. The important thing is to grasp what is being said. Questions about truth content, process of composition, or historical reliability may indeed be addressed to a story, and some stories positively invite such questions, but they are distinct from the task of understanding and entering into what the story is saying and may, in general, be left aside until the primary task of understanding has been accomplished. One should not, however, separate the questions of understanding and truth too sharply, for it is often precisely by appealing to a reader's sense of what is "true to life" that the story involves the reader in what is being said. Utilizing, then, the notion of "story" one can concentrate in the first instance on a straightforward reading of the text and postpone explicitly addressing the issue of the precise nature of the story's contents.

To carry out such a procedure with Ex. 32-34 fits well with the tenor of the argument so far. For most pentateuchal genre discussions tend to be concerned with either the historicity or the traditio-historical development of the material rather than illuminating the meaning of what is being said. This may be seen by briefly considering the two main genre classifications that have been suggested for the Sinai material.

The first classification is that of *Sage* or legend.[73] Although the notion of *Sage* may direct one to aspects of story-telling hitherto unappreciated, for example by the application of Olrik's Epic Laws, interest in *Sage* tends to be concerned with the fact that if a story is *Sage* then one must be cautious in searching for underlying historicity; for such stories will tend to consist of largely unhistorical accretions upon a possibly historical nucleus, although the degree to which a Sage is considered unhistorical may vary considerably.[74]

The designation of "cult legend" has also been suggested. This is a particularly slippery notion to grasp and is discussed at length in ch. 3. Suffice it to say at present that language about a narrative "reflecting" a cult-festival in the life of Israel can easily lead to confusion between what the text now is and says and what it once may have been and said. Some such confusion may perhaps be discerned in Mowinckel's pioneering work on the genre of the Sinai material when he says,

> Ce que J et E rapportent comme récit des événements du Sinaï n'est autre chose que la description d' une fête cultuelle célébrée à une époque plus récente, plus précisément dans le temple de Jérusalem.[75]

The Sinai narrative is an account of happenings at Sinai. It is not a description of a cultic festival in the Jerusalem temple. Even if the constituent elements of the narrative were entirely drawn from the Jerusalem cult, this would not alter the fact that now they are being used to describe a ceremony at Sinai; that is what the text is about. If Mowinckel were right, his view would have many implications for one's understanding of the origins and development of the text. But for understanding what the text now is and is saying his statement is misleading.

Von Rad's discussion of the genre[76] is more nuanced than Mowinckel's. He argues not that the narrative is an account of a post-Sinai cultic ceremony but that cultic practices have deeply influenced the development of the narrative. Yet for all the cultic influences which von Rad discerns in the Sinai pericope and elsewhere in J, he says:

> There is a wealth of ancient cultic material built into the work of the J writer, but it would be true to say that there is not one single instance in which the original cultic interest has been preserved. The many hieroi logoi have no longer the function of legitimating and guaranteeing the holiness of an actual site, nor have the cult legends of Exod. 1-14 or Exod. 19ff. and 24 retained their ancient sacral purpose, which was exclusively concerned with providing the basis and shaping the pattern of an ancient Yahwistic festival. The materials have been "historicized": their inner content has actually

> been removed bodily from its narrow sacral context into the freer atmosphere of common history.[77]

The recognition of the "historicized" nature of the text and of the fact that any original sacral context has receded into the background means that discussion of the Sinai material as a cult legend will necessarily focus on the prehistory of the text rather than on its present form. Insofar as one is interested in the origins and development of the Sinai traditions it is valuable to ask in what sense they may be a cult legend. But as long as one is concerned with the basic task of understanding what the present text is saying, such traditio-historical concerns may be appropriately postponed.

The concept of "story" is of value in helping to release the scholar from undue concern with questions of genre and prehistory. But it would be wrong to acquiesce in an undiscriminating appeal to "story" which does not differentiate types of story and story-telling. In particular, it is important to be sensitive to distinctive perspectives which may mould the telling of a story and especially the theological perspectives characteristic of many Hebrew writers.

In Ex. 32-34, for example, there are many of the elements of dramatic story-telling, the clash of contrasts, the creation of suspense, the use of climax, etc. In the light of these one may justifiably suppose that a dramatic presentation is integral to the story. Yet in the midst of such a narrative there is the block of laws in 34:11-26 which from a literary perspective do not enhance but detract from the drama on the summit of Sinai. The fact that the writer was prepared to sacrifice the principles of good story-telling where he deemed it necessary shows that his purpose was not simply, or even primarily, to tell an interesting story. His concern is profoundly theological, to do with the nature of Yahweh and the nature and basis of Yahweh's covenant with Israel. For such the inclusion of the laws is of first importance.

Again, the clear depiction of a central figure, a hero, is another characteristic of good story-telling.[78] In one sense this can be seen in Ex. 32-34 in that Moses is the leading, indeed the only significant, human protagonist throughout. The role of Moses as mediator and intercessor is a constant theme all through the chapters, and the closing scene (34:29-35) rightly leaves him in sole possession of the stage.[79] Yet in the most important part of the narrative as a whole, its dramatic and theological climax, it is Yahweh alone to whom attention is directed (33:18-34:9). Yahweh's self-revelation is the highlight of the narrative. It is remarkable how in the intercession of Moses (33:12-23), although at first all the initiative seems to lie with Moses in his efforts boldly to win a concession from Yahweh, yet at the culmination of the prayer (33:18ff.) Yahweh completely takes over and Moses recedes from view; the heroic intercessor becomes the passive recipient (33:22f.). Who then is the hero, Moses or Yahweh? The answer is both. One is confronted in Ex. 32-34 with a fine theological balance between the human and the divine. The story functions consistently on both the human and divine level; it is the story of both God and man. Of course human and divine are intermingled in much ancient Near Eastern literature. But the fine balance between the two in such a way that the narrative is forced out of conventional literary patterns is a characteristic one must be particularly sensitive to in this narrative if one is to do justice to its nuances and particularities.

SUMMARY AND CONCLUSION

After this brief general outline of methodological considerations, a summary statement of exegetical approach, with special reference to the following exegesis of Ex. 32-34, may be offered.

First, it is clear that some justification must be offered for deciding upon just three chapters as the section for study. Upon what grounds may they be treated as distinct from their surrounding context? This decision is not based upon the customary source-critical analysis of the Sinai pericope. It is important that one's decision should, at least initially, conform to the divisions that the text itself presents. As such there can be no question that the content, structure and style of Ex. 32-34 are distinct from that of the surrounding material. And a comparatively superficial reading of Ex. 32-34 reveals that it contains a rounded, and to a certain extent self-contained, story. It is reasonable, therefore, in terms of the presentation within Exodus to treat Ex. 32-34 as a narrative in its own right, whose contents are to be interpreted primarily in relationship to themselves. At the same time, however, the narrative must be taken as it is presented as a part of a larger whole. One must consider the exegetical significance, in order of priority, of the larger Sinai context, Ex. 19-24, 25-31, 35-40; the preceding exodus narrative, Ex. 1-18; the larger pentateuchal context; the literature of Israel as a whole; and ancient Near Eastern literature of non-Israelite origin.[80]

Having decided upon the compass of material under consideration (a decision subject to possible modification in the light of a further understanding of the text), the primary exegetical task is to determine the meaning of the text. This is mainly achieved through a literary, theological and historical exegesis of the units of meaning in their context.

The work of text criticism, which is a prerequisite of exegesis, need not be discussed since its role is not controversial. Admittedly not all text-critical work is prior to exegesis, for sometimes exegetical considerations are determinative for text-critical conclusions. But this is not of significance for the present discussion.

The exegesis of the text will be literary in that it will attempt to take seriously the narrative as a work of literature. The unity of the work will be assumed, until shown otherwise. One will attempt to discern a plot or theme and to discover those elements which impose structural pattern on the material. Literary devices such as foreshadowing, irony, suspense, climax, symbolism, etc. will constitute part of the nature and meaning of the narrative. All this is in principle straightforward. Sometimes it may lead later to controversy with source-critical interests, given the possible role of assumption and allusion outlined above.[81] Sometimes, as Licht observes, one will run the "risk of misinterpreting a scribal error as a deliberate stylistic feature, or awkward editorial manipulations as structural features".[82] Only experience as a literary critic can lessen the dangers. But even when one does misinterpret textual data it is still the case that, as Licht puts it, "one is still commenting upon actual phenomena in an actual text, which is certainly preferable to commenting upon hypothetical constructions of one's own".[83]

The exegesis will be theological in that the exegete will be open to theological meaning both in the content of the narrative and in its presentation. This requires sensitivity to the perspectives and emphases which may be characteristic of a theological mind. For instance, the tendency of theological language to resort to paradox has already been mentioned. Theological exegesis naturally runs the same risk as literary exegesis of finding significance where none should be found. But this is no less than the risk of denying significance where it is present. The literary and theological merit of the pentateuchal narratives is unquestionably great. In exegesis it is preferable that there be no bias or error at all. But if one is to err it would seem to me less reprehensible to err in the direction of seeing too much in the text, than in seeing too little.

The exegesis will be historical not in the sense of attempting to reconstruct the underlying historical events but in the sense that the meaning attributed to the text must not be historically anachronistic. This will be on the whole straightforward, given a sound overall grasp of the history of Israel in its environment, but occasionally will be controversial where the resolution of an historical problem is at issue. For example, one contention of the present exegesis of Ex. 32-34 is that the narrative presupposes instructions to build a movable sanctuary. It is this movable sanctuary which is referred to when Yahweh speaks of his "presence going" with Israel (Ex. 33:14,16) and also when Moses prays for the accompanying presence (Ex. 34:9a). If such a meaning is to be historically valid, then the concept of a movable sanctuary must be familiar and meaningful at the period when the writer was composing his work (insofar as this can be determined with any likelihood). This does not mean that there must also be an actual historical referent in the period the narrative relates. Nonetheless the verses would constitute evidence, available to be assessed historically, in favour of such an actual movable sanctuary.

These steps outlined constitute the primary exegetical task of ascertaining the meaning of the text. As a result of the exegesis the exegete will turn to an investigation of the origins, prehistory and composition of the text, insofar as the textual data permit this. There will be several goals in view. The first will be to add a "depth dimension" to the reading of the final text through discerning the underlying traditio-historical development wherever this is possible. Once it is accepted that the present text is the end-point of a process of composition, then, whether the process be long or short, it will clearly add nuance to one's reading to have some understanding of this process, and to be able to locate the narrative within the historical experience of Israel. This is best approached by focussing upon the genre of the material, and thus gaining a clearer understanding of the sort of material one is dealing with.

Secondly, the penetration behind the text may be part of a study in the development of early Israelite literature and traditions for its own sake, with less regard to how this may illuminate the final text. This is primarily the domain of the technical article and lies beyond the scope of the present study.

Thirdly, one may enquire into the historical value of the traditions contained in the text. This may be done from more than one perspective. It may be the concern of the historian who seeks to reconstruct the early history of Israel for its own sake. Equally one may approach from the perspective of the classical form of biblical theology, that is the at least partial dependence of theological content upon historical factuality. Such a dependence both justifies and requires an enquiry into the nature of the text's origins and development and an enquiry as to whether some historical basis to the text in question can reasonably be maintained. If it appears that no historical basis can plausibly be maintained in terms either of the evidence of the sources or of the literary genre, then this constitutes an issue for one's understanding of the relationship between theology and history, a question which requires separate treatment. It has not yet been possible to proceed to the stage of drawing conclusions about the historical worth of the traditions in Ex. 32-34, for much preliminary groundwork remains to be done. But the general tenor of the arguments in this study is to allow at least a greater openness to the possibility of discerning underlying historical events than is often the case.

This statement of method and approach, while primarily a justification for the following treatment of Ex. 32-34, also goes far beyond the scope of the present work. For while the exegesis of the text is intended to be fairly thorough (although numerous technical details which do not affect the flow of the story are passed over), the treatment of the secondary questions to do with the sources, development and historicity of the material cannot claim to be more than a preliminary and selective clearing of the ground, leaving a vast amount of further work to be done. The purpose of this selective discussion is threefold.

First, it is an attempt to show the sort of difference that it may make to preface historical-critical analysis with an exegesis of the final text. While the demonstration of a literary and theological coherence in the final text obviously cannot be allowed to prejudge or obviate the need for penetration behind the text, it equally obviously must have some bearing upon the way this penetration is done, especially when one is looking for signs of the incorporation of different sources. In the discussion of whether Ex. 34 should be seen as the J parallel to the E theophany/covenant in Ex. 19-20, it is argued that the coherence and distinctiveness of Ex. 34 as seen in the exegesis remove the support for many of the arguments commonly adduced.[84] Alternatively, in the discussion of Ex. 33:7-11 attention is drawn to the way in which analysis varies according to how far context is allowed to determine meaning.[85] The discussion is trying not simply to resolve outstanding problems but also to show how the resolution one proposes may be influenced by the assumptions implicit in the way one tackles the question.

Secondly, this study attempts to reconsider questions worthy of reconsideration in themselves, even though the textual exegesis may have only indirect bearing upon them. The cult legend hypothesis, for example, although widely held, has never received sufficient clarification. The probing of the assumptions of the hypothesis is not dependent upon the exegesis of the preceding chapter. Yet the exegesis still has some bearing upon the hypothesis by insisting that the postulated complex traditio-historical development should take into account the literary and theological coherence of the final product. Alternatively, the arguments for the antiquity of the tradition in Ex. 32:1-6 are quite independent of the exegesis, apart from the fact that it was the realization that the plural "these are your elohim" in 32:4 was most likely dependent upon its context and not on 1 Kings 12:28 that prompted the enquiry in the first place. In general it may be said that while the literary and theological coherence of Ex. 32-34 of itself says nothing about the antiquity and development of its traditions, it is nonetheless a latent, and sometimes potent, factor in discussions about these factors. For one must be able to show not only how, in the light of the evidence of the text, the narrative may be composed from different elements from different periods, but also how these diverse elements have been moulded into a coherent whole. This will be no easy task.

Finally, it will be noted that much of the argumentation is somewhat negative, with more stress on showing the inadequacy of commonly-advanced arguments than on replacing them with positive alternatives. This is partly to clear the ground. But although demolition is easier than construction, construction is ultimately more important and so it is unsatisfactory to leave the matter there. Some tentative proposals are therefore advanced as to the sort of direction that further study might take. But the lack of more thorough proposals does not simply result from the exigencies of space. It also results from a growing unease as to the ability of our modern critical tools to perform the task they are employed for. That is, the prolonged study of the contents of Ex. 32-34 has left this reader at least with a growing sense of their impenetrability. This is not to say that the chapters constitute a kind of seamless robe for they do not, although the seams are fewer than is commonly thought. But it is to wonder whether the text really affords sufficient evidence for the kind of thoroughgoing critical analysis that is customarily attempted. This is not to deny that diverse sources and traditions may underlie the text, but it is to ask whether we are still in a position to recover them and do more than point to possible hints of their presence. No doubt numerous such analyses will continue to be presented. But there are times when it may perhaps be best to say "We just do not know".

Chapter 2

AN EXEGESIS OF EX. 32-34

We may turn now to a practical demonstration of the exegetical approach advocated. Ex. 32-34 will be interpreted as a literary narrative, meaningful in itself. Discussion of genre and prehistory will be postponed to subsequent chapters.

Since attention is being directed to the final form of the text, the non-specific term "the writer" will be used for convenience throughout. This is not intended to beg questions of composition and redaction, but simply to postpone them on the grounds that such questions are not part of the primary task of interpretation.

In the course of the exegesis reference will also be made to other parts of Exodus as "presupposed" by Ex. 32-34. For it is consistent to treat the book as a whole as an entity in its own right. Again it must be stressed that this exegesis of the final form of the text is not intended to prejudge the historical-critical questions which may be raised.

Narrative Presuppositions in Ex. 32-34

One of the principles of interpretation outlined above is that one must be open to things which a writer did not make explicit because he assumed them. Initially, therefore, it is appropriate to specify those presuppositions which may plausibly be seen to underlie the writer's treatment of his story in Ex. 32-34. A prolonged study of the story has suggested four particular assumptions which can illuminate the reading of the text. The justification for these assumptions will lie in their heuristic value in the subsequent reading of the text.

First, Ex. 32-34 presupposes the substance of Ex. 19-24. That is, Yahweh, having brought the people of Israel out of Egypt and led them to Sinai, has there entered into a new and formal relationship with them.[1] At the heart of this new relationship stands the giving of the decalogue, a revelation of the character of Yahweh and the moral and religious basis of the future life of the people. In addition to this a selection of laws provides in greater detail than the decalogue the paradigmatic basis for the just and orderly life of the newly-constituted people of Yahweh. The people have then accepted their role as the exclusive people of Yahweh.

The second presupposition is that after the covenant ratification ceremony in Ex. 24, the people were in principle ready to move off from Sinai to the land which Yahweh would give them where they would live as his people. Already in Ex. 23, after the last of the detailed laws in v. 19, attention shifts to the future journeyings of the people of Israel and their consequent occupation of the land which Yahweh is giving them (vv. 20-33).

As the people are ready to leave Sinai, they will need certain things as they journey on. Two such things in particular are assumed in Ex. 32-34. The first arises from the fact that, although the people are to leave the place where their commitment to Yahweh was made, there is to be a permanent reminder of its meaning and significance. When the covenant ratification is concluded, Yahweh says to Moses that he will give him tables of stone which will contain the laws just given (24:12). The recording of the commandments will give them a permanent validity. As L. Alonso Schökel puts it,

> According to ancient custom, the writing of a contract conferred on it a juridical status ... Thus the writing of a text is not merely the graphic notation of what is spoken: it is a new act constitutive and meaningful, which makes a word into a juridical instrument, an immutable norm, or a witness for the future.[2]

It may be suggested that the tables of the law are to be seen as in some way analogous in significance to the stone of witness erected by Joshua at Shechem (Josh. 24:26f.).

Finally, because the relationship between Yahweh and Israel has now been regularized and set on a formal basis, a new[3] symbol of Yahweh's presence among the people is needed. This is to be a portable shrine. The presence of Yahweh among his people is a central concern in the OT.[4] Since, at least in the early period, Yahweh's presence was not so much conceived abstractly as connected with some visible symbol or manifestation (cf. e.g. Num. 5:3, 10:35f., 2 Sam. 7:6), and since Yahweh's relationship with Israel has been set upon a permanent and regular basis, some permanent symbol of Yahweh's presence among Israel is now appropriate. It is the ark and tabernacle (Ex. 25-27) which fulfil this role.[5]

With a knowledge of these presuppositions, it is now possible to turn to the interpretation of Ex. 32-34.

Ex. 32:1-6

The opening paragraph sets the scene and describes the sin of Aaron and the people. The truculent mood of the people is conveyed by their emphatic imperative to Aaron, "Up, make us 'elōhîm", and by the threatening implications of the expression "to gather to" (qhl ᶜl, cf. Num. 16:3, 20:2). The people exert pressure upon Aaron. Although Ex. 32 stresses Aaron's responsibility for the calf, the people are implicated too.[6] The rapid succession of verbs in v. 6 expresses the restless and orgiastic nature of the proceedings.[7] A calf[8] is made,[9] and the people worship before it[10] - an act regarded in later times (as indeed in the present text, as will be seen) as the paradigm of apostasy.[11]

The problem arises out of the prolonged absence of Moses on the mountain. The people's request for 'elōhîm on the grounds that Moses has now disappeared is notable in that it implies that the 'elōhîm are a replacement, in some sense, for Moses. A similar implication can be seen in the parallelism of v. 1bß with v. 4b:

> v. 1. ... "This Moses, the man who brought us up out of the land of Egypt ..."
> v. 4. ... "Here are your 'elōhîm, O Israel, who brought you up out of the land of Egypt".

A similar antithesis in vv. 7-8 also points to the supplanting of Moses by the 'elōhîm.

That the 'elōhîm are a substitute for Moses need not imply that Moses himself had been to the people as an 'elōhîm.[12] Two points, rather, are clear. The first is that Moses is the one who uniquely mediates Yahweh's guidance and leadership to the people. It is in and through Moses that Yahweh is known and his saving deeds experienced. The second is that the calf is a challenge to Moses' leadership; it is a rival means of mediating Yahweh's presence to the people. It is significant that both these ideas will be picked up again in the closing scene of the narrative, 34:29ff.; Moses, with his shining face, is the man through whom God's glory is seen, and the use of qeren (34:29, 30,35) echoes the calf and suggests that Moses is to the people what the calf had been intended to be.[13] With this use of the Moses theme at beginning and end the writer constructs an inclusio for the narrative.

Although the calf functions as a challenge to Moses, the parallelism is not exact, nor does it begin to exhaust the calf's significance. For it seems clear that the calf was actually intended as a symbol of the divine presence in a more real and direct way than Moses could be. That the calf was seen as a real embodiment of the divine presence is indicated by v. 5 (ḥag lyhwh), and also the designation as 'ᵉlōhîm in vv. 1,4,8.[14] In vv. 4f. the acclamation of the calf as the divine agent of the exodus may seem slightly discordant with the concern for having 'ᵉlōhîm to go before the people. But the point is to establish a continuity between the people's past experience and this new representation of the deity. The calf does not represent any new god, but is identical with the one, that is Yahweh, who has brought the people to Sinai and entered into a relationship with them on the basis of which he will continue to go with them in future. It may be significant that the only previous usage of the phrase in v. 4f. is in the preamble to the decalogue in Ex. 20:2 (echoed also in 29:46). If the shout is taken as a deliberate reminiscence of 20:2,[15] this supports the view that the people were concerned to affirm the continuity between the calf and Yahweh the God of the exodus who had revealed himself at Sinai.

One further aspect of the calf lies in some notable parallels between 32:1-6 and 25:1-9, the preliminary directions for building the ark and tabernacle. In 25:1-9 Yahweh provides that a symbol or vehicle of his presence should be constructed out of offerings from the people, willingly contributed, and containing gold and other precious substances. The construction should follow his specifications and so he will dwell among the people (25:9). In ch. 32, although they are not obeying the commands in Ex. 25, the people do willingly offer ornaments of gold (32:3). Aaron, representative of Moses (and also designated as priest, 28:1ff.), and so in a position to act with Yahweh's authority, fashions the object which is then interpreted as conveying the divine presence (32:4b,5b). The calf thus functions not only as a parallel to Moses, but also to the ark/tabernacle. These two are not incompatible for Yahweh's presence is mediated in more ways than one.

It is clear that although the calf is intended as a symbol of Yahweh, this is to be understood as a grotesque parody. This is made most clear by the use of 'ᵉlōhîm with plural verb and demonstrative in 32:1,4,8. For it is customary in the OT to convey a pagan understanding of deity by the use of 'ᵉlōhîm with a plural verb, as in, for example, 1 Sam. 4:8, the words in the mouth of the Philistines, or Gen. 20:13, Abraham's words to the Philistine king, perhaps out of deference to Abimelech's presumed polytheistic views. This is not indeed the only signification of *ʾelōhîm* with plural verb or predicate. In several contexts, e.g., Gen. 35:7, Deut. 4:7, 2 Sam. 7:23, any pagan implications would be out of place.[16] But in the present context the intention is clear. When the present phrase is used without polemical intent, as in Neh. 9:18, it can be used with an ordinary singular verb. This pagan implication is best conveyed in English by the rendering "god". For it is not plurality of gods but a false conception of the one God that the writer is conveying.[17]

The whole account of 32:1-6 can thus be seen as heavily ironic. This is clearest in the juxtaposition of 32:1-6 with 25:1-9. Not only is there irony here but also theological reflection on the nature of sin. The people want a symbol of Yahweh's presence. In their impatience they demand and make for themselves what Yahweh has already made provision for and is about to give them. What Aaron and the people do is in many ways similar to what Yahweh has specified. Yet because they push ahead without waiting for Yahweh's directions through Moses their work is but a parody which, far from assuring Yahweh's presence and accompaniment, simply forfeits it. Likewise the people's attempt to affirm the identity of the calf with Yahweh by echoing Ex. 20:2 is to be seen as a parody of the true nature and purposes of Yahweh.

Finally it is worth noting the request for a god that will go "ahead" of the people (*lpnynw*). In the present context it is just a general request for divine leadership. Later in the narrative a particular significance accrues to the notion of going ahead; the angel who goes ahead (*lpny*, 33:2, cf. 23:20,23) becomes an inadequate substitute for Yahweh "in the midst" (33:3,5). But the difference between "ahead" and "in the midst" only becomes significant in the context of Yahweh's judgment on Israel's sin when ordinary conditions do not pertain. It should not be read back into 32:1. One may perhaps say that 32:1 introduces a motif in anticipation of its later significance. Forms of *pnym/pny* are also of importance in Ex. 32-34, and at a purely verbal level 32:1 introduces these.

Ex. 32:7-14

The second paragraph, 32:7-14, presents a dramatic contrast to the first. The theme of contrast between what happens on the mountain, where the divine perspective is seen, and what happens down below, where human sin and weakness is evident, forms an important part of the literary structure of the chapter.[18] The paragraph also introduces the theme of Moses as intercessor, and provides a theological framework for the subsequent narrative.

The words of Yahweh in vv. 7-10 fall into two parts. In vv. 7-8 he commands Moses to descend from the mountain and describes the people's sin, while vv. 9-10 recount Yahweh's reaction to the sin and what he will do with the people. The use of a second introductory formula (v. 9a) within the same speech functions to signal the shift of content.[19]

Yahweh's command to Moses to descend is somewhat brusquely expressed, reflecting the urgency of the situation and the shattering of the calm on the mountain that had existed hitherto.[20] The situation is that the people has "acted sinfully" (šḥt, Pi.) and "quickly turned aside from the way (drk) ..." The word derek in the OT characteristically refers to Yahweh's commandments and the proclamation of his will which prescribes the way of life for his people. It is in this sense that it is used here,[21] and so points to the sin as being a transgression of the laws already given at Sinai, in particular the first two commandments of the decalogue (cf. Ex. 20:4a, 20:23). Although one might argue that Israel's sin was only against the second commandment,[22] the prohibition of idolatry, it is likely that for the writer the first two commandments were regarded as in practice inseparable.[23] Such a close connection between the first two commandments is most clearly visible in [illegible]teronomy, especially in Deut. 6-11.[24] This linkage [illegible]t be labelled as specifically "deuteronomic" for there is [illegible]ence of any other OT writer who would have disagreed [illegible]ade any sharp separation between the two commandments.[25]

The designation of the people as "stiff-necked", which forms the basis for Yahweh's anger and judgment, introduces one of the key motifs[26] of 32-34 (cf. 33:3,5, 34:9), which will be discussed at 34:9.

The problem which 32:7-14 deals with is whether or not Israel, in the light of their sin, can continue to be the people of God. The way in which it is resolved is important for the narrative of 32-34 as a whole. Yahweh seems to repudiate the people by referring to them before Moses as "your people" (ᶜammᵉkā, v. 7) whom "you brought up" (heᶜᵉlêtā)[27] or else as "this people", a designation which frequently carries hostile overtones.[28] Moses responds to this by pleading the fact that

Israel is Yahweh's people, "thy people" (^{c}amm^{e}kā, vv. 11,12) whom "thou didst bring (hôṣē'tā) out of Egypt". That this variation in suffixes is significant[29] is indicated by the closing word of the paragraph "to his people" (l^{ec}ammô) which the writer uses to indicate Yahweh's acceptance of Moses' plea. Yahweh accepts that Israel is his people and so not to be destroyed or cast off.

The theological basis for this acceptance of Israel by Yahweh is presented as lying within the character of Yahweh himself, a theological truth which is later developed as the fundamental message of the whole story (cf. 33:19, 34:6f.,9). It is remarkable that at the same time as Yahweh announces his judgment of the people, he makes his action in some way dependent on the agreement of Moses - "Now therefore let me alone that ... I may consume them" - and so paradoxically leaves open a possible escape. This paradox in no way diminishes the seriousness of the situation or the reality of the wrath and judgment incurred,[30] but reflects rather the character of Yahweh as a God both of judgment and of mercy. Further, this possible way of escape is developed in 32:10 by Yahweh making a promise to Moses almost identical in wording to the original promise to Abraham in Gen. 12:3.

Gen. 12:3: w^{e}'e^{c}eskā l^{e}gôy gādôl
Ex. 32:10: w^{e}'e^{ce}seh 'ôt^{e}kā l^{e}gôy gādôl

Yahweh's faithfulness to his promise, to which Moses appeals in v. 13, becomes the reason why Yahweh spares the people; and this theme of promise is introduced by Yahweh himself.

The faithfulness of Yahweh as the basis for mercy is further developed in the course of Moses' intercession. Nowhere does Moses excuse or mitigate what the people have done, but bases his appeal entirely on the character and purposes of Yahweh,[31] the God who brought the people out of Egypt (v. 11), the God whose reputation is at stake (v. 12), the God who has made promises to his people (v. 13). In v. 13 Moses appeals to both the main elements of Yahweh's patriarchal promises, both descendants and possession of land, and also uses the special name "Israel" instead of Jacob,[32] thus claiming God's promise in all its fullness. The fact that Yahweh accedes to Moses' plea on these terms reveals a theological understanding of mercy as dependent on God's character and his promises.

In addition to this appeal to God's faithfulness, another striking aspect of Yahweh's words in 32:10 lies in the fact that, apart from the paradox of judgment and mercy within Yahweh himself which they reveal, they open the way for the man Moses to play a decisive role within the purposes of God. A further paradox. It is God's faithfulness alone which is the basis for forgiveness; and yet this faithfulness is only revealed and made actual when Moses' bold intercession calls it forth. This divine-human balance plays a central role in the following narrative.

The importance of Moses' role in these chapters and elsewhere has frequently been underestimated through a slightly exaggerated emphasis on divine sovereignty. A typical position is that of von Rad:

> Not a single one of all these stories, in which Moses is the central figure, was really written about Moses. Great as was the veneration of the writers for this man to whom God had been pleased to reveal Himself, in all these stories it is not Moses himself, Moses the man, but God who is the central figure. God's words and God's deeds - these are the things that the writers intend to set forth.[33]

A similar statement is made by P.F. Ellis:

> There is no human hero in the Yahwist saga - not Abraham or Jacob or Joseph or Moses. There is no human hero because the protagonist of the saga is the Lord God.[34]

G.W. Coats[35] has attempted to redress the balance by pointing out the fine theological tension between the divine and human which exists in many of the Moses stories. It is neither God alone nor Moses alone who is responsible for the welfare of Israel but both together:

> For Pentateuchal theology the balance is crucial. Moses is not simply the blind servant, dancing his minuet of obedience to the sound of an all-encompassing divine drumbeat. To the contrary, for Pentateuchal theology Moses is <u>both</u> servant of God <u>and</u> heroic giant.[36]

Admittedly some Exodus narratives, particularly the victory at the Red Sea (14:1-15:21), do stress Yahweh's action to the exclusion of human involvement. Coats warns against an exclusive stress on Yahweh's act and sees a tension between ch. 15 which describes the event totally in terms of divine activity and ch. 14 in which Moses enters the account as an efficient agent.[37] Yet even in ch. 14 the overwhelming emphasis is on Yahweh's action and when Moses does act it is at Yahweh's behest and not on his own account.[38] The fact that this narrative, at the culmination of the paradigm act of salvation, so stresses Yahweh's action alone constitutes the significant exception which proves the rule. In the last resort it is Yahweh alone upon whom salvation depends. Yet this should not overrule but rather heighten the significance of those narratives in which both divine and human action play an integral role.

It has frequently been noted that there is a certain tension between 32:7-14 and the rest of ch. 32, particularly in Moses seeming unaware of the people's sin as he descends the mountain despite his having been told by God, and in his seeking forgiveness (vv. 30ff.) as though it had not yet been granted (v. 14). Childs has shown, however, the necessity of at least some earlier form of the tradition as integral to the narrative, and has also argued persuasively that the literary moulding of the story into a pattern of contrasting scenes gives a character to the narrative which makes it somewhat impervious to criticisms based on logical and chronological considerations.[39] Three further observations may be added to this.

First, just as 32:1-6 presents a paradigm of sin and apostasy, so 32:7-14 can be seen to present a paradigm of judgment, intercession, and forgiveness. Both scenes have a certain exemplary quality, the juxtaposition of which forms an effective contrast.

Secondly, the theme of Yahweh's faithfulness to his promise despite seemingly impossible obstacles is evident in other JE stories, most notably the Abraham cycle (Gen. 12-25) and probably also the Balaam cycle (Num. 22-24) where Num. 22:6 indicates an interpretation of the cycle in terms of a challenge to Yahweh's promise in Gen. 12:3 and the way in which the challenge is overcome. This suggests an interpretation of Ex. 32-34 also in terms of a challenge to Yahweh's promise and the vindication of his faithfulness. The challenge is particularly potent in that it arises not from external danger, as in Num. 22-24, but from the sinfulness of God's own people and their inherent inability to live in the way that God has prescribed. That Yahweh can deal with this problem is indicated at the outset of the narrative (v. 14). Yet this need in no way lessens the drama or tension of seeing his faithfulness being tested and confirmed through the rest of the story.

Thirdly, 32:7-14 not only presents, in nuce, the major themes of sin, intercession, and forgiveness, the mercy of God and the role of Moses which the rest of the narrative goes on to develop but it also provides a theological perspective from which the rest of the narrative should be read. For it presents a context of God's grace in which the episodes of judgment in 32:15-33:11 are to be read. In particular this can be seen in the juxtaposition of v. 14 with vv. 15-20. The smashing of the tablets by Moses is generally considered to signify the termination or annulment of the covenant relationship. Noth, for example, says,

> Moses' breaking of the tables ... means that he now declares the covenant between God and the people to be broken and therefore null and void.[40]

In itself the action would suggest such a finality given the significance of the tablets outlined above.[41] Yet in the light of v. 14 the reader knows that Yahweh has not rejected his people. Therefore the covenant is not abrogated, despite the people's unfaithfulness, but somehow God will be merciful and restore his people.

Ex. 32:15-20

The third paragraph, 32:15-20, recounts Moses' descent from Mt. Sinai. The reader has seen the people's sin below the mountain. He has also seen the divine perspective on the mountain top. But what will happen when the two meet?

The paragraph is short, consisting of only 92 words.[42] After an introduction of 5 words, 23 words, that is a quarter of the total, are given to a description of the tables of stone, and 25 words are given to the distinct but threatening sound from the camp. After a further 5 words recounting Moses' final approach, the actual confrontation is told swiftly and brusquely in 34 words.

Although the reader knows of Israel's sin with the calf, his attention is directed first to the divine splendour of the tablets, described more fully here than anywhere else. It is stressed that they are the work of God and that the writing on them is the writing of God. There is perhaps a contrast implied between these and the man-made idol of the people. Then a noise is heard from the camp whose meaning is unclear. Joshua guesses wrongly at its significance, thus serving as a foil for Moses whose superior insight into the character of the people is brought out. Moses responds[43] with a play on words which shows that he understands the true significance of the sound even though all details are still unclear.[44] The metrical cola of v. 18, by attracting attention to the word play, continue to build up suspense for the moment of actual confrontation with the people. When the confrontation comes its initial presentation is brief and consists of the brusque actions of Moses in smashing the tablets - despite the divine workmanship! - and thoroughly destroying the calf,[45] the remains of which are scattered on the water for the people to drink as punishment.[46] The less dramatic account of Deut. 9 takes time to designate the calf as a "sinful thing" and to explain that there was a brook that flowed out of the mountain (Deut. 9:21); such expansion is extraneous to the taut narrative of Ex. 32:20.

Ex. 32:21-24

The story turns next to the role played by Aaron. As Childs has shown,[47] if one compares Aaron's account of the making of the calf with the earlier account in 32:1-6, the way in which Aaron designates the people as "set on evil" and dwells on their role at length while minimizing his own involvement reveals Aaron as guiltily trying to evade his responsibility. The contrast between him and Moses could hardly be greater:

> Aaron saw the people "bent on evil"; Moses defended them before God's hot anger (v. 11). Aaron exonerated himself from all active involvement; Moses put his own life on the line for Israel's sake. Aaron was too weak to restrain the people; Moses was strong enough to restrain even God.[48]

It is of further interest that there is a certain parallel between the manner of Aaron's excuse and that of Adam in Gen. 3.[49] There are no verbal links, but the behaviour of Aaron corresponds to that of the archetypal pattern in Gen. 3. As in Gen. 3, the attempt to excuse does not mitigate but increases guilt; and as in Gen. 3 the story moves on from Adam's excuse to the woman who incited him, so here the story moves from Aaron's excuse to the people who incited him.

Ex. 32:25-29

The episode of the Levites is told with a brevity that leaves some of its details unclear, in particular the problematic v. 29, although the general tenor is unambiguous. It continues the theme of Yahweh's judgment upon the people, and again the use of contrast is evident, the contrast between the faithful Levites and faithless Aaron, and also implicitly the contrast between the faithful few (remnant?) and the disobedient many.

The key to understanding the episode is to appreciate that its central concern is a life-or-death faithfulness to Yahweh. It is a classic example of the faithfulness commanded in Deut. 13. This theme will recur again, especially in Ex. 34:11ff.

That faithfulness is the issue in 32:25-29 (cf. Deut. 33:8-9) can also be appreciated through a comparison with Num. 25:6ff. Unlike that narrative, where Phinehas' slaying of the unfaithful Israelite and Midianite is given atoning significance, there is no hint in Ex. 32 of such a meaning given to the Levites' action. Indeed the words of Moses in v. 30 about his seeking to make atonement himself exclude it. The primary significance of the story is to show that death is the penalty for unfaithfulness to Yahweh and the covenant, whereas blessing (v. 29b) is the reward for faithfulness. Although the aetiological element of the ordination of the Levites is present in v. 29a, little weight is laid upon it by the narrator (one may contrast Deut. 33:8-10); it is the Levites' faithfulness, and the cost of this, to which attention is directed.

There is some ambiguity over which people were slain by the Levites, whether fellow Levites or Israelites from other tribes. While the words of v. 29, "each one at the cost of his son and of his brother", in themselves suggest a slaughter within the ranks of the Levites, the command to go right through the camp (v. 27), as well as the setting of the scene as a whole (v. 25), suggests that offenders in every tribe are punished. There is some evidence that everyone who stood within the covenant was a brother or kinsman to his fellow, e.g. Lev. 25:46, Deut. 3:18, 24:7, Jdg. 20:13, Num. 25:6,[50] and the point of designating those slain as brothers and sons[51] may be to stress the costliness of faithfulness to Yahweh.[52]

It is interesting to reflect on this role of the Levites in the light of the larger pentateuchal context. The violence of the Levites is a theme in Genesis, but there it is condemned (Gen. 34, 49:5ff.). Here, by contrast, it is commended. What is the difference? In a not wholly dissimilar way G.W. Coats has shown how in Ex. 32-34 both Moses and the people in some way resist the will of Yahweh, and yet it is only Moses' opposition in the way in which he boldly intercedes with Yahweh, and not that of the people, which is commended.[53] Such ambiguity suggests that for this writer it is not so much the action performed as the motive underlying it which is of central importance. What distinguishes the Levites' slaying is that it is done out of faithfulness to Yahweh (32:26), while Moses appeals to Yahweh's glory as bound up with the fate of the people (32:12, 33:16), showing concern for Yahweh and not for himself. It is loyalty to Yahweh that for this writer is the crucial factor in assessing the worth of an action.

Three notes on v. 25 may be added. First, although there is some uncertainty over the precise meaning of *pārua^{c}* and *šimṣāh*, the context makes their general significance clear. Secondly there is a word play in the double use of *pr^{c}* in v. 25 which echoes the preceding narrative;[54] cf. v. 22, *b^{e}rā^{c}*,[55] v. 17, *b^{e}rē^{c}ōh*, v. 14, *hārā^{c}āh*, v. 12, *b^{e}rā^{c}āh*. The archaic spelling with *h* at the end in v. 25 and v. 17 seems deliberately to focus attention on the word play.[56]

Thirdly, emphasis is laid on Aaron's responsibility for the people (v. 25b), as in v. 21. It is remarkable that despite this emphasis there is no mention of any punishment for Aaron. A resolution to this is provided by Deut. 9:20, which possibly represents an element of old tradition omitted by the writer of Ex. 32-34 whose concern is for the fate of the people as a whole.

The positioning of vv. 25-29 is significant for the literary development of the story. One might expect the account of a dramatic punishment to follow immediately after Moses' initial confrontation with the people, and that only later would Moses remonstrate with Aaron. Yet by holding back the account of the slaying of the people while Aaron's excuses are made first, its impact and the contrast with Aaron is heightened. There is also then an alternation of themes in the narrative between highlighting the role of Moses (vv. 21-24) and the execution of judgment (vv. 25-29), the role of Moses (vv. 30-34), and Yahweh's words of judgment (32:34-33:6).

Ex. 32:30-33:6

The next twelve verses are not easy to interpret. In the first place the literary divisions are unclear, and the construction of these verses appears to be looser than anywhere else in Ex. 32-34. There is indeed a certain thematic continuity in the material. The basic framework is a dialogue between Moses and Yahweh. The issue at stake throughout is the future of Israel which is under Yahweh's disfavour: in particular the question is how Israel will experience Yahweh's presence as it moves on from Sinai to Canaan.

The precise division of material depends largely upon the interpretation of 32:35. On the one hand v. 35 may be taken as the conclusion of the narrative recounting the calf and its immediate aftermath before the focus shifts in ch. 33 to a second problem caused by the calf, the forfeiting of Yahweh's presence "in the midst" of the people. On the other hand, 32:34 introduces the theme of Israel's departure from Sinai, a theme developed in 33:1, and 32:34 handles this theme in a way similar to 33:1ff. by linking the journeying with the expression of Yahweh's disfavour. 32:35 can be seen then as a parenthetical note recording the fulfilment of 32:34b within a developing sequence initiated by 32:34a and continued in 33:1ff.

Such a difficulty in dividing the material means that any proposed divisions are somewhat artificial. 32:35 does conclude the sequence of punishments directly inflicted on Israel (the punishment implied by 33:3f.,5 is of a different order), yet the continuity into ch. 33 should also be appreciated.

The section begins with Moses' intercession in 32:30-33. The scene resumes the narrative contrast between the happenings on the mountain top and in the valley below. The sin which Israel has committed is a serious one (<u>hṭ'h gdlh</u>, vv. 30,31, cf. v. 21) and Moses recounts it in words reminiscent of the prohibition in Ex. 20:23:

32:31, <u>wy^cśw lhm 'lhy zhb</u>
20:23, <u>w'lhy zhb l' t^cśw lkm</u>

In the light of this Moses can offer no plea except to present himself as a recipient of God's judgment along with the people. Moses declines to be part of a future which does not include Israel also.[57] This is similar to 32:10-14 where also Moses declines a future for himself which does not include contemporary Israel. Such a total commitment of Moses to Israel is a central feature of his role as mediator and intercessor. Interestingly, however, the writer does not dwell on it at this point, although he develops it later (33:11ff.), but directs attention to the response of Yahweh, where concession is mingled with warning.

The precise force of 32:33 is again difficult to determine. There are two main alternatives. The one is that the words represent a concession which limits future judgment to something less than a total elimination of Israel, yet they are at the same time a strong statement of the righteousness of God such as seems to leave little room for mercy to the guilty - a problem which is resolved in the following narrative (33:19, 34:6f.). The other alternative is that the words are to be interpreted wholly in the light of v. 32b. That is, the words are not a general statement about God's righteous character, but an answer to Moses' prayer, using the terms that Moses had introduced. As such they could represent an accession to Moses' plea. For Moses declined to live unless Israel did also. God responds that he cannot blot out Moses for Moses has not sinned against him (to paraphrase v. 33). V. 33b could refer back not to the sin of Israel but simply to the lack of sin in Moses. If then Moses, who has bound his future to Israel's future, is to live then it would follow that Israel will live also. God responds favourably to Moses' sacrificial commitment to Israel. This latter interpretation, though less obvious than the first, deserves consideration. It would receive further support from the fact that v. 34, with its directions to lead the people away from Sinai, seems to presuppose that Israel has a future as a nation and as such could follow from a favourable interpretation of v. 33. On balance, however, the first interpretation seems more likely.

However one interprets the precise emphasis of v. 33, the point at issue seems to be that Israel is to have some future yet is subject to God's disfavour. That is, Israel's sin has further implications and its restoration, if there is to be one, will be in several stages. Even if one gave the more favourable interpretation to Yahweh's response to Moses, one could still compare various other passages in the OT where pardon for sin is accompanied by further punishment for it, e.g. Num. 14:20ff., 2 Sam. 12:13f. It is important not to impose an alien or anachronistic understanding of forgiveness upon the text.[58]

Yahweh's acceptance of some future for Israel is implied by 32:34a. Yet Israel will still suffer for its sin as the sudden warning in v. 34b makes clear. The point is reinforced by a play on the meaning of pqd, first in a neutral, then in a hostile sense. This is best conveyed in English by "visit ... visit sin". It gains effect from earlier uses of pqd in Ex. 3:16, 4:31, 13:19 (cf. Gen. 50:24f.) where it is uniformly used of God's visiting Israel in a favourable sense. Because of Israel's sin, God's action with Israel is changed from blessing to curse.

The idea of Yahweh "visiting" Israel introduces the theme of the divine presence which is central to ch. 33. The tacit assumption is that Israel's sin has caused the withdrawal of the divine presence. But as God begins to draw close to Israel again, in response to Moses' intercession, his presence, even if only partial,[59] cannot but have serious consequences for sinful Israel.

That v. 34b is no idle warning is brought out by v. 35. The punishment, "And Yahweh smote the people (with a plague)" fits a common pattern of divine judgment in the wilderness narratives. Although it is possible that this is to be viewed as a summary of what has happened thus far, it is more likely that it is an additional act of judgment while the people were still at Sinai, since v. 34b implies something subsequent to the time of speaking. It is often felt that v. 34b implies an indefinite future time such as makes v. 35 an awkward continuation. But this need not be so. The closest parallel in construction, where b^eyôm is followed by a perfect consecutive, is Gen. 3:5a where the serpent's statement is followed by an immediate fulfilment. The word and act of judgment in vv. 34b-35 concludes Yahweh's immediate response to Israel's sin.

Two notes may be added on the interpretation of 32:35. First, this punishment where Yahweh acts as direct agent has often been contrasted with 32:20, where Moses is agent, and 32:25-29, where the Levites are agents, as representing alternative traditions. It is hard to see this as a genuine difficulty. That judgment should be administered in more than one way is not unnatural. And given the divine-human balance in the narrative, there need be no problem in the fact of judgment administered through both divine and human agency.

Secondly, there is the problem of the last three words of v. 35 which are widely regarded as a gloss on account of their contradictory content; did the people or Aaron make the calf? Again, the difficulty may be more apparent than real. For although the writer has made Aaron primarily responsible for the calf, in 32:1-6 the initiative and involvement of the people in the calf-making is clearly presented. Assuming that v. 35b is to be translated "because they made the calf which Aaron made",[60] the seeming contradiction can be seen as an attempt to express the dual responsibility for the calf, that neither Aaron nor the people alone but both together are responsible for their sinful behaviour. Underlying this is perhaps reflection on the question of the interaction between, and respective responsibility of, a people and its leader.

The dialogue between Yahweh and Moses resumes in 33:1.

Although it picks up and develops the theme introduced in 32:34a, it is perhaps to be envisaged as a separate occasion from Moses' intercession in 32:31ff., because of the intervening note in 32:35. In this section of the narrative (32:30-33:6), however, the writer shows no interest in developing the story in terms of space and time. All attention is directed to Yahweh's words and their consequences.

33:1-3a resumes the theme of the people leaving Sinai for the promised land. Unlike the brief treatment of this in 32:34a, here it is at first described in the richest colours possible. In v. 1b the land is that which God has promised to the patriarchs. This is perhaps deliberately taking up and acknowledging Moses' plea in 32:13; Yahweh now acknowledges Israel as his people and as the inheritors of the promise. Secondly there is the promise of divine guidance and assistance as they travel and occupy the land. This reaffirms the original promise of 23:20ff. It is also stated more fully, and so more emphatically, than in 32:34. Thirdly, there is a further description of the land in ideal terms, a land "flowing with milk and honey". This recalls the promises of Moses' original commissioning (Ex. 3:8,17). There is a certain unevenness in the resumptive 'l-'rṣ in v. 3a. This probably reflects the difficulties inherent in the piling up of different phrases to convey a favourable impression. One may compare Ex. 3:17 where there is also a resumptive "to a land flowing with milk and honey" after a list of the inhabitants of the land. The difference in 33:1-3a is that the preceding promises are expanded.

The impact of 33:1-3a is strongly favourable. Yet suddenly this is countered in v. 3b by a word of denial and warning. Such is the nature of the people - "stiff-necked" - that, despite his promises, were Yahweh to be "in their midst" then he could not but destroy them. The promised land and the divine guidance to it is not denied; but it is severely qualified by the absence of some particularly intimate role of Yahweh's presence "in their midst" that otherwise might be expected.

After this hard word the people respond with grief and do not put on their ornaments. Gen. 35:4 recounts the stripping of ornaments in the context of the renunciation of foreign deities, and the action here probably has a similar significance. The people remove those objects connected with the construction of the calf. The people's "mourning" ('bl, Hithp.) should not, as is sometimes suggested,[61] be interpreted as showing repentance; for the parallel use of the verb in Num. 14:39, where the people continue to be disobedient, shows that it is remorse rather than repentance that is envisaged. Although the people's attitude has improved, it is not yet right.

The importance of this denial of Yahweh's presence "in the midst" is emphasized by vv. 5-6 which repeat and expand the contents of vv. 3b-4. The crucial factor that the people are stiff-necked[62] is stressed again.[63] As a result Yahweh cannot go "in the midst" of the people even for a single moment, which strengthens the previous denial of v. 3b. Moreover the people's action of v. 4, which might have signified at least some change for the better among the people is now construed as the result of God's disfavour towards the people. So the section ends with a repetition of the fact that the people stripped themselves, and it is now given a further meaning. For the verb nṣl (Hithp.) is used, which has been used twice previously in the narrative of Exodus for the "spoiling" of the Egyptians (3:22, 12:36; the Pi. form is used each time). The suggested meaning is that the triumphant character of the Israelites who "spoiled" others lasted only till Sinai; henceforth mēhar ḥôrēb, because of their sin, they are, in themselves, no better off than the Egyptians.

It should be noted, however, that although the predominant note of 33:1-6 is that of Yahweh's disfavour, yet there is still a note of hope implicit in v. 5bß. The fact that Yahweh is still undecided what to do leaves the way open for Moses' intercession that follows; as will be seen, in 33:12ff. Moses prays for the restoration of the presence denied in 33:3,5. The theological balance of 33:5 is thus closely akin to that in 32:10.

In the light of this exegesis it is possible to ask in what way Yahweh's presence is envisaged as being among, or removed from, the people of Israel. The question is usually posed with reference to the angel (ml'k)[64] who is promised (32:34, 33:2). In the original promise the angel embodies the divine presence (23:21,23), yet here this does not seem to be so, inasmuch as the presence of the angel is compatible with a denial of Yahweh's presence "among" (bqrb) the people. Childs[65] rightly criticizes a harmonization which distinguishes between two different kinds of angel, only one of which is a form of the divine presence, as going beyond the biblical text, but himself leaves the problem unresolved, the general sense of Yahweh's withdrawal of his presence being in any case clear.

Before offering any detailed discussion of the problem, it is important to set it in a broad theological context, a context necessary for ch. 33 as a whole. This context is the theological problem of the presence of God. The presence of God, while of central importance both in religious experience and theology, is extremely difficult either to conceptualize or to systematize. Theologically reflective accounts of the divine presence will frequently resort to the language of paradox.[66] The problem is how to describe God both as omnipresent and yet as present in some ways and places more, or differently, than in others. Insofar as theological language reflects religious experience this problem will be inescapable and, at the conceptual level, in some ways insoluble. When God's presence is associated in some special way with physical objects the problems in offering a rational theological explanation are acute. The debates over Christian eucharistic doctrine are a classic illustration of this.

Ex. 33 is the most extended treatment of the issue of God's presence in the OT. Although the writer is thinking of God's presence primarily in specific terms of angel or shrine, the subtly allusive language used shows that the writer is at the same time wrestling with the larger theological problems inherent in giving an account of God's presence. Any interpretation must take account of these difficulties.

Beyond these general theological considerations, the narrative context of Ex. 32:30-33:6 is an important factor for interpretation. The meaning of what is said will be affected by the situation in which it is said.

When the promise of the angel from 23:20ff. is repeated in 32:34, 33:2, there are two significant differences from its original giving. The first is the sin of Israel and the rupture of the covenant. This introduces an abnormal dimension into Israel's relationship with Yahweh. This abnormal dimension may mean that that which usually conveys Yahweh's presence will not now do so, or will not do so in the normal way. The angel, therefore, will not necessarily mediate Yahweh's presence in the same way as in 23:20ff.

Secondly, instructions concerning a shrine as the means of Yahweh's presence among Israel introduce a factor not present in ch. 23. This shrine, whereby Yahweh will be present in Israel's cult, means that Yahweh will be "in the midst" of Israel (w^{e}šākantî b^{e}tôkām, 25:8, cf. 29:45f.; cf. also Num. 14:42,44 for the ark). On any reckoning the shrine is a mode of Yahweh's presence distinct from that in the angel.

Given these two contextual considerations, the references to

Yahweh's presence in 32:34-33:6 may be coherently interpreted. In 23:20ff. a general promise of Yahweh's presence and help is given, expressed in the form most appropriate for a people about to journey and enter a new land. The fact that the angel goes "ahead" (lpnyk) implies no distancing from the people; it is simply an appropriate expression of guidance. In 32:34ff., although Yahweh has accepted Israel for the future, the people are still in his disfavour. He will indeed guide the people in a general way - this is the significance of the angel here. But the special presence of Yahweh in his shrine "in the midst" of the people is now denied, the directions for the shrine are abrogated. Although Yahweh can give a sinful people general guidance without difficulty, he cannot be specially present among them without their sinfulness provoking him to act against them. One may compare Num. 16-17 (tent of meeting) and 1 Sam. 6:19f., 2 Sam. 6:6ff. (ark) for the dangers of Yahweh's presence in a shrine amongst the people. Yet the special presence of Yahweh among Israel is one of the major signs of their covenant status (cf. 33:16, 34:9), and to deprive them of this would leave them with no significant future. Israel's sin in making their own vehicle of the divine presence has made them forfeit the true one. For this reason they mourn and wait to see what God will do with them.

Ex. 33:7-11

In this next section Moses erects a tent as a temporary medium of Yahweh's presence prior to the full restoration of the divine presence for which he subsequently intercedes.

This unit lies at the mid-point of 32-34 and marks the turning point in the story. It continues and concludes the theme of Israel as under God's judgment and prepares for the revelation of God's grace as the theme of what follows. The centrality of Moses' role is carried further; indeed it may be that 33:11, where Yahweh speaks with Moses "face to face" is the specific moment of transition in the narrative structure as a whole.[67]

The continuation of the theme of judgment is seen in the positioning of the tent "far off" (hrḥq) from the camp. The simple fact of the tent being outside the camp would not in itself necessarily have significance. But when the words "outside the camp" are repeated within one verse, and the tent is said to be not only outside the camp but far off from it, the writer is clearly drawing attention to this fact. As a continuation of the preceding verses which have stressed that

God cannot be "in the midst" of the people lest he destroy them, this distancing of God's presence from the camp fits naturally. Further, the preceding verses have effectively repealed the instructions given in Ex. 25ff. for the construction of the shrine designated as the tent of meeting (<u>'hl mwᶜd</u>).[68] So when Moses calls this tent "the tent of meeting" (<u>'hl mwᶜd</u>, twice in v. 7), it is natural to see this as a substitute for the proper tent in the middle of the camp, pending the restoration of Yahweh's favour and the renewal of the covenant. For the reader familiar with the idea of ch. 25ff. that the tent of meeting was in the midst of the camp there is irony and reflection on the result of sin in the wording "And every one who sought Yahweh would go out to the tent of meeting, which was outside the camp".

The identity of this tent is much debated but either of two alternatives would fit well. The first possibility is that the tent is Moses' own tent[69] which has been mentioned earlier in Ex. 18:7.[70] This might be supported by the expression <u>wᵉnāṭāh-lô</u> where the pronoun probably refers reflexively to Moses.[71] Alternatively the definite article in <u>hā'ōhel</u> could be indefinite in sense and should be rendered "a tent".[72] This would fit well with the context[73] since the point is precisely that this tent is a provisional substitute for the promised tent of ch. 25ff., and not a permanent sanctuary in its own right.[74] Either way the problem over the apparently abrupt and unprecedented reference to the tent in v. 7 need not be a problem if one takes seriously the context of 33:3,5 where admittedly no explicit reference is made to a tent but the writer may simply presuppose familiarity with the notion of a shrine designated "tent of meeting" which conveys Yahweh's presence "in the midst of" his people.

A notable feature of the section is its use throughout of verbs in the imperfect which have a clearly frequentative force. This is significant for two reasons. First, the verbs imply that the tent was constantly put up and taken down. Although this is usually taken to refer to Moses' habitual practice at successive encampments in the wilderness, there are difficulties with such an interpretation.[75] The verbs in context suggest the impermanence of the tent. Although the tent is not taken down as soon as Moses has finished with it the implication is that it is set up only for limited periods of time. This gains point through the contrast with the shrine that should have permanently mediated Yahweh's presence in the midst of the people. This tent is a temporary substitute which is not only outside the camp but is only available intermittently to seek Yahweh; it is not permanently established as Yahweh's official shrine would be.

Secondly, the imperfect verbs convey the sense of a passing of time, and are a literary device to slow the narrative at this transitional point. After the tense and sombre narrative preceding, this section provides a pause before the renewed heightening of tension in the intercession of Moses. The implied passing of time, combined with a picture of the life of the people as returning to an orderly and reverent pattern of existence conveys a certain sense of calm and gives the impression that Yahweh's disfavour will not be his final word but that the way is open for a restoration of Israel.

The transition from judgment to mercy, suggested by the general tenor of 33:7-11, is based largely on the role of Moses. Not only is he treated with great deference by the people (v. 8) - a contrast to 32:1! - but, most important, he enjoys the favour of a unique and intimate relationship with Yahweh (v. 11a). It is this which forms the basis for a renewed intercession of unparalleled boldness.[76]

That Yahweh should speak to Moses "face to face" (pānîm el-pānîm) is not only of deep significance for understanding the relationship between Moses and Yahweh (cf. Num. 12:8, Deut. 34:10), but also has more general implications for the relationship between God and man. That the writer has this larger issue in mind is evident from the juxtaposition of 33:11 with 33:20:

> 33:11, "And Yahweh spoke with Moses face to face ..."
> 33:20, "But (Yahweh) said, 'You cannot see my face,
> for man shall not see me and live'."

This juxtaposition of apparently conflicting statements has long troubled commentators. The fact that the LXX uses different words for "face" in vv. 11,20[77] probably reflects an attempt to resolve the contradiction. Likewise the Targums to 33:11 replace "face" by "speech" (mmll) and render the idiom "speech for speech".[78] It is common among modern commentators to argue that these two verses represent conflicting conceptions of man's access to God and that these different conceptions belong to different sources or traditions.[79]

Such exegetical moves are surely unnecessary once the verses are set in the context of the theological problems inherent in discussing the presence of God. For it is necessary to affirm both that God can be known as intimately present and that he is beyond human reach and knowledge. This problem, that is immanence and transcendence, is inherent in language about God and cannot, as such, be resolved. Indeed what matters is not to dissolve the tension but to recognize it as a paradox and to describe it correctly. It is precisely such a theological reflection on the problem of immanence and transcendence that 33:11 points to. As such it is an important part of the total theological treatment of the presence of God in ch. 33. It is characteristic also of the subtle narrative technique of Ex. 32-34 that it is not made explicit as a reflective comment upon the story but is integrated smoothly into the development of the narrative.

The use of pānîm in 33:11 is significant not only in juxtaposition with 33:20. For the use of pānîm in 33:14f. is also clearly part of the same theological treatment. And the pānîm motif recurs in the final section of the story, 34:29ff. The development of nuances and implications of pānîm is an important aspect of the present narrative.

Finally it may be noted that the access of Moses to God in the tent suggests that it is the tent which should be understood as the setting for the prayer of 33:12ff. (although the question of location is of limited significance). The only evidence against this would be v. 21a hinnēh māqôm 'ittî which could be interpreted demonstratively, thus implying the presence of Moses on the mountain. But hinnēh need not have demonstrative force, and if Moses were already on the mountain one would expect the theophany to take place directly rather than for directions about it to be given. Whenever Moses is found on the mountain, this is preceded by a reference to his going up there (ᶜlh) first. There is no such reference in 33:12, rather a natural sequence giving content to the close relationship in the tent of 33:11.

Ex. 33:12-23

The content of the next section, 33:12-23,[80] is the most dense and compressed in the whole of 32-34. It recounts the bold and successful intercession of Moses before Yahweh, and while the general tenor is not difficult to discern some of the detail is problematic and some of the terminology is deliberately multivalent. The section divides into two main parts, vv. 12-17 and vv. 18-23. The favourable response to God in v. 17 concludes the first part of Moses' prayer, while the renewed petition of v. 18 marks a new stage of the intercession.

The character of the section, at least of vv. 12-17, 18, as an intercession is clear. A correct understanding is less immediately obvious and depends on first determining the problem with which the intercession in concerned. The problem is frequently considered to be that of whether or not Yahweh can leave Sinai: such was the spatial mentality of the ancient Near East, which saw an intimate relation between gods and their holy places, that it was difficult to conceive of Yahweh as leaving his holy mountain of Sinai.[81] This same essential problem can be differently nuanced by saying that the concern of the narrative is from the perspective of life in Canaan, seeking to establish "that the God who once revealed himself fully and for the first time on Sinai was now present with his people in Canaan too".[82] There are obvious difficulties with this view,[83] the most important of which is the tradition of the exodus in which Yahweh revealed his might in Egypt and is depicted as being superior to the Egyptian gods even on their own ground (cf. Ex. 7:8-13). It may further be asked whether any ancient Near Eastern high-god was considered to be spatially restricted to a limited area; a particular attachment to a locality need not imply any restriction to it. If the answer to this question is negative, then it becomes less likely that the God of the Israelites was ever conceived of in such a restricted way.

In addition to these difficulties with the supposition that the problem of 33:12ff. is whether or not Yahweh was able to leave Sinai, the main objection to this premise is that it arises largely through discounting the present context which has provided good reasons of its own for Yahweh's reluctance to go with the people. The problem in the present context is not spatial or metaphysical,[84] concerning the possibility of Yahweh's presence away from Sinai, nor is it to do with the affirmation of the identity of the Israelites' God in Canaan with the deity of Sinai, but it is the moral problem of how a holy God can abide with a sinful people. The recognition of this enables a coherent understanding of the material as a whole.

The development of Moses' intercession may be outlined as follows. 33:12-17 are Moses' response to 33:1-6 after the way has been prepared by 33:7-11. Moses seeks the restoration of Yahweh's accompanying presence with the people. Although this is couched in allusive terms, it is reasonably clear that a concrete realization of Yahweh's presence, that is a shrine, is envisaged. The term used for Yahweh's presence in vv. 14f. is pānîm, a word characteristically used of the divine presence in the cult.[85] It is such a divine presence that makes Israel distinctive, and this Yahweh grants (v. 17). Yet this favourable response still does not resolve Moses' problem. For the fundamental fact of the sinfulness of Israel, which was the cause of all the trouble, remains unchanged. The possibility is thereby raised that the renewed presence of Yahweh with his people would simply lead to his further wrath and judgment against them as the inevitable result of any future sin. The restoration of the shrine as the means of Yahweh's presence could of itself yet lead to the destruction of Israel.[86] Something further is needed, and this Moses seeks in vv. 18ff.; this is nothing less than a deeper and fuller revelation of the character of Yahweh as a God whose very nature it is to be gracious and merciful (33:19, 34:6f.). Only on this basis can the covenant be renewed because now even the sin of Israel can be accounted for within the mercy of God and need not lead to the people's destruction. Hence the need for the theophany in which God reveals his graciousness and mercy; hence also Moses' final response in 34:9 in which, on the basis of this revelation, he prays finally for the presence of Yahweh even with a continuingly sinful people.[87]

In the light of this general outline,[88] a more detailed analysis of the intercession may be undertaken. It has often been queried whether any coherent development of thought can be traced within 33:12ff.[89] It is important to recognize that the logic and development of Moses' prayer corresponds to the logic of plea and petition, not that of sober, rational discourse, and must be judged accordingly. As Childs puts it,

> Perhaps the logical consistency of the dialogue should not be overworked. There is an emotional tone of the highest intensity throughout the conversation as Moses seeks unswervingly to wrest from God a further concession.[90]

Muilenburg[91] likewise stresses the "urgency and passion" which characterize the prayer.[92]

The structure of the intercession in vv. 12-17 falls into two parts. Vv. 12-13 constitute the first plea which meets with a favourable, but still partial and somewhat enigmatic, response in v. 14. In vv. 15-16 Moses renews his plea, strengthening it by appeal to this concession and developing it yet further, and this plea is granted in v. 17.

The situation presupposed in vv. 12ff. has been outlined thus far. Moses in v. 12 refers back to God's command to leave (33:1). The words with which his statement of the problem continues, "You have not told me whom you will send with me" (so, roughly, most EVV), have occasioned difficulty. In another context the words could simply constitute a request for a human companion or guide who would know the way through the wilderness.[93] Since, however, such an issue has not been raised hitherto, either in the Sinai pericope or in the journeyings to Sinai, nor is it raised at any later stage in the wanderings,[94] it is unlikely to be the concern here.

There is also an apparent tension with the promise of the angel in 32:34, 33:2. God has said he will send an angel. But in fact the problem here is the same as in 32:34ff., that is there is a distinction between different modes of Yahweh's presence, one more and the other less intimate. The angel represents Yahweh's general guidance of his people which, while important, is inadequate if not combined with his special presence in his shrine. It was this shrine that was denied in 33:3b-6 and which Moses now seeks to restore. It is misleading to render 33:12a$^{\gamma}$ 'ēt '^{a}šer tišlaḥ ^{c}immî by "... whom you will send with me" for the Hebrew is not specifically personal and could equally well be impersonal: "... what you will send with me", with reference to a shrine of Yahweh's presence.

The use of the preposition "with" (^{c}im) in v. 12 (cf. v. 16 'immānû) is also of significance in determining the nature of Moses' request. The preposition implies close personal contact, being reminiscent of the words at Moses' commissioning (Ex. 3:12), "But I will be with you" (ky 'hyh ^{c}mk). Further, it probably has a force, particularly in v. 16, similar to that of bqrb in 33:3,5. The prepositions in 33:12-17, as in 33:1-6, carry great weight. A general promise of guidance, which could still imply some distance between God and the people (cf. lpny) is inadequate. Nothing less than the immediate and close presence of God (bqrb, ^{c}m) will suffice. With this insight one can understand the difference between the two responses of God in vv. 14,17. In v. 14 he promises to "go" (hlk) but the precise nature of this going is still unclear; no preposition is used, to distinguish whether Yahweh will go ahead of or amongst the people. So Moses prays further that Yahweh will not only go (v. 15), but will go "with us" (^{c}immānû). It is this extra factor (gm 't-hdbr hzh)[95] which is then finally granted (v. 17).[96]

After stating the problem in v. 12a, Moses goes on in v. 12b to appeal to his special relationship with Yahweh, which is made the basis for his following plea. The special position of Moses is based on two things: first, that Yahweh "knows him by name", and secondly that "he has found favour in his sight". This latter is the key expression in the prayer, occurring five times and binding the prayer together by its use at both beginning and end. What do these expressions mean? And to what do they refer? The introduction of them by "yet you have said" (wᵉ'attāh 'āmartā) implies some previous occasion at which Yahweh designated Moses in this way.

The verb "to know" in Hebrew idiom has a variety of meanings, one of which is to know a person in an intimate relationship. When used of God's relationship to man it can have the force of "to elect"; cf. Gen. 18:19, Am. 3:2, Hos. 13:5, Jer. 1:5.[97] Likewise "by name" implies intimate knowledge of a person and his character; cf. Is. 43:1 ("I have called you by name (bᵉšimka) - you are mine"), 45:3, 49:1. This combination of "know" and "by name" is without parallel elsewhere in the OT and points to the uniquely intimate relationship between Moses and Yahweh.

The idiom "to find favour in N's eyes" is highly flexible and can convey a variety of different connotations, being used of both man and God.[98] Sometimes "if I have found favour in your eyes" may be simply an expression of deference,[99] or it may be a formula for strengthening a request.[100] It may be a request not to be angry.[101] It may mean positively enjoying someone's goodwill and approval.[102] And it may refer to such goodwill with an eye specifically towards its practical consequences.[103] It may also refer to some specific word or deed of goodwill already bestowed upon the recipient.[104] With such a wide range of nuances, variable according to situation and intention, one need not expect the phrase to be univocal in its usage in 33:12ff. Of the five occurrences in 33:12ff., the use in v. 13a[a] resembles the purely deferential expression, whereas the use in v. 13a[c] is similar to the uses in Gen. 32:5, 33:8, seeking a goodwill which will have practical expression. In v. 16a the expression means the enjoyment of goodwill and approval. V. 17b is a re-affirmation of v. 12b and has a similar force. The initial use of the phrase in v. 12b is the most important. It has a close parallel in Gen. 6:8. The link of Ex. 33:12 with Gen. 6:8 is the more notable because these are the only two instances in the OT where it is said absolutely of individuals that they "found favour" with God.[105] Of the usage in Gen. 6:8 Zimmerli comments that it "implied the mystery of the free divine decision".[106] In Ex. 33:12, then, as in Gen. 6:8, what is set forward is effectively the special election of Moses by God.

To what previous occasion ("yet you have said") does this refer? There are four possibilities. First, it could refer to some previous saying of Yahweh which used these same words. Secondly, it could intend some previous saying not using these words, but the tenor of whose content could be aptly conveyed thus. Thirdly, it could refer more generally to the special position enjoyed by Moses since his commissioning in Ex. 3. Fourthly it could refer to the immediate context of 33:11a.

If the first possibility is adopted, then there are two alternatives. Either one has to say that the tradition has not preserved this word, or that Yahweh's words in 33:17b originally preceded those of Moses in 33:12b but were subsequently re-arranged. This latter alternative faces the difficulty not only of the general principle that one should not rearrange the text (where the problem is not that of textual corruption) unless it cannot make satisfactory sense in its present order (which is yet to be demonstrated), but also that it creates new problems of its own. For if the words were transposed to the beginning of the prayer, even though in the present text there is no obvious location for them, they would disrupt the whole movement of the narrative. Hitherto Yahweh's words have been words of judgment; not solely judgment for notes of hope have been sounded (32:10, 32:33, 33:5), but words of disfavour have been the consistent theme. To have an explicit word of Yahweh's favour at this point, when this is what Moses is seeking to elicit, would greatly weaken the development of the intercession.

The second possibility could allow that Moses is referring back to 32:10 where the Abrahamic promise is offered to him. A promise of such import could well be seen as a special election of Moses. Two considerations support this. First, it has been seen that "finding favour" can refer back to some word or deed of goodwill already bestowed (cf. Gen. 19:19), and so there could be a similar intention here. It is possible too that Gen. 6:8 may contain some reference back to the oracle concerning Noah's future significance in Gen. 5:29, though this cannot be pressed, particularly since the oracle is not pronounced by God himself. Secondly, the offer of 32:10b is not taken up by Moses in the intercession at 32:11-13. He does appeal to God's faithfulness to his promises to the patriarchs (32:13), but does not link this with the offer just made to him, unless perhaps by implicitly declining it. In 33:12ff., however, the way in which Moses seeks to bring the people into the same favoured position that he enjoys (cf. below on vv. 13b, 14b, 15b, 16) makes good sense if interpreted as Moses having accepted God's offer but insisting that it should be precisely the historic people of Israel, and not anyone else, who should be the fulfilment of the promise of the great nation. The fact that Moses seeks to bring the people to share in his favoured position is clear and is not dependent upon presupposing 32:10. But the interpretation of Moses' plea in terms of 32:10 undoubtedly adds force and point.

The third possibility, of a reference to Moses' special position since Ex. 3, may also be present and need not be set in contrast to the second interpretation. For Moses' receipt of the promise in 32:10 can be seen as focussing and distilling the role which he plays elsewhere.

The fourth possibility, of a reference back to 33:11, is likewise not exclusive of the previous two interpretations. In terms of the narrative development of the story Moses' special relationship in 33:11 clearly prepares for the following intercession, and the account of the intercession adds content to 33:11. In this sense v. 12b is linked with v. 11. But inasmuch as v. 11 can be interpreted not as introducing something new but as crystallizing the favoured role that Moses already enjoys, its presence does not exclude wider reference back to both 32:10 and the role of Moses throughout the narrative hitherto.

These considerations suggest that the fact of Moses' being known by God and having found favour in his sight refers to the grace of God bestowed on Moses in having admitted him to a uniquely intimate relationship, probably with special reference to the promise of 32:10. It is this that forms the ground for Moses' following plea and is the ground also on which God finally grants it.

The actual plea of Moses in v. 13 begins with the adversative *w^{c}th*, preparing for some contrast with what has gone before.[107] There is also perhaps a word-play with v. 12, *'attāh* ... *w^{e}'attāh* ... *w^{e}'attāh* ... *w^{ec}attāh* .... As observed above, Moses' second use of the "finding favour" expression is akin to the familiar deferential usage which introduces a petition. But the use in the previous verse lends it extra significance here as the writer develops different nuances of meaning in the expression. It is notable too that the verb *yd^{c}* is used twice in this verse, as it was in v. 12, and so could be said to form one of the leitmotifs of the prayer as a whole.[108]

Moses asks to be shown God's "ways" (*d^{e}rākekā*).[109] "Ways" often denotes a person's character or the course of behaviour that he adopts,[110] and so the request would appear to be to know God's character. This is indicated also by the following *w^{e}'ēdā^{ca}kā*, "that I may know thee". (There may, however, be a double entendre in the use of *derek*, hinting at its literal meaning of "route for a journey"; Moses seeks to know the route by which Yahweh will go with his people. Such a nuance is not impossible.)

If a request to know God's character is the meaning of Moses' petition, it might be asked how this concern for *revelation* fits in the context of seeking God's *accompaniment*. But to contrast revelation and accompaniment as in any sense antithetical would be insensitive to the fundamental concern not only of this prayer but also of the surrounding context which is the moral problem of reconciling God to a sinful people, a general problem of which the question of God's accompaniment of the people in his shrine is a specific manifestation. Moses' request should be interpreted as an attempt to press behind the immediate problem to the heart of the matter; to solve the impasse of Yahweh's refusal in terms of seeking a fuller and deeper knowledge of Yahweh's character and purposes than has hitherto been revealed, confident that this will lead to a deeper relationship with him ("that I may know you") and the practical enjoyment of his goodwill ("and find favour in your sight"). *Who* God is determines *how* he will act.

If Moses is already known by God and has found favour with him it may seem strange that this should be the object of his petition. Yet this is in keeping with the logic of prayer evident elsewhere in the OT, most notably 2 Sam. 7:18ff. There, Nathan has just brought a promise from Yahweh, the fulfilment of which is not contingent upon David's response. Yet in both v. 25 and v. 28f. David prays for the confirmation and establishment of this promise.[111] This attitude follows from an understanding of a relationship with Yahweh as not static but dynamic. That is, past favours cannot be appealed to without their being continually reappropriated and made an existential reality. It is such a present experience of Yahweh and his goodwill that Moses seeks.

In v. 13 Moses seeks this experience primarily for himself, in terms of the favour he already enjoys. Yet significantly he adds to the end of his request "and consider that this nation is your people" (ûr^{e}'ēh kî ^{c}amm^{e}kā haggôy hazzeh). Moses seeks to extend the scope of God's favour beyond himself to include the people. He appeals to Yahweh to consider Israel as "your people" in a way similar to the prayer of 32:11ff. At this stage no special favour for the people is sought; simply a reaffirmation of the fact that they are Yahweh's people.

The response in v. 14 has often been taken as a question but the context demands rather that it should be a positive affirmation.[112] Yahweh grants Moses' prayer. Yet, as noted above, there is a deliberate vagueness about the affirmation in that no preposition is used after "will go" to indicate the nature of Yahweh's going, whether with the people in their midst, or not. To say, as Eichrodt does,[113] that pānāy yēlēkû should be completed by the addition of l^{e}pānêkā is entirely to miss the subtlety of the omission and to miss the contrast between lpny and ^{c}m. Likewise the addition of the words "with you", as in all English translations, makes a concession which is absent from the Hebrew. Moreover the promise of rest[114] is given to Moses alone (lāk, second person singular suffix), and Moses is seeking the divine favour not for himself alone but for the people too. There is need therefore to pray further to obtain a fuller concession from Yahweh.

This general sense of the verse is clear, whatever the precise interpretation of Yahweh's "presence" (pānîm).[115] The use of pānîm is significant for the several different nuances that the word can convey.[116] First, it can convey the personal sense of Yahweh's accompaniment, for pānîm with a suffix is used elsewhere as a periphrasis for the personal pronoun. A striking example is 2 Sam. 17:11 where Hushai urges Absalom that he go (to battle)[117] in person (ûpānêkā hōl^{e}kîm baqrāb).[118] When pānîm is used thus of God, it stresses his direct personal involvement. Such a usage, in the context of 33:11,20, would appropriately fit into a theological reflection on the presence of God.

On the other hand it has already been seen[119] that pānîm is frequently used in connection with the cult, so that a shrine, a place for the divine presence (cf. Ex. 29:42-46), is probably being alluded to.[120] Moreover, it is because the shrine is movable that it is possible to speak of Yahweh's pānîm "going".[121]

Moses' request thus far has received a favourable response, but this concession is still only partial and so he resumes his intercession again to seek a full concession from God. First, he takes up and claims the partial concession already made (33:15). He uses the same words that Yahweh has used, being content at this stage to add no preposition and to leave vague the relationship of the divine presence to the people; this concession in itself is a major step. But on the basis of this Moses immediately extends his request - "If your 'presence' does not come, *do not take us up from here*". Hitherto Moses himself has been given the task of taking up the people (vv. 1, 12). He now, so smoothly that it is easy not to notice it, makes Yahweh the subject of the verb, and not so much requests as takes for granted that it is Yahweh who will take them up. Further, the suffix after the verb is plural, "us". This resumes Moses' theme, introduced in v. 13b and not taken up in the concession of v. 14, that not just he but also the people as a whole should be the recipients of Yahweh's favour. Gathering boldness, Moses then takes this further and in v. 16 twice links himself with the people "I and your people" (*'^{a}nî w$^{e\,c}$amm^{e}kā*), uses a plural suffix "with us" and a plural verb "we are distinct", stressing that they be distinct *as a people* among other peoples.[122]

In addition to this Moses takes up again the promise that Yahweh's "presence" will "go", which previously (v. 15) he was content to leave vague, but now in his climax he specifies as going *with us* (*^{c}immānû*). Nothing less than the presence of Yahweh in the shrine in the midst of Israel will show that Israel is the recipient of the divine favour and is set apart from all other people. Moses appeals to no desert or repentance on the part of the people but solely to God's favour and his granting of his presence in empirical and accessible form. To this request Yahweh grants a full concession (v. 17) and gives as reason the special position of Moses. From a literary point of view this forms an inclusio with v. 12 and rounds off the unit. Theologically it not only confirms Moses' special status, but makes the favoured position of Israel both mediated through, and dependent upon, Moses. As will be seen later,[123] the restoration of Israel and the renewal of the covenant does not put Israel in a position identical to that before its sin. Henceforth it is dependent upon the mercy of God mediated through Moses as the primary recipient of that mercy.

Moses' bold intercession has thus far been granted. Yet, as

observed above, this is still not sufficient, for the fundamental problem of the sinfulness of Israel, which would most likely provoke Yahweh again to destroy them in anger, still remains. Moses therefore makes one final supreme request that Yahweh should reveal himself in a fuller way than hitherto; only in the very depths of God can a final solution to the people's sin be found.

Moses makes one final short request and then, significantly, has to say no more. At the supreme moment of answering Moses' prayer and undertaking to reveal himself Yahweh completely takes over. No longer does Moses need boldly to wrest concessions from God. God now takes the initiative himself and Moses becomes the passive recipient. When God prepares to show himself, Moses' role is suddenly transformed from daring interlocutor to receptive servant.

The whole of 33:18-23 constitutes a rich treasury of terms for expressing the character of God. The variety of terminology - glory, goodness, name, face - represents an attempt to express the inexpressible, the experience of God. This attempt strains the ordinary usage of language, and the writer brings together such varied terms as will best convey the sense of the importance and depth of what Yahweh is revealing of himself.[124]

Moses asks to see[125] Yahweh's glory (kābôd). The precise nuance of the term, which in general means God's majesty, those qualities which call forth worship, must be determined from the context. The word appears again in v. 22 where it is effectively synonymous with God himself, for the context is describing Yahweh himself passing by and ba^{c}abōr k^{e}bōdî is parallel to ^{c}ad-^{c}obrî. Moses thus asks to see Yahweh himself. Another nuance in the request may possibly be seen in connection with the concern for the restoration of the shrine. Elsewhere the glory of God is connected with the tabernacle (29:43) and signifies the presence of God there (29:42-46, 40:34-35). Perhaps Moses is seeking an experience of God such as will later characterize the regular cult where Yahweh will meet with his people in both judgment and mercy.

To this Yahweh responds affirmatively in v. 19 and yet alters the wording of the concession at the same time in that he will make all his goodness (ṭûb) pass before Moses. Although there is no exact parallel to this usage of ṭûb elsewhere in the OT, the word is generally used to signify God's benefits experienced by Israel,[126] and such a meaning fits well the present context. For a certain synonymity between "goodness" and "glory" is indicated by the parallelism between v. 19, <u>'a^{c}a^{b}îr kol-ṭûbî</u> and v. 22 <u>w^{e}hāyāh ba^{c}abōr k^{e}bōdî</u>. The point is that Yahweh is presenting an understanding of the divine glory in terms of the divine goodness. God's glory is experienced in his graciousness. This is the more significant in that elsewhere in the pentateuchal narratives the appearance of Yahweh's glory is characteristically in the context of judgment on the people (e.g. Num. 14:10-12, 16:19ff.), although in Ex. 16:9ff. the expected judgment does not materialize and the people are given manna instead. The fact that at the supremely critical moment in Israel's existence it is Yahweh's "goodness" rather than judgment which is brought to the fore is of great theological importance.

Yahweh will also proclaim his name (<u>šēm</u>) before Moses. This prepares for the theophany of 34:6f. It also echoes vv. 12, 17 where there has been mention of Moses' name. (This link is verbal, on the literary level, and no connection of theological content is intended.)

The use of the formula <u>qr' bšm yhwh</u>[127] with Yahweh himself as subject is most striking and is unique to this verse and 34:5f. Elsewhere it is always used of the worshipper calling upon Yahweh (cf. Gen. 4:26 etc.). And it does initially seem odd to have Yahweh calling his own name. Consequently it has been suggested[128] that the text should be emended here to make Moses the subject, and that Moses should be construed as the subject in 34:5f. But such emendation is unnecessary, and indeed misses the point. For the point surely lies precisely in the inversion of the usual use of the formula. The writer reverses the customary use of the formula so as to stress the initiative of Yahweh here; men can only call upon the name of God and rehearse his attributes, as they customarily do in the cult, because at the critical moment in Israel's history Yahweh revealed himself and proclaimed his name first. It is a striking conception of the basis of Israel's worship.

In v. 19b Yahweh gives Moses a solemn assurance about the meaning of his name and the character which it reveals which both forms a preview, as it were, of 34:6f. and also forms part of an immediate answer to the request to see God's glory. The use of the <u>idem per idem</u> formula is notable.[129] The repetition of the verb emphasizes the verbal idea. "The second verb serves as a predicate, and thus, like a cognate accusative, emphasizes the verbal action".[130] When, as here, the formula is repeated with two verbs of related meaning, then the statement of the verbal meaning - the mercy of God - is as emphatic as the Hebrew language can make it. At the same time the expression contains a certain ambiguity or indeterminacy which preserves the idea of freedom and choice on the part of the acting agent. As Driver puts it, the idiom is "employed where either the means, or the desire, to be more explicit does not exist".[131] While Freedman may be correct in arguing that the element of arbitrary choice is not inherent in the expression and that in 33:19 "there appears to be no suggestion of wilfulness or arbitrary free choice in the Hebrew",[132] this does not mean that the idea of freedom and choice is not present at all. Choice can be free without being either wilful or arbitrary.[133] The formula in 33:19 not only stresses that Yahweh will be gracious but that there is a mystery about it such that it depends entirely upon Yahweh himself as to who will be the recipient of his grace. The context makes clear that Israel will receive Yahweh's grace - emphatically so; yet this is so expressed as to make clear that this is not something automatically granted which can in any way be presumed upon.

Further, there is a certain finality about the expression. An idem per idem formula is often used to terminate debate (cf. "That's that!").[134] As such the formula fittingly concludes what the present section has to say about the gracious character of God before shifting to a different theme in v. 20.

The use of the idem per idem formula here is reminiscent of Ex. 3:14, and probably a deliberate recollection of the earlier passage is intended. Both verses come at crucial moments of Yahweh's self-revelation. Ex. 3:14 reveals the God who is about to act on behalf of his people in bringing them out of Egypt. In the account of the exodus it is remarkable that there is little explicit moral concern; the emphasis is on Yahweh's triumphant acts of deliverance. Neither the grumblings of the Israelites nor the opposition of Pharaoh are designated as sin. (The exceptions which prove the rule are Pharaoh's self-accusations in 9:27, 10:16f., and the comment in 9:34, but little weight is attached to these.) The writer stresses the actions of Yahweh on Israel's behalf and the glory which accrues to him for this. Pharaoh is an opponent whose opposition is overruled by the true Lord of the Israelites. The Israelites are weak and fearful and their God's acts of power are the greater by contrast. In Ex. 15 Yahweh's salvation (yšw^{c}h' v. 2) is portrayed entirely in nonmoral terms, the deeds that he has done on Israel's behalf.

Yahweh's character is very much that of the victorious warrior; "Yahweh is a man of war, Yahweh is his name" (15:3).

The covenant at Sinai has changed the situation and added a moral dimension, both extensive and profound, into the relationship between Yahweh and Israel and this gives the problem of sin a new meaning and importance. The making of the calf may be described as Israel's first sin. Hence in 33:19, in the context of Israel's sin as the problem to be dealt with, Yahweh's character is revealed entirely in moral terms, showing how he deals with sin and the need for forgiveness in the life of Israel. One can see then that there is an essential complementarity between these two stages of Yahweh's self-revelation in Ex. 3:14 and 33:19.

If this analysis is correct, it has important implications. Hitherto Ex. 3:14 has received far more attention than 33:19 in attempts to explicate the meaning of the divine name. Yet since it seems clear that 3:14 is not offering an account of the origins or etymology of YHWH in terms of the verb hyh but pointing to an understood connection of meaning between the two in terms of dynamic activity,[135] there is no good reason for concentrating on this passage to the exclusion of others which also develop aspects of the character or "name" of Yahweh. For the meaning of the name is the meaning it was given in Hebrew thought and usage as reflected in Ex. 3:14, 33:19, 34:14 and elsewhere, and not some "basic" meaning derived from the verb hyh.

In v. 19 Yahweh has given the positive answer needed by Moses; Yahweh is to reveal his goodness and mercy and this will answer the problem of Israel's sin. In v. 20, although there is a continuity with v. 19 in that it is the same theophany being treated, there is a significant shift of theme. It has already been noted that the idem per idem formula can terminate the treatment of a particular topic. A change of subject is also indicated by the interposition of a second introductory speech formula.[136] That there is a duality of theme which creates a certain tension in the narrative is important to recognize for a correct understanding of the flow of thought. This may be considered in relation to J. Barr's statement that in Ex. 33,

> the problem which interests the writer is not that of anthropomorphism and transcendence but that of sin and atonement in relation to (a) the accompanying presence

and (b) the vision or appearance of Yahweh.[137]

As the discussion of Ex. 33 as a whole, and of the relationship of 33:18ff. to the preceding intercession in particular, has attempted to show, the fundamental concern is indeed that of sin and forgiveness. But this need not exclude a concern with the question of immanence and transcendence also; or, in other terms, the question of the accessibility of God to man. The juxtaposition of the different uses of <u>pānîm</u>, commented on already, points to such an interest. This interest may arise from the fact that although the theophany is on behalf of sinful Israel, it is revealed to Moses whose relation to Yahweh is not disturbed by sin. One could say that v. 19 presents the theophany as it relates to the moral character of Yahweh in relation to Israel's sin, while vv. 20-23 concern the access to God by mortal man and the limitations imposed by human finitude as such. Even when man's relation to God is not hindered by sin, which is the fundamental cause of Yahweh's wrath and his distancing himself from his people, there are still limits upon man's access to God, not because man is inherently sinful but because he is <u>man</u> and not God.

Of course one must <u>not</u> pose this distinction between v. 19 and vv. 20ff. too sharply, either theologically or in terms of the present context. Theologically there is a continuity between the two concerns. The removal of sin must come first, but this leads on inevitably to the question of what approach to, and relation with, God is possible once sin ceases to be the problem. The movement from v. 19, where sin is treated, is smooth and natural theologically. In terms of the narrative vv. 20ff. should not be too sharply separated from v. 19 since the fact that Moses is only permitted a partial or limited vision of God is probably intended to relate to the revelation of the moral character of God so as to convey the meaning that the revelation of the grace and mercy of Yahweh in 33:19, 34:6f. is but a glimpse of the divine character and that the fulness is yet more extensive and profound (cf. Job 26:14).

It is difficult to comment upon the content of 33:20-23 without laying solemnly prosaic hands upon one of the most profound and mysterious passages in the whole OT. The verses use resonant and memorable imagery, such as are clearly intended to appeal to the imagination. The literary impact is poetic. Such an imaginative appeal is all the more striking in the light of the customary reserve of the OT in describing

Yahweh and his activity. The emphasis is usually on the verbal content conveyed by the divine revelation.[138] Yet the singular importance of the context allows the use of a daring anthropomorphism in an attempt to describe the presence and experience of Yahweh in the concrete way characteristic of the Hebrew mind.

33:20-23 recount how Yahweh will so reveal himself to Moses that there will be a genuine revelation and yet it will be but partial, both bringing Moses close and preserving the distance at the same time. This tension is expressed by saying that Moses will see Yahweh's back and not his face. The anthropomorphism here is unparalleled elsewhere in the OT. Yet at the same time it is used with a certain restraint. As Childs puts it,

> Of course, a tremendous anthropomorphism is involved, but the extreme caution with which it is used is an eloquent testimony to the Hebrew understanding of God. Even to be allowed to catch a glimpse of his passing from the rear is so awesome to the man Moses that God himself - note the strange paradox - must shield him with his own hand.[139]

The use of pānîm here recalls the earlier uses in vv. 11, 14, 15 and, as already observed, conveys the paradox inherent in attempts to speak of man's communion with God. Moses can speak with God intimately, "face to face". Yahweh's presence, or "face", in his shrine in the midst of Israel is a real possibility. Moses' request for a fuller divine revelation than hitherto is granted. And yet ... the distance between God and man must be preserved. Even Moses the mediator, whose relationship with God was unparalleled in the OT (cf. Deut. 34:10) must observe the limitations inherent in humanity.[140] In 33:20f. the generalized form "man" (hā'ādām) is used, rather than a specific address to Moses in the second person, so that a general theological point is clearly being made. It is striking how the OT, in this and related passages, resists moves towards mysticism or divinization by insisting on the qualitative and ontological difference between God and man. Yet the paradox is clear in the fact that it is precisely those passages which say that man cannot see or hear God which affirm that just such has indeed happened. So too Ex. 33:20 provides the necessary theological balance to what has preceded.[141]

It is difficult to say why the idea of seeing God's "back" was introduced here. The closest OT parallel is Gen. 16:13, but this is of little help.[142] There is no background of ancient Near Eastern parallels such as could provide a matrix within which, or against which, to interpret its Hebrew contextualization. Most likely the idea of Yahweh's back was introduced for this particular context where Yahweh's "face" is given such prominence, as forming a natural contrast to it, given the licence of the bold anthropomorphism.

It is important to appreciate the way in which the contrast between "face" and "back" is developed. The unmediated impact of the divine face would be fatal. Yet the writer does not say that Yahweh will therefore hide his face or turn his back, for these are customarily figures of speech conveying disapproval.[143] Any static imagery, however, which pictured Yahweh before Moses as a king before his subject or else retained the imagery of 33:11, could hardly describe Yahweh's averting his face without conveying the misleading implications of the idiom. The dynamic imagery of "passing by" avoids this difficulty. It preserves the sovereign freedom and activity of Yahweh and need not describe his turning away, for the picture is rather of Yahweh leading on ahead with man capable only of following and looking on from behind. The splendour of Yahweh is present in all its fulness but Moses needs to be protected from this for his own sake. But as Yahweh dynamically moves on, Moses may look after him and see the "afterglow". Interestingly, the word for Yahweh's "back" (<u>'āḥôr</u>) is not the usual term for "back" in the physical or anatomical sense (<u>gaw</u>, <u>gēw</u>), but more vaguely means "hinder part",[144] thus conveying the idea of a view from behind, while being less explicit about exactly what is seen. As Yahweh presses on ahead Moses can only see the traces left behind. Thus the impact of the imagery is to enhance the qualitative superiority of God over man.

Beyond this general import of the imagery of 33:20-23, there is little that need be said here about other details in the verses. V. 20 states the general principle of God's distance from man; vv. 21-23 tell in concrete terms how Yahweh will make provision for Moses upon the mountain so that he may to some degree see him. There are some similarities to accounts of theophanies elsewhere,[145] but such are only to be expected and do not greatly illuminate the particularities of the present account.

One peculiarity of the present text is that it may envisage the theophany in two parts. First, in v. 21, Moses enjoys the close presence of Yahweh (<u>māqôm 'ittî</u>) and takes his stand in the open, upon the rock (<u>ᶜal-haṣṣûr</u>). In some sense Moses is already with Yahweh. But when the moment of "passing by" comes, Yahweh has to hide and protect Moses within the rock. A similar pattern may be seen in 34:5f. where first Moses stands in Yahweh's presence (34:5a$^{\beta}$)[146] and then subsequently Yahweh "passes by" (34:6a$^{\alpha}$). Each time it is unclear whether an actual chronological sequence is envisaged or whether this is again an attempt to relate the theological tension that Moses was both "with" Yahweh, implying a close relation, and that he was the passive and partial onlooker before the dynamic motion of the divine splendour, in which the gulf between God and man is stressed. But this slight uncertainty does not affect the general tenor of the account which remains clear.[147]

<u>Introduction to Ex. 34</u>

The intensity of 33:12-23, with its deep theological content, forms one of the high points of the narrative. By the end, when Yahweh has so completely taken the initiative and the theophany is evocatively described, one has almost forgotten that this is all part of Yahweh's response to the urgent intercession of Moses on behalf of sinful Israel who have broken the covenant. Yet it is the issue of covenant breaking and renewal which remains fundamental and it is with this that the story continues. Moses' intercession has been met with the response that Yahweh will reveal the grace and mercy which are inherent in his being and which will constitute the basis for the renewed covenant relationship; it remains to tell how this promise is fulfilled. The writer reverts to the straightforward narrative style appropriate for such.

The outline of the material is as follows:

vv. 1-4	Moses' preparations for the theophany.
vv. 5-7	The theophany.
vv. 8-9	Moses' response to the theophany and final prayer.
v. 10	Yahweh's response to Moses' prayer: the renewal of the covenant.
vv. 11-26	Covenant stipulations.
vv. 27-28	The recording of the covenant conditions and the writing on the tablets.
vv. 29-35	Moses' final descent from Sinai.

Ex. 34:1-9

34:1-4 recounts the preparations necessary for the reception of Yahweh's promised theophany. They form an effective contrast with the preceding verses. The change of content is marked by the use of a further introductory speech formula (v. 1a$^{\alpha}$). The mysterious theophany description is balanced by basic, down-to-earth preparations which Moses must carry out. First, Moses is to cut two tablets of stone upon which Yahweh will write in replacement of the first. The tablets have not been alluded to since 32:15f., 19. Because the tablets had written on them those commandments which form the heart of the covenant,[148] and function as witnesses to the covenant, their replacement is an essential part of the renewed covenant. No great attention is drawn to the tablets, beyond the references in vv. 1, 4, 28, because they do not present an issue in themselves. Unlike the question of Yahweh's accompanying presence in his shrine, which was fundamentally challenged by the calf and so is treated at length, the tablets were not inherently connected with the people's sin in the same way; rather, because they contain the basic covenant stipulations, they are only relevant to be mentioned when the question of the existence of the covenant is at issue. Insofar as grounds are established upon which the covenant can be renewed, then the way is also made clear for the replacement of the tablets.

Apart from being commanded to replace the tablets, Moses also receives directions as to how to prepare for the coming theophany. An appreciation of the preparations in 34:1ff. has usually been impeded by the standard source-critical approach which has reconstructed a J theophany account with material drawn from both Ex. 19 and Ex. 34. The close linking of Ex. 34 with Ex. 19 has obscured the distinctive features of each respective account, as a brief comparison will show. First, throughout Ex. 19 the theophany is public.[149] The people are constantly in view; the theophany is for their sake (v. 9), they are to consecrate themselves (vv. 10ff.), they tremble with fear (v. 16), they stand at the foot of the mountain (v. 17), and they are the cause of an extra warning from Yahweh to Moses (vv. 21ff.). In Ex. 34 the people are nowhere in view. Yahweh appears to Moses alone. There is close verbal similarity between 34:3 and 19:12-13a and each time the holiness of the mountain is stressed. But whereas in 19:12-13a detailed directions are given, presupposing some actual danger of the people ascending the mountain, in 34:3 the point is simply that Moses must be alone.

Secondly, in Ex. 19 the phenomena accompanying the theophany are all appropriate (and necessary) for a public theophany. Volcanic and thunderstorm phenomena are widely visible. In Ex. 34, although the cloud is mentioned (34:5a), no stress is laid upon it. The emphasis is on the close, even intimate, presence of Yahweh (34:5a$^{\beta}$ *wayyityaṣṣēb ^{c}immô šām*; whether Moses or Yahweh is the subject of the verb does not affect the point). In the climax of the theophany (34:6) no visible phenomena are mentioned. The details of ch. 34 are all appropriate for a private theophany. Even the partial vision of 33:20-23 is strikingly different from the visible phenomena of Ex. 19, being again more appropriate for the private nature of the occasion.

The theophany itself is recounted in 34:5-7. There are three essential exegetical questions. First, who are the subjects of the verbs (*wytyṣb*, *wyqr'*, v. 5; *wyqr'*, v. 6)? Either Yahweh or Moses could be the subject of each verb. Secondly, how does v. 5 relate to v. 6? Is v. 5 pleonastic when followed by v. 6? Thirdly, how do vv. 5-7 relate to 33:18-23? Vv. 5-7 are not a simple fulfilment of all that is promised in 33:18-23.

In order rightly to answer these questions it is necessary first to appreciate the numerous verbal and substantive links between 34:5-7 and 33:18-23:

v. 5a$^{\alpha}$ wayyēred yhwh be^{c}ānān

cf. 33:18,22. There is no explicit mention of *^{c}nn* in these verses but *kbwd* is customarily linked with *^{c}nn* which surrounds it (cf. Ex. 16:10, 24:15-18), so that reference to the latter may imply the former also.

v. 5a$^{\beta}$ wayyityaṣṣēb ^{c}immô šām

cf. 33:21, hinnēh māqôm 'ittî w^{e}niṣṣabtā ^{c}al-haṣṣûr

34:2b, w^{e}niṣṣabtā lî šām ^{c}al-rō'š hāhār

v. 5b wayyiqrā' b^{e}šēm yhwh

cf. 33:19, w^{e}qārā'tî b^{e}šēm yhwh l^{e}pānêkā

v. 6a wayya^{ca}bōr yhwh ^{c}al-pānāyw

cf. 33:19, '^{a}nî 'a^{ca}bîr kol-ṭûbî ^{c}al-pānêkā

33:22, w^{e}hāyāh ba^{ca}bōr k^{e}bōdî ...^{c}ad-^{c}obrî

v. 6a wayyiqrā' yhwh yhwh

cf. 33:19, w^{e}qārā'tî b^{e}šēm yhwh l^{e}pānêkā

v. 6a 'ēl raḥûm w^{e}ḥannûn

cf. 33:19b, w^{e}hannōtî 'et-'^{a}šer 'āḥōn w^{e}riḥamtî 'et-'^{a}šer '^{a}raḥēm

1) If one allows the context to have due weight then these parallels make clear that Moses is to be taken as the subject of wytyṣb (v. 5) and Yahweh as the subject of wyqr' (vv. 5, 6). Although this means that there is alternation of subject among the three verbs of v. 5, this need not be too difficult if the writer considers that the context will make his meaning clear. There is no inherent objection to Yahweh being the subject of wytyṣb. After the anthropomorphism of 33:21-23, this anthropomorphism would be mild, and is attested else- where.[150] But when the verb for "standing" (nṣb in 33:21, 34:2, yṣb in 34:5) has been used hitherto only of Moses, and that in the context of what Moses will do on the mountain top, it is most natural to take v. 5 as the fulfilment of what has been directed. Likewise, if Moses was the subject of wykr' in v. 5 this would accord with the usage of the formula qr' bšm yhwh elsewhere in the OT. One could then interpret v. 5a as an anticipative summary of vv. 6-7, with v. 5b looking forward to vv. 8-9. Not only, however, does the flow of the narrative in v. 6 demand that Yahweh should be the subject of wyqr',[151] and it would be difficult to have a different subject for wyqr' in v. 5, but also the clear instance in 33:19a of Yahweh as subject of the formula qr' bšm ywhw must be decisive for interpreting Yahweh as the subject of wyqr' in both v. 5 and v. 6.

2) The relation of v. 5 to v. 6 has already been raised in the discussion of 33:21-23,[152] and nothing need be added here once it is appreciated that it is the same "two-stage" theophany being described in both contexts. In v. 5b wyqr' does not envisage a proclamation different from that of v. 6. By using the same formula as in 33:19 it functions as showing that the theophany is the fulfilment of the promise in 33:19. It also states in introductory form what vv. 6f. will explain and expand - the meaning of the name of Yahweh.

3) There are two main factors which make 34:6f. different from 33:18ff. First, the theophany of 33:21-23 is not recounted as such. There is no reference made to visible phenomena (apart from the cloud of v. 5a), nor to Moses seeing anything. Secondly, the content of v. 7b is to do with judgment, a theme apparently absent from 33:19. These differences probably arise largely from the demands of the developing narrative. When the verbal links make clear that 34:5ff. is the fulfilment of 33:19ff. it would be poor style to repeat the details of 33:21-23 when nothing of substance could be added to them; the reader is to take for granted that Yahweh did what he said he would do.

Moreover it has been seen that the central theme of 33:20-23 is not that of sin and forgiveness but a further issue arising out of it, that of the degree of proximity to God which man may attain when sin is no longer at issue. This has, however, already been sufficiently treated by the writer in ch. 33. The narrative must return to a concern with the prior and more urgent problem of sin and forgiveness, and its relation to the covenant with Israel. To dwell further on Moses' access to God would detract from this. Therefore the writer excludes it.

The judgment theme of 34:7b is not wholly lacking in 33:19 inasmuch as the formula used there has been seen to leave open the freedom of Yahweh to be merciful as he chooses in a way that cannot be presumed upon. The real possibility of incurring judgment is implicitly present in 33:19. Furthermore, the context of Ex. 32-34 as a whole, in particular the judgment theme of 32:15-33:11, shows that the experience of divine wrath in all its seriousness is a real possibility for Israel. Both 33:19 and 34:6f. strongly emphasize the mercy of God, yet do so in such a way as not to deny or abrogate his wrath and judgment. The point is not that the people experience either wrath or mercy, but that both wrath and mercy are in the character of God though it is his mercy which is ultimately predominant in his dealings with his people.

It is unnecessary for present purposes to offer detailed examination of the terminology employed in 34:6f., the general meaning being clear.[153] It is worth noting, however, that K.D. Sakenfeld, who has provided the most recent treatment of one of the key terms, ḥesed, says that the meaning of ḥesed in 34:6f. may be interpreted as signifying that Yahweh is "so great in faithfulness that he is willing even to forgive breach of relationship".[154] This accords well with the theology of the section.

The theological significance of 34:6f. can be best appreciated through a comparison with Ex. 20:5f. Since 34:6f. is usually taken as the primary form of a cultic formula upon which 20:5b-6, together with many other passages elsewhere in the OT which echo the formula, is secondarily dependent, 20:5b-6 has been interpreted in the light of 34:6f. rather than vice versa. If one retains the textual order as the basis for interpreting the interrelationship between the two passages, three points emerge. First, the sequence of the two poles of judgment and mercy is reversed, mercy being put first in Ex. 34. Secondly, the mercy theme is greatly expanded in Ex. 34 over the basic statement of 20:6a. Thirdly, and perhaps most significantly, the stipulation of an obedient response on the part of Israel as the condition for receiving Yahweh's ḥesed (20:6b "to those who love me and keep my commandments") is absent from 34:6f. In the context of Yahweh's reaction to Israel's sin of Ex. 32 this is of fundamental importance, for it means that Yahweh's mercy towards Israel is independent of their responding in the right way. Even when Israel is disobedient it is still the recipient of the divine goodness. The comparison with 20:5f. shows pointedly how profound a statement of God's grace is contained in 34:6f.

Moses' response to this revelation of God is in two parts. First, he bows down and worships. Such is the appropriate response of man before God. In addition to this Moses offers one final prayer. This prayer gathers together major themes from the preceding narrative:

9a$^{\alpha}$, 'im-nā' māṣātî ḥēn b^{e}^{c}ênêkā '^{a}dōnāy; cf. 33:12-17. Formally the usage of the idiom is akin to the merely deferential introduction to a request. Yet to this, as to 33:13a, the use in 33:12b lends a potentially more significant nuance. As in 33:12ff. Moses' special position is the basis of his prayer.

9a$^{\beta}$, yēlek-nā' '^{a}dōnāy b^{e}qirbēnû; the use of bqrbnw echoes 33:3,5 with its reference to the shrine. Since 33:3,5 were taken up in Moses' intercession of 33:12ff., one may see here a further reference back to this earlier intercession. This is supported by the use in 34:9a$^{\beta}$ of the verb hlk which was used in 33:14, 15,16 whereas in 33:3,5 ^{c}lh was used.

9b$^{\alpha}$, kî ^{c}am-q^{e}šēh-^{c}ōrep hû'; cf. 32:9, 33:3,5. This is the most significant phrase and will be discussed below.

9b$^{\beta}$, w^{e}sālaḥtā la^{ca}wōnēnû ûl^{e}ḥattā'tēnû ûn^{e}ḥaltānû; there are no special links between these words and the preceding narrative, although ḥt' has been used several times (32:30,31,33, cf. 32:21). It is of note that Moses seeks not only forgiveness but also the positive restoration of Israel in a right relation under Yahweh such as is implied in being taken as Yahweh's possession.[155]

It is perhaps initially a little surprising that Moses prays for Yahweh's presence in the shrine again, after the favourable response in 33:17 to his earlier intercession.[156] Yet it is not inappropriate, since the logic of prayer and petition is not that of sober discourse, and repetition and assurance play an important role. Moreover this request is not identical to that in 33:12-17. There the shrine was sought and given, but it brought the potential danger of Yahweh's renewed judgment, which had to be met by something further, the revelation of God's character as gracious and merciful. This has now been given. So Moses links these two things in his prayer, "Let the Lord, I pray, go in the midst of us ... and forgive our iniquity and sin". It is for God's presence and forgiveness together that Moses prays.

The most crucial words in the prayer are the reference to Israel as a stiff-necked people. Each of the three previous occurrences of this phrase has been at an important moment in the narrative. Each time it has been made the explicit reason for Yahweh's judgment upon Israel. In 32:9f. it is the reason why Yahweh purposes to destroy the nation. At 33:3 Yahweh will not go in the midst of the people because (ky) they are stiff-necked. At 33:5, apart from the emphatic repetition of the impossibility of Yahweh going with the people, it is made the reason why Yahweh despoils Israel, as the Egyptians were despoiled. What is remarkable about the phrase in 34:9 is that not only is it used in the context of Yahweh's mercy, after the theophany, but, apparently, it is the reason for Yahweh's mercy to be experienced in the restoration of the shrine in Israel's midst as a sign of the renewed covenant, since the connective particle ky is commonly causative in force. One is thereby presented with the paradox, verging on contradiction, that the same factor, the sin of Israel, which causes Yahweh's wrath, also brings about his mercy.

The interpretation of the particle ky is clearly of great significance; yet it is problematic. There are at least three possible ways of construing it.[157] 1) It may be causative, "for", or "because". Not only is this its most common meaning, but it has already been used in this sense in conjunction with "stiff-necked people" in 33:3. Since 34:9 presupposes this earlier usage, and since a word play on a particle may be deemed to be unlikely, this would suggest the same causative sense in 34:9 as in 33:3.[158] 2) The particle may be concessive, "although". This is less common than the causative sense but is still attested.[159] It is preferred by several translations (e.g., RSV, NIV, Childs, Exodus, p. 602). 3) The particle may be an emphatic concessive, to be rendered "however much" or "although indeed". This is argued for by Vriezen[160] whose German rendering is "wie sehr auch". Such an interpretation is conveyed in JB and NEB.

Of these renderings the straightforward concessive has least to commend it. It is adopted on account of the apparent inappropriateness of the causative sense. But when it is indisputable that some paradox is intended, the concessive tends to evade the issue. Between the causative and emphatic concessive senses it is harder, but perhaps less important, to choose. Both draw attention to the fact that Israel still is stiff-necked, and the stress on this is the important factor. Probably the emphatic concessive offers the best English rendering - "Although they are indeed a stiff-necked people, yet forgive ...".

The paradox is striking. Superficially, it would seem to mean either that Yahweh is inconsistent or that one should "sin in order that grace might abound". Closer consideration, in the light of the context and theological emphases discerned thus far, shows this phrase to contain a theology of the grace of God unsurpassed in the OT. A central concern of Ex. 32-34 is sin and forgiveness. When Israel sins, can this mean the end of the covenant? If not, then on what terms can the covenant be renewed and continue? The answer of 34:9 is that the terms lie entirely in the character of God. The point that is made by the forceful ky is that Israel has not changed but remains as sinful as at the time of making the calf. Any change which could herald something other than their being cast off must therefore be on the part of God. The people remain sinful; yet not only do they receive from God the judgment they deserve, but also they receive the grace and mercy they do not deserve. God will show mercy, a mercy experienced supremely in his accompanying presence, because it lies within the character of God not only to inflict judgment but also to show mercy - even to a continuingly sinful people.

This interpretation of 34:9 is supported by the fact that nowhere in 32-34 is any reference made to a repentance of Israel which might occasion Yahweh's renewed favour. It has already been noted[161] that the mourning of 33:4 is remorse rather than repentance, and nowhere else is any word for repentance, such as šwb or nḥm, used of Israel. The lack of repentance supports the interpretation that Israel is continuingly sinful - yet it is to such that Yahweh is merciful.

The connection in 34:9 between Yahweh's going in the midst of the people and the fact that they are still a stiff-necked people reflects the same concern as is in 33:12-17, 18-23 where the problem is that if the shrine were to be in the midst of Israel then Yahweh might be provoked again to wrath against a sinful people. The answer was seen to be in a deeper revelation of the character of God. 34:9 takes this further, in the light of the actual revelation, by posing the same problem and inverting it through pleading Israel's sin as in some sense the reason why Yahweh should go with Israel and forgive them. The same point is made as in 33:19, but in more striking and paradoxical form. Not only is it the character of God to be merciful, but it is precisely to the sinful who ought to be destroyed that this mercy is extended. The theme of the grace and mercy of God, already set forward in 32:14, 33:19, 34:6f., is brought to its climax in 34:9.

The bold theological conception of 34:9, although unsurpassed, is not unparalleled in the OT. It occurs in one other passage also, in the context of the flood narrative of Gen. 6-9. It can be seen in the juxtaposition of Gen. 8:21 with Gen. 6:5. Gen. 6:5 gives the reason why Yahweh brings the flood, that is the evil of man's heart, and Gen. 8:21 tells why in future Yahweh will show mercy:

6:5, wkl-yṣr mḥšbwt lbw rq r^{c} kl-hywm
8:21, ky yṣr lb h'dm r^{c} mn^{c}ryw

The wording is less emphatic in 8:21 than in 6:5 - kl, rq, kl-hywm are omitted. This is appropriate in the context of ch. 8 where the nature of man need not be dwelt on in the same way as in ch. 6. But the basic point remains the same. Here there is the same paradox as in Ex. 34. The cause of God's judgment apparently becomes the cause of his mercy - the same ky is used in Gen. 8:21 as in Ex. 34:9. That the ky clause in Gen. 8:21 is meant to have the same force as in Ex. 34:9 can hardly be disputed, once the parallelism is seen.[162] The paradox in Genesis has often been noted,[163] that in Exodus occasionally.[164] But hitherto no interpretation of both together has been offered.

In addition to the parallel paradox in Gen. 8:21 and Ex. 34:9, other parallels between the flood and Sinai narratives can be seen.

1) The overall structure of Ex. 32-34 is sin and judgment followed by mercy and renewal. So too in the flood narrative.[165]

2) Throughout Ex. 32-34 the favoured position of Moses before Yahweh is a constant factor. So too does Noah enjoy a favoured position from start to finish.

3) Noah's favoured position marks the specific turning point in the story, Gen. 8:1; God remembers Noah and then the waters begin to recede.[166] Similarly one may see Ex. 33:11a as the specific turning point in Ex. 32-34; hereafter God reveals his

mercy.
4) Only in Gen. 6:8, Ex. 33:12 is it said absolutely of an individual that he "found favour in the sight of Yahweh".[167] Noah and Moses are unique in their standing before God.
5) In each narrative the final revelation of Yahweh's paradoxical mercy is the result of the chosen man's intercession, the prayer of Moses (Ex. 34:9), and the sacrifice of Noah (Gen. 8:20).

This striking similarity between the flood and Sinai, between Noah and Moses,[168] is of great theological significance for the interpretation of each story. For each story is a critical moment. First the future of the world, then the future of Israel is in the balance. The world, while still in its infancy, has sinned and brought upon itself Yahweh's wrath and judgment. Israel has only just been constituted a people, God's chosen people, yet directly it has sinned and incurred Yahweh's wrath and judgment. Each time the same question is raised. How, before God, can a sinful world (in general) or a sinful people, even God's chosen people (in particular), exist without being destroyed? Each time the answer is given that if the sin is answered solely by the judgment it deserves, then there is no hope. But in addition to the judgment there is also mercy, a mercy which depends entirely on the character of God and is given to an unchangingly sinful people.

And not only this. Both Ex. 32-34 and the flood narrative contain another theological paradox that God's mercy, given to a sinful people and dependent on himself alone, is yet mediated through a man. Obviously the role of Noah as mediator is rudimentary in comparison with that of Moses, yet it is Noah's special position that ensures that man will not be totally destroyed (Gen. 6:8), God remembering Noah is the turning-point of the story (Gen. 8:1), and God responds to the acceptable sacrifice of Noah as to the prayer of Moses (Gen. 8:20f.). Both narratives display the same theological tension that on the one hand God's mercy is shown to continuously sinful man and is dependent upon himself alone, and on the other hand this mercy is shown through a man who is chosen by God and whose right response to God, whether through sacrifice or prayer, constitutes the necessary medium through which this mercy is shown.

It is clear, then, that Ex. 32-34 is a profound interpretation of the basis of Israel's existence as the chosen people of God. No sooner are they constituted as such than they sin and deserve to forfeit their position. They do not forfeit it, but henceforth Israel is as dependent as the rest of the world upon the mercy of God. Yet it is through the faithful man of God that this mercy is given. God's mercy does not override man, but man is given an indispensable role within God's purposes. Such is the understanding of Yahweh's dealings with his people expressed by Ex. 32-34.

Ex. 34:10

After Moses' prayer, Yahweh's final answer is given; the covenant is renewed. The connection of v. 10 with what precedes is generally considered to be somewhat loose. Certainly this is the first time in Ex. 32-34 that the technical term for covenant, berît, is used. But this is because the narrative is concerned not with the word but with the content of what actually constitutes the relationship with God, and this is supremely two things: God's presence in his shrine and his laws. God's words in 34:10 bring these two together, for that Israel should have God's presence (34:9a) and his laws (34:11ff.) means that they are in a covenant relationship. When God grants these, he thereby renews the covenant.

The specific designation "covenant" is in fact prepared for in the last word of v. 9, ûn^{e}ḥaltānû. Being Yahweh's possession is very much a covenantal idea, implying the status of a vassal under its overlord.[169] Moses effectively prays that Yahweh should renew the covenant relationship. And Yahweh does.

There is some uncertainty over who is the addressee in v. 10. In v. 10a it is clearly Moses; the people are "your people" (^{c}amm^{e}kā).[170] The LXX reads ego tithēmi soi diathēkēn, thus making Moses the primary recipient of the covenant. This agrees with v. 27, but is probably not original to v. 10a. It is, however, not out of keeping with the flow of v. 10a. In v. 10b, by contrast, it seems that Israel is the addressee. It is more natural to think of Israel rather than Moses as being in the midst of other peoples, and the final "with you" (immāk) reads more easily as Israel.[171]

That there should be a transition from Moses to Israel is in fact appropriate. For Moses is being addressed on behalf of Israel to whom he is to proclaim the following covenant stipulations, and so, in a sense, Israel is being addressed through Moses. The reference to "all the earth and every nation" enables a smooth transition to Israel the people as addressee. Moreover, the shift to Israel in v. 10 enables a smooth transition to the paraenesis of vv. 11ff., which is all in the second person singular, as was the decalogue, and which is for the benefit of Israel rather than Moses.

The interpretation of v. 10 depends on the meaning given to the "marvels" (npl'wt) and the "fearful thing" (ky-nwr' hw') which Yahweh is to do. These words customarily refer to Yahweh's mighty acts bringing salvation to Israel and judgment on her enemies,[172] and if that is their significance here then the meaning would be that Yahweh will resume his acts of salvation on behalf of his covenant people. This is a possible interpretation.

An alternative rendering may, however, be preferable. This is that the significant statement is "Behold, I make a covenant", and the rest of the verse simply sets out the unique and marvellous nature of this fact. There is no exact parallel elsewhere to a "fearful thing" in the singular (v. 10b), and it is something Yahweh does with (ᶜm) his people.[173] This suggests that it is the fact of covenant renewal with a sinful people which is the "fearful thing". The work of Yahweh which people will see is the restoration of sinful Israel. If this is so then "marvels" would have a similar meaning - the marvellous acts of mercy and restoration. This slightly unusual sense is not impossible for the renewal of the covenant with a sinful people can be seen as the quintessence of Yahweh's wonderful acts. It is notable that the unusual word br' is used in 10a, a word which suggests that "that which Yahweh creates has the character of the wonderful, of the entirely new".[174] The restoration of Israel could well be so described. The verbs in the verse, the imperfect 'eᶜᵉseh (10a) and the participle (ᶜōśēh) refer either to that which is at present happening or is conceived of as imminent. Since the participle kōrēt is probably a present tense, a similar meaning is likely for ᶜōśēh as well: as Yahweh renews the covenant, he is in the process of doing something marvellous. That Yahweh makes the covenant "before all your people" reflects the fact that this action is being done on Mt. Sinai with Israel encamped around below.

If this analysis is correct one may paraphrase the verse thus. The renewal of a covenant with a sinful people is something quite without parallel in history (v. 10a). It will, therefore, constitute a powerful testimony to the character of God and the nature of his dealings with people (v. 10b).

Finally, the significance of 34:10 thus interpreted is further enhanced by a comparison with 20:2, the introduction to the first law-giving. There the introduction is factual in form, recounting that sequence of events which led up to, and formed the basis for, the following decalogue. In keeping with the context there is no unnecessary elaboration of the point. But the context of 34:10, which serves as an introduction to the laws of vv. 11-26, is quite different - the sin of Israel has intervened. That God should again make a covenant and give laws to such a people is now not simply stated but is appropriately designated as an unparalleled marvel.

Ex. 34:11-26

The statement that the covenant is being renewed is followed by an exposition of the stipulations which are integral to it. First, there is a general paraenesis (vv. 11-16), then a series of detailed prescriptions (vv. 17-26). A detailed treatment of the laws lies beyond the scope of the present task where the purpose is to determine their literary and theological function within the development of the narrative.[175] A few brief observations must suffice.

The inclusion of a legal corpus at this point may be objected to on both literary and theological grounds. The literary argument is that the inclusion of the laws destroys the flow of the narrative. Far from prolonging the climactic moment of covenant renewal, it seems to deaden it. For most modern readers this may well be the case. Nonetheless, as argued above,[176] the laws are of great importance for the writer and his conception of what matters in the story. It might also be said that the feeling that the laws are anti-climactic is largely a cultural difficulty. A Jew who delighted in Torah might well find the objection difficult to grasp.

Theologically the propriety of this legal corpus here has been queried by Driver and McNeile. Driver cites with approval McNeile's comment that a fresh body of laws is not required because

> a covenant having been formed (24:7f.), and based upon laws which are given earlier in the book (20:22-23:33), and then having been broken by sin, all that can conceivably be required is repentance and forgiveness. The original covenant laws must unalterably hold good.[177]

This is insensitive to the seriousness of the sin of Israel and the writer's awareness of Israel's continuingly sinful nature. The point of these laws is not to renew the covenant on conditions different from those previously obtaining (Ex. 20-24) - their continuing validity is taken for granted - but to select and emphasize those particular aspects which are relevant to the sinful tendencies which Israel has displayed. That is, Israel has been unfaithful to Yahweh and sinned against the first two commandments of the decalogue in particular,[178] and both the paraenesis and the prescriptions of 34:11-26 are, in different ways, more or less relevant to the observation of these same commandments. That is why the laws of 34:11-26 are cultic in emphasis. The first two commandments are cultic commandments and Israel's sin with the calf was a cultic sin. As Yahweh renews the covenant he does so by demanding obedience in the area where Israel has already failed and where it will be under continual temptation in the promised land to sin again.

Theologically the demand for Israel's obedience at this point is of significance. For it comes directly after the exposition of the mercy of Yahweh which is as absolute and unconditional as it could be. Without any sense of incongruity the writer juxtaposes with this a strong demand for total obedience on the part of Israel. The writer thus reveals a striking understanding of "faith and works". On the one hand Israel's position is entirely dependent upon Yahweh and Moses and in no way upon themselves; even their sin does not forfeit their position. On the other hand they can only live as the people of Yahweh if they faithfully obey him in all they do. Theologically it is not a case of "either - or" but of "both - and".

The paraenesis of vv. 11-16 starts by looking ahead to the fact that Yahweh is going to lead the people into the promised land. As mentioned above, the assumption that once the covenant making at Sinai is complete the people are to move on into the promised land underlies the narrative. It is appropriate therefore to take up the theme here, particularly because it raises what is likely to be the next moment of acute temptation for Israel to apostasize from Yahweh, the time of contact with the culture and religion of Canaan.

The wording, "Behold I will drive out ..." (hinnî gōrēš) is significant in the light of what has preceded. The promise of 23:20ff. was that the angel, mediating the presence of Yahweh himself, would lead the people as they moved on. After Israel's sin, not only would the angel no longer mediate Yahweh's presence in the same way as before, but the crucial issue became the restoration of Yahweh's presence in the shrine in the midst of Israel. Now Israel's sin has been dealt with, the covenant renewed, and permission to build the shrine restored. Therefore the future guidance of Israel is no longer a problem. Because Yahweh is in the midst of Israel he can also lead them and fight for them. To stress the point, the angel is not mentioned here even though it would fully mediate the divine presence again, since after 32:34, 33:2f. it might still be taken to imply a "second-best". None but Yahweh himself (hnny) will fight for the people.

Vv. 12-16 present a strong demand for exclusive commitment to Yahweh alone. This is not a novel element within Ex. 32-34 since this demand is a presupposition for Israel's sin in Ex. 32. In particular it has been seen that in 32:25-29 there is a "deuteronomic" theology of faithfulness to Yahweh. This aspect of the covenant commitment is more fully developed in the present context.

34:14 is an important verse. The comparison of 34:14b with 20:5b$^{\alpha}$ shows a development and expansion of the earlier text not dissimilar to that in the relationship of 34:6f. to 20:6:

34:14: ky yhwh qn' šmw 'l qn' hw'
20:5: ky 'nky yhwh 'lhyk 'l qn'

The basic principle is enunciated in the context of the decalogue. It is now reiterated in far more emphatic form, as was the principle of Yahweh's ḥesed, because of the situation obtaining after Israel's sin. Nowhere else in the OT is Yahweh's "jealousy" made so emphatic (compare Deut. 4:24, 6:14f., Josh. 24:19f.). The fact of Israel's unfaithfulness calls forth the emphatic restatement that such unfaithfulness is incompatible with the nature of Yahweh,[179] and therefore with being Yahweh's covenant people. Faithfulness to Yahweh must be all or nothing. This develops the writer's theological balance mentioned above. On the one hand Yahweh's mercy is revealed more fully than hitherto, but on the other hand his demand upon Israel is likewise intensified.

One other interesting feature in v. 14 is its reference to "another god" ('l 'ḥr) in the singular.[180] This singular is unique in the OT, the customary designation being plural, 'lhym 'ḥrym. It is possible that this reflects the specific sin with the calf in ch. 32, for which the generalizing plural would be slightly less appropriate. The fact that the calf was designated with a plural verb and demonstrative in ch. 32 does not tell against this, since that was the most effective way in context of conveying the pagan nature of the occasion.

The laws which follow in vv. 17-26 are to be understood as an illustration of the general principles of vv. 11-16. They seek to ensure purity of theological meaning and ritual practice within the cult of Israel. It is true that there is little explicit reference to a concern for purity in vv. 17-26, but this can be seen as a further case where the writer assumes that the context will make his meaning clear. The context of vv. 11-16 has set forward the distinctiveness of Yahwism from Canaanite religion in strong terms. If there is a close connection between vv. 11-16 and vv. 17-26, and such a connection is evident at least in v. 17, then the way to interpret the laws would naturally be in terms of their being a detailed application of the general principles preceding.[181]

If it may be attempted to reconstruct the writer's theological understanding as reflected in vv. 11-26 without, I hope, "simply producing a modern midrash",[182] the pattern of thought may be roughly as follows.

Israel's sinful tendency to compromise its commitment to Yahweh and to express its faith in the symbols of the surrounding religious culture rather than in the way prescribed by Yahweh has already become evident even while the people are still at Sinai. Now that the covenant is being renewed the people are to move on to the land of Canaan which Yahweh has promised to give them (v. 11). But here the pressure to form treaties with the Canaanites, with the inevitable adoption of, or at least accommodation to, alien religious practices (vv. 12,15), will lead to a religious compromise unacceptable to Yahweh who demands exclusive commitment from his people (vv. 13,14). The temptations in Canaan will be far greater than those experienced at Sinai. They must therefore be resisted uncompromisingly if Israel is to survive as the people of Yahweh (v. 13). Even social intercourse leading to inter-marriage will be destructive of commitment to Yahweh and must be rejected (v. 16).

It is one thing to enunciate general principles. It is another to work them out in practice. It is in official cultic worship that Israel's commitment to Yahweh is necessarily focussed and finds its true expression. Therefore the details of this worship, or at least a representative selection of them,[183] must be carefully prescribed so that Israel's worship may be true to Yahweh. It is important in the first instance that there should be no cultic idols, for such idols, like the calf, are antithetical to the basic nature of Yahweh's revelation of himself (v. 17). This practical prescription for true worship is made that much more difficult by the fact that there will inevitably be certain formal similarities between the cultic worship of Israel and that of the Canaanites. Although the Canaanite mode of worship is to be rejected, the framework of feasts through the year is a right and necessary pattern of worship for a people who will be living in an agricultural society (vv. 18,22,23). Since Yahweh is the giver of the land (v. 24), it is right for the people to offer back to him the fruits of the land. The meaning of these feasts will be different for Israel than for the Canaanites. The feast of unleavened bread will no longer be of purely agricultural significance but will recall Yahweh's acts of salvation on behalf of Israel (v. 18c).

Despite the rejection of Canaanite practices, it must be stressed that Yahweh makes no less demand upon Israel than the Canaanite gods do upon their adherents. Although Yahweh does not require human sacrifice, the first and best of Israel is his by right (vv. 19,20). The need to provide an offering for Yahweh (v. 20b$^{\beta}$) does not mean that work must override Yahweh's provision for rest (v. 21). The other two major festivals of the year, in addition to that of unleavened bread, are also to be observed (v. 22), as part of the general principle of regularly coming before Yahweh in worship (v. 23). There need be no practical difficulty over coming before Yahweh at festival time because Yahweh is God of the land and will protect a man's inheritance during his absence (v. 24). An appendix of four brief cultic commandments is added to stress the importance of correct Yahwistic practice at the festivals (vv. 25,26).

This outline is not the only way to interpret these laws, and its accuracy in detail is secondary to the task of showing at least a certain overall coherence in the selection of the laws. A few points of detail do, however, require further elaboration in support of the outline offered.

First, it is notable that the prohibition which stands first, in the position of importance, relates specifically to the sin of Israel in Ex. 32. This emerges the more clearly from a comparison with the parallel in Ex. 20:4.

34:17: '^{e}lōhê massēkāh lō' ta^{ca}śeh-lāk
20:4: lō' ta^{c}aseh l^{e}kā pesel

The more general term psl is replaced by mskh.[184] In Ex. 32

Israel's sin has been to make a molten calf (ᶜgl mskh) to which they refer as 'lhym (32:4). The specific prohibition of 'lhy mskh relates to the sinful tendency towards false worship already displayed.

Secondly, the inclusion of the dedication of the firstborn to Yahweh makes sense as an example of the distinction to be preserved between Yahwism and Canaanite religion even when there are similarities. Canaanite religion could involve the practice of sacrificing not only the firstborn of animals but also a firstborn son.[185] Such a human sacrifice is incompatible with Yahwism. But the point is that Yahweh demands no less than the Canaanite gods, and so if he chooses to forego his claim then the Israelite must still remember that his son is to be redeemed and belongs to him not by right but by gift. Yahweh's authority over life is emphasized by the statement that the firstborn of animals are all his.

The offering of the firstborn is also mentioned in Ex. 13:2,12f. Here Yahweh's right to the firstborn is connected with his having slain the firstborn of Egypt but spared the firstborn of Israel. Although not made explicit in 34:19f. this tradition is probably presupposed. This is suggested by its placing after the reference to the exodus in v. 18c. Israel's response to Yahweh is characteristically linked with the tradition of Yahweh's saving acts.

Thirdly, the positioning of the sabbath commandment may well be to deal with a possible difficulty occasioned by the demand of v. $20b^{\beta}$, in a way not dissimilar to the link between v. 24 and v. 23. The importance of providing an offering for Yahweh could be taken to imply a need at times to neglect Yahweh's provision for rest if the offering is to be brought. V. 21 denies that this should be the case. Even at the important times of ploughing and harvest rest is to be observed. This observance of rest will not mean that the Israelite will not be able to bring a sufficient offering at the requisite times. On the contrary, it will ensure it.

Fourthly, a possible link between 34:26b and the Ugaritic text 1.23:14 has long been noted. This Ugaritic text, taken to refer to boiling a kid in milk, would suggest that the force of the Hebrew prohibition lies in an anti-Canaanite polemic; even though Israel is to keep the same feasts as the Canaanites, their ritual practice at the feast is to be different - perhaps specifically in the rejection of fertility magic.

In three recent studies,[186] both the generally accepted

restoration of the Ugaritic text and the cultic interpretation of the text as a whole have been seriously questioned, and it now appears that the parallel with the biblical injunction is invalid.[187] Haran argues that the point of the biblical text is to prevent a practice considered morally revolting on the basis of humane considerations. But even if this is correct, some implication of anti-Canaanite polemic may not be entirely lacking in the biblical precept, in accordance with the tenor of the laws as a whole.

Ex. 34:27-28

We see in vv. 11-26 that as the covenant is renewed Yahweh demands faithfulness to himself as a necessary part of the covenant. Vv. 27-28 then bring to a conclusion Moses' sojourn on Mt. Sinai. A permanent written record of the covenant is to be provided, to serve as a reminder and witness in the future.[188]

These two verses may at first sight appear to be straightforward. God tells Moses to write down the laws he has just given, and Moses complies. Such would be a simple and apparently appropriate conclusion to the preceding narrative. This seemingly "obvious" reading, however, raises two problems when taken in the context of Ex. 34 as a whole.

The first problem arises from the fact that v. 28b specifies that the "ten words" (*^{c}śrt hdbrym*) were written on the tablets, yet v. 27 clearly envisages that the terms for the renewal of the covenant which are to be recorded are those specified in the preceding section, vv. 11-26. And there is no decalogue obviously present in these verses. How then can the "ten words" be related to what precedes?

The second problem lies in the tension created between v. 28b and v. 1b. If Moses is the subject of *wyktb* in v. 28b, how is this to be reconciled with v. 1 where it is said that Yahweh will write upon the tablets? Although one could interpret v. 28b in the light of v. 1 as showing Moses "functioning as the writing finger of YHWH",[189] this is not a natural reading of the text.

It is the first of these problems, in some form, that has most occupied modern scholars since Goethe;[190] what is intended by "the ten words", when they are set in conjunction with vv. 11-26? This will therefore be the best point at which to begin our study of vv. 27-28.

The great majority of scholars have accepted the reference to the "ten words" as original to the text. It is possible that the words are a marginal gloss. If so, they would best be understood as an attempt to express the deuteronomic conception of the decalogue as standing apart from all other laws and constituting by itself the basis of the covenant, a distinction which did not exist in the earlier tradition.[191] The main motive, however, for seeing the words as a gloss is the belief that they do not cohere well with their context.[192] It must therefore be decided whether or not this is actually the case.

Of those scholars who accept "the ten words" as original, some have argued on that basis for the presence of a decalogue in vv. 11-26 as they now stand.[193] Others have argued that, as there is no decalogue to be found in vv. 11-26 the reference to "the ten words" is evidence that a decalogue, identical or similar to that in Ex. 20, did once stand in the text of Ex. 34 but that it was displaced and that the present laws are a substitute for it.[194]

Rather than assess these arguments in detail, two points may be made. First, such is the variety of proposed reconstructions of a decalogue in vv. 11-26 that the whole attempt to find one becomes unconvincing.[195] The situation is in no way comparable to that in Ex. 20 where, although there has always been difficulty over the precise numbering of the decalogue, it has hardly ever been seriously doubted that it is a decalogue with which one is dealing.[196] The laws of Ex. 34 do not, however, look like a decalogue. And were it not for "the ten words" of v. 28 it is unlikely that much attempt would have been made to find one.

Secondly, the proposals for either a present or a displaced decalogue both share one crucial assumption, that v. 28b (what was written on the tablets) is to be read as the fulfilment of v. 27 (what Moses was commanded to write). But is this necessary? The tension between v. 28b and v. 1b has already been noted. In the light of v. 1 it would be possible to read v. 28b with Yahweh, not Moses, as subject.[197] And if Yahweh "wrote", then one would expect him to write something other than what he has just told Moses to write. That is, "the words of the covenant, the ten words" in v. 28b may refer to something other than the laws of vv. 11-26 which Moses is told to write in v. 27. This possibility demands a careful reappraisal of the relationship of v. 28b to v. 27.

In favour of the view that v. 27 and v. 28b are to be taken in close conjunction, with the latter as the fulfilment of the former, there are three main arguments. First, it seems natural in context that v. 28b should specify the carrying out of the preceding command in v. 27 (cf. 34:4 with 34:1). Secondly, there is the use of berith in both verses. Thirdly, since Moses is the subject in v. 28a, he should naturally still be the subject in v. 28b.

In support of the independence of v. 28b from v. 27 there are also good exegetical arguments. First, v. 27 twice designates the words Moses is told to write as "these words" (hdbrym h'lh). In v. 28b what is written is not thus designated, but as "the words of the covenant" and "the ten words". V. 27, by the use of h'lh, clearly identifies the words to be written with the preceding laws of vv. 11-26. But neither "words of the covenant" nor "the ten words" in themselves necessitate identification with vv. 11-26.

Secondly, v. 27 does not mention the tablets of stone whereas v. 28b does. V. 27, in itself, could envisage Moses writing on a scroll or some covenant document (cf. 24:7), while this is excluded in v. 28b.

Thirdly, there is the interposition of v. 28a separating the surrounding references to the covenant. V. 28a reads naturally as the conclusion to the preceding narrative, rounding off the time of Moses' sojourn on Sinai. If Moses is the subject in v. 28b and he is fulfilling the command of v. 27, one would expect the note in v. 28a about the duration of his stay on Sinai to come after v. 28b and not before. V. 28b, coming after v. 28a, reads like an additional note, added to tie up a remaining loose end in the narrative, rather than as a continuation and fulfilment of v. 27. As such, the focus in v. 28b could have moved away from Moses, reference to whom is now complete, to Yahweh.

Fourthly, the alternation of verbal subject in v. 28, changing from Moses as subject in v. 28a to Yahweh as subject in v. 28b, would not be unnatural. A parallel can be seen in 34:5, where there is likewise an alternation of verbal subject. The subject is not specified each time, for it is assumed that the context of the preceding verses makes sufficiently clear who does what. The considerations relevant to interpreting 34:5 can apply also to 34:28.

Fifthly, there is the verbal parallel between v. 1b and v. 28b:

34:1: wktbty ᶜl hlḥwt 't-hdbrym

34:28: wyktwb ᶜl hlḥwt 't dbry hbryt

This verbal parallel is closer than that between v. 27 and v. 28, and argues for interpreting v. 28b in the light of v. 1 rather than v. 27.[198]

The balance of exegetical probability, simply considering v.

28b in relation to v. 28a and v. 27, seems to support the independence of v. 28b from the previous verse. If this is correct, it must further be shown how a reference to Yahweh writing on the tablets something other than the laws of vv. 11-26 would be appropriate at this point in terms of the larger narrative context. This can be seen if one may again conjecture the likely perspective and assumptions of the writer. For, as already argued, the writer of Ex. 32-34 assumes a knowledge of the larger Sinai context and so need only make brief allusions where he considers the meaning to be clear. Thus the writer presupposes that the decalogue was previously given (Ex. 20) and that the decalogue was written by God upon the tablets which were smashed (32:19) but whose replacement, with identical content, was promised (34:1). That is, the writer assumes the tradition made explicit in Deut. 10:1-4 that the tablets (a) contained the decalogue, and (b) were written by Yahweh himself. That the tablets contained the decalogue is not actually specified in so many words anywhere in the Sinai pericope (apart from 34:28!), but this could be because it is taken for granted. Since the only tradition the OT records about the tablets is that the decalogue was on them (unless one interprets 34:28b to the contrary, which is the point at issue), no one would have questioned the tradition and the writer need not make explicit what he considers obvious. That the tablets were written by Yahweh himself is emphasized in 32:15f. and again in 34:1. This suggests that when the writer refers briefly to the tablets in 34:28b, he takes for granted that the reader knows what "the ten words" are and that therefore he would not attempt to find them in vv. 11-26. He further takes for granted that the reader is familiar with 34:1 and the tradition of Yahweh writing on the tablets, and so will naturally read v. 28b as the fulfilment of v. 1, with Yahweh as subject.

The flow of vv. 27-28 is therefore as follows. After Israel's sin with the calf, Yahweh has renewed the covenant with them, presupposing the validity of the laws previously given yet singling out for emphatic repetition those which pertain to the sin of Israel and which must particularly be observed to ensure faithfulness to Yahweh when the covenant relationship is restored. These laws he commands Moses to record. Although the ground for the renewed covenant lies in the gracious character of Yahweh revealed in 34:6f., for Israel's part the covenant is renewed on terms of total faithfulness and loyalty to Yahweh being demanded of them - "in accordance with these words (i.e. the exhortations and laws requiring faithfulness) I have made a covenant ...". This theme is then drawn to a conclusion by the note about the duration of Moses' stay on Sinai and the conditions he endured. The writer then adds a concluding note stating that the decalogue on the tablets, which Yahweh had promised to write again (34:1), was in fact written by him. That these are still the heart of the covenant is taken for granted by the writer who designates them "the words of the covenant". The preceding section has been essentially an exposition, appropriate to the particular situation, of the demand for covenant faithfulness to Yahweh as enshrined especially in the first two commandments. The writer thus adds this note to make clear that in addition to giving the prescriptions for the particular situation of renewal, Yahweh also fulfilled his promise of 34:1 to restore the tablets, which are a witness to all the demands of the covenant. To make clear that these "words of the covenant" are not to be identified with the words of v. 27, the writer adds the clarifying note that the words on the tablets[199] are the already-known "ten words".

There remains one other point of interest in vv. 27-28, and that is the wording that Yahweh is making the covenant "with you and with Israel" (v. 27b, krty 'tk bryt w't-yśr'l). The positioning of "and with Israel" seems awkward. Was the covenant originally with Moses alone, so that "and with Israel" is a later gloss? Or if the reference to Israel is original, why is it placed secondary to Moses?

The first suggestion has little to commend it. On the one hand it disregards the immediate context since there is no reason for Yahweh to make a covenant with Moses "according to these words" when the content of these words is the injunctions and laws concerning faithfulness to Yahweh, which in Moses' case has not been in doubt. On the other hand it disregards the larger context where the problem is that of Israel's covenant relationship and the way Israel has broken the covenant.

The present wording with Israel in secondary position points to an understanding of the renewed covenant as being not only mediated through, but in some sense necessarily dependent upon, Moses. This coheres well with 33:12-17, 34:9 where the special position of Moses is essential to the restoration of Israel. The original covenant-giving was itself mediated through Moses, but was not dependent upon him in the way it now is when Moses alone has stood out against the people's sin. So the position of Israel in the restored covenant is not identical to what it would have been had the people never sinned. Henceforth their life as a people depends not only upon the mercy of God but also upon the intercession of God's chosen mediator. This accords with the fine divine-human balance already observed in the narrative. It also prepares for the closing scene in which the people see the glory of God on the face of Moses.

Ex. 34:29-35

The final scene, 34:29-35, brings the narrative to the quiet close that is a common characteristic of a good story. The presence of God is restored among the people and the previous tensions are resolved.

It is notable how several important themes of the preceding narrative are woven in. First, there is the descent from the mountain, a striking contrast to 32:15ff. Each time Moses descends with the tablets in his hand. But whereas the first time he was confronted by sin and apostasy, now he is met with awe and reverence. A right relation between Yahweh, Moses and the people has been restored.

Secondly the motif of "face" (pānîm), so central in 33:11,12-23, is echoed here. Moses sought not only that Yahweh's "face" should go with the people but that he might see Yahweh's glory. This latter was partially granted. Now the implication is that the Israelites see the glory of Yahweh in the face of Moses. As Moses was not able to see the face of Yahweh, so the Israelites can hardly endure to look on the face of Moses (v. 30); though insofar as Moses is man and not God, and the glory is reflected, they are able to behold him.

Thirdly, there is a contrast with the tent section in 33:7-11 where it was stressed that the people beheld and worshipped from afar off. Now the people can draw close to Moses (vv. 31a, 32a - the repetition may be intended to emphasize the fact of approach), and when Moses goes in and out of the tent (v. 34) no mention is made of the people having to maintain any distance. Since, however, all the emphasis is upon the role of Moses and the people serve as, in a sense, a foil to him, one cannot lay much weight upon this.

Fourthly, there are the significant implications of Moses' shining (literally "horned") face, discussed below.

Apart from these echoes of the preceding narrative, these

verses are important for the central role of Moses. It is a principle of popular narrative that the story should end with reference to the hero, and that is the case here. Although the high points in the course of the narrative focus on Yahweh (33:18-23, 34:6f.) rather more than on Moses (32:30-33), in the final scene it is Moses alone who holds the stage. Again one is aware of the balance between the respective human and divine roles in Ex. 32-34. Both Yahweh and Moses are the central characters. It is the mark of Moses' unique relationship with Yahweh that he is the sole important character in the closing scene, which has no real duality of persons as in some other scenes in the narrative.

The passage not only stresses the status of Moses in himself, but draws attention again to his role as mediator through whom Yahweh's glory is seen (vv. 29,30) and his commandments given (vv. 34f.). It has often been noted that whereas vv. 29-33 recount the single event of Moses' descent and encounter with the people, vv. 34f. are imperfect in tense with a frequentative meaning, describing a recurring situation. The implication is that Moses' mediating role was ongoing. His access to God and receipt of commandments was not limited to the time spent on Mt. Sinai but was a continual reality in the life of the people.

The usual focus of interest in vv. 29-35 has been on two interrelated issues, first the veil (masweh)[200] which Moses puts on and off, and secondly the odd word for shining (qrn, literally "to have horns") used of Moses' face. It has become customary to interpret the veil in terms of the widespread ancient practice of the priest wearing a mask - "the priest assumes the 'face' of his deity and identifies himself with him".[201] Such a mask would commonly have been a horned mask.

There are three difficulties with this. First, such a mask is unattested elsewhere in the OT.[202] Secondly, and more important, the veil here functions in the opposite way to priestly masks, in that Moses takes it off when speaking both to God and to the people and puts it on again only when he ceases to perform his mediatorial function. The present passage can only be assimilated to the practice attested elsewhere at the cost of precisely that element to which the writer draws attention. Thirdly, it is important to be clear at which level one is interpreting the text. Whatever the ancient Near Eastern parallels, there can be little dispute that the text as it now stands is not describing either a priestly mask or horns. In context qrn must mean "shine" and the significance of the mswh must be that of a veil to cover the shining. The parallels are adduced to reveal a traditio-historical development of the story; originally there was a version different from the present which was sometime changed, presumably in the light of later Yahwistic sentiments that such a priestly mask was incompatible with Yahwism.[203] The appeal to priestly masks does not provide an alternative rendering of the present text, but offers an hypothetical account of its origins. This issue lies beyond the scope of the present exegetical task and is discussed later.[204]

The adducing of ancient Near Eastern parallels, is, nonetheless, still of relevance to the exegetical task, for they provide a background against which one's appreciation of the singularity of the present narrative may be enhanced.

It will be helpful to deal with the veil and the "shining"/"horns" separately. First then, the veil. It may well be that the writer's meaning lies in the explicit contrast to a known practice. That is, whereas other gods were represented by a mask with the priest's face hidden, Yahweh uses no such mask but shines directly through the face of his servant. No mask is needed to communicate Yahweh's presence; it is a man and not an object who has the role of mediating Yahweh. That it should be the uncovered face of a man which lets the divine glory shine through reflects the same profound theology of the role of man within the purposes of God as has been discerned elsewhere (cf. also Gen. 1:26). The veil (not a mask for the writer) is only put on when Moses is not speaking either to Yahweh or to the people. No reason is given for this and one can but speculate. The writer either considers it unimportant, the point lying in the fact that the face is uncovered when Moses speaks, or he assumes its significance will be obvious to the reader. Possibly it was to protect the people from too much exposure to the reflected glory of Yahweh. Alternatively (and less likely) it may have been to distinguish those times when Moses spoke as mediator from other occasions when he did not function in this capacity. Either way the nature of the veil is of secondary importance to the point of the glory of God shining in the face of Moses.

The writer's choice of the verb qrn has long been puzzling. On philological grounds the use of qrn in Ex. 34 should mean that Moses had horns[205] yet the context demands the sense of "shine".[206] The question must be asked why the writer chose the unusual qrn when the more common verb 'wr was available. While it is customary to seek religio-historical parallels outside the OT, one need not go so far afield, for a sufficient reason is provided by the context of Ex. 32-34, that is the account of the calf with which the narrative opens. It has already been noted that 32:1-6 implies that the calf was a challenge to Moses and his authority. This closing scene harks back to the opening scene of the story. In the ancient world the power of a bull was frequently symbolized by its horn, indeed, "In cult the horn tends to stand for the bull and to supplant it".[207] The writer's use of qrn, therefore, is a clear echo of the calf and constitutes a daring parallelism of Moses with the calf. It is daring to take the symbol of the false god and use it of Moses, but the true role of Moses has already been made clear to the reader so there should be no danger of misunderstanding.[208] The writer makes the point that Moses was to the people what they wanted the calf to be - a leader and mediator of the divine presence. The fact that Yahweh, and his presence in his shrine, is also this to the people in no way excludes the attribution of a similar significance to Moses, such is the harmony between Moses and Yahweh in the writer's understanding.

The use of qrn is thus most revealing of the writer's method and intention. From a literary point of view the echo in the final scene of a motif in the opening scene constitutes a skilful structuring of the story. Theologically it points again to the importance of Moses as leader and mediator and further highlights the nature of the calf as a gross parody of Yahweh's true intentions for his people.

Conclusion

On this note the narrative of Ex. 32-34 draws to a close. Only one or two observations still need to be made. Although Ex. 32-34 constitutes a coherent and clearly defined unit it has been seen that it does not stand in isolation from the context in Exodus which precedes it, but that there are many links with the narrative elsewhere, including Ex. 25-31. It is right, therefore, briefly to consider Ex. 35-40 also, insofar as these chapters relate to Ex. 32-34.

First, there is the obvious fact that these chapters recount the building of the shrine, that is the tabernacle, which is made possible by the restoration of Israel within the covenant. Perhaps the extensive repetition from Ex. 25-31 reflects the significance of the fact that this construction should be possible at all after Israel's sin.

Secondly, what is of importance in the coming of Yahweh's glory to the tabernacle (40:34f.) is that it serves to extend the Sinai experience,[209] that is, "the presence of God which had once dwelt on Sinai now accompanies Israel in the tabernacle on her desert journey".[210] This is in direct continuity with one of the central themes of Ex. 32-34, that of Yahweh's accompanying presence as the people move on from Sinai. It was this, as a basic part of the covenant relationship, that was jeopardized by Israel's sin, and it is for this that Moses urgently pleaded, that despite the people's sin Yahweh should yet go with the people in a movable shrine and be present in their midst. After Yahweh has granted this prayer of Moses it is right that it should then be told how this was actually carried out. The restoration of Israel is then complete when the covenant is renewed and the empirical symbol of the covenant becomes a reality.

Thirdly, there is a striking emphasis in Ex. 35-40 on the eager readiness of the people to contribute to the work (35:20-29, 36:2-7). No explanation of this is offered within Ex. 35-40. Could it be because of Ex. 32-34? The notable feature that no reference is made to any repentance on the part of the people has been mentioned already. This silence highlights the presentation of Israel's restoration as entirely the work of Yahweh. Could then this picture of the willing offering of the people be intended as their response to what Yahweh has done? It is at least possible that the people's free offering reflects a theological understanding that it is the experience of God's mercy which elicits a true and worthy response on the part of Israel.

In conclusion it may be said that if the exegesis offered here is at least substantially correct, then the importance of Ex. 32-34 emerges in a new light. The chapters can be freshly appreciated as a literary composition of considerable skill and a theological work of great depth.

There remain many questions to be asked concerning the origins and formation of the chapters, the examination of which will now be carried out in the light of the perception of the balance and pattern of the final text, a perception which may well require a re-appraisal of certain existing analyses. But whatever the results of the more speculative task of enquiring behind the text, such a task should not be allowed to detract from the appreciation of the literary and theological achievement which the present text of Ex. 32-34 represents.

Excursus One: Ex. 32:18

The exegetical problem of Ex. 32:18 lies in the interpretation of ^{c}nwt in the third section of the verse. There are basically three approaches that have been adopted.[1]

i) One may retain the MT and its pointing. This means that there is a play between the Qal and Pi. of ^{c}nh, a contrast between noise and some special kind of noise or singing (cf. Is. 27:2, Ps. 88:1).[2]

ii) One may retain the MT, but repoint it. One can then read the name of the goddess Anath.[3]

iii) One can emend the text on the assumption that a word has dropped out. Numerous candidates for the missing word have been suggested, of which a few are: wine/drunkenness, Heb. yyn;[4] harlotry, Heb. znwnym;[5] revelry, Heb. ṣḥwqh;[6] some substantive denoting cultic singers derived from ^{c}nh or a homonym;[7] festival, Heb. ḥg;[8] "in honour of Anath", Heb. l^{c}nt.[9]

It is no easy task to choose between these, but at least one can indicate which alternatives are less unlikely.

i) Estimations of the effectiveness of the word-play vary. Dillmann calls it "das feine Spiel".[10] Edelmann, on the other hand, says that "in his highly emotional outcry Moses would hardly have thought of grammatical subtleties",[11] and Holzinger considers that "Das Wortspiel mit zweimaligen ^{c}^{a}nôt und ^{c}annôt ... ist selbst für einen punktierten Text fast zu dunkel".[12] Given the Hebraic fondness for intricate word-play, and the evidence of word-play elsewhere in Ex. 32-34,[13] the objection to a word-play of this kind here is not very cogent.

ii) The advantage in reading "Anath" is that this apparently fits well with Israel's apostasy in 32:1-6. For Anath was often represented by a cow or heifer. There are, however, two difficulties with this. First, there is no reason to introduce a female deity at this point. The bull-calf was a symbol of male deity, and the bull-calf of 32:1-6 was intended to represent the male deity Yahweh. Secondly the spelling in the MT is ^{c}nwt and not ^{c}nt, and one has to account for the extra *waw*. Simply to say that the extra *waw* "must be a secondary addition made by the *soferim* for some reason"[14] is unsatisfactory. Whybray offers the explanation that *^{c}nwt* represents a dialectical variant of *^{c}nt*, as in Josh. 15:59, *byt-^{c}nwt*. But if this were so, and the pointing were originally *^{c}nwt*, then this third *^{c}nôt* would simply be indistinguishable from the previous two, and there would be no way of telling that it was meant to be the name of a goddess rather than the infinitive of a verb. Or if the spelling were originally *^{c}nt*, there would be no reason subsequently to modify this to a variant spelling which obscured the point - unless it was done by accident or the point had already become obscure. This is not a satisfactory explanation of the *waw*.

iii) The advantage of a textual emendation is that one can provide some definite contrast to the preceding *gbwrh* ... *ḥlwšh*. There would then be no word-play on *^{c}nwt*, but all the emphasis would fall on the missing word. There are two difficulties with this solution. First there is little MSS support for the omission of a word. The variations in the early versions look like attempts to explicate a difficulty rather than evidence for an alternative reading. Secondly, if the whole point of v. 18 depended on this extra word, it is difficult to explain how it could have dropped out of the text. If the word was similar in form to *^{c}nwt*, this might provide an explanation; hence the suggestions of a substantive from a homonym of *^{c}nh*, or *l^{c}nt*. The latter faces the same objection to the mention of a female deity already specified. The former, though attested in Ugaritic, is without parallel in the OT.

Conclusion

Of the three approaches, the proposal to repoint the text to introduce a reference to Anath has least to commend it and may, in my judgment, be discarded. Between the other two it is harder to choose. That a word has fallen out of the text cannot be ruled out. Nonetheless, the retention of the MT and its pointing encounters fewest difficulties and offers a word play which may well have been more effective for an ancient Hebrew audience or readership than it has been since.

Excursus Two: Gen. 8:21

The study of ky in Ex. 34:9 has shown that the particle should have either causative or else emphatic concessive force. Since the paradoxical use of ky in Gen. 8:21 is an exact parallel to that in Ex. 34:9, the meaning of the particle may reasonably be assumed to be identical in each instance. The purpose of this excursus is, therefore, twofold. First, it is to check whether the meaning of Gen. 8:21, decided on the basis of a parallel, can also be sustained by a study of the Genesis passage in its own right. Secondly, the interpretation of Gen. 8:21 in its context, especially when this has been much discussed,[1] will serve as a test for the exegesis of Ex. 34:9 which has not, as yet, been subjected to a similar intensive scrutiny.

The debate about the interpretation of Gen. 8:21 is complex because it has focussed on 8:21 not only in relation to 6:5 but also in relation to the larger context of the primeval history and the curse of 3:17.

The central exegetical problem is whether to construe the ky clause in 8:21 as epexegetic of h'dm or lqll. The former possibility which makes the ky clause descriptive of man, tends to minimize its theological significance, whereas the latter, which makes the clause the reason for Yahweh's decision, sees it as theologically crucial.

That the ky clause is to be taken with h'dm has been argued by Rendtorff, who sees 8:21 as the conclusion of the Yahwistic primeval history which repeals the curse of 3:17 and initiates a new age of blessing; Yahweh will no more treat the earth as accursed as he has done hitherto. The ky clause is of little theological importance since it is retrospective, describing man's state in the past as the cause of judgment, and does not represent a significant post-flood assessment of mankind. The theological emphasis is on the repeal of the curse. Despite illuminating insights in Rendtorff's thesis, the thesis raises serious difficulties, both linguistic and contextual. First, it is dubious to interpret qillēl in a declarative sense ("treat as cursed"), when it does not bear that meaning in its only other occurrence in J (Gen. 12:3). Secondly, the varying position of ᶜwd in 8:21a,b affects its meaning. In 8:21a it qualifies lqll and must mean that the curse remains valid but will not be added to. In 8:21b it qualifies l'-'sp and means that God will not destroy again, will not act in the same way for a second time. Only if ᶜwd qualified l'-'sp in v. 21a could it bear the meaning which Rendtorff attaches to it. Thirdly, the development of Gen. 1-11 as a whole demands the end of the primeval history in ch. 11 and not in ch. 8. A conclusion in ch. 8 would leave chs. 9-11 ill-fitting in their context and would not explain the continuity of the theme of human sin throughout Gen. 3-11.

It remains possible to interpret the ky clause as epexegetic of h'dm without adopting Rendtorff's interpretation. It is difficult to see, then, why it should have been added to its present context. That the clause is a J redactional addition is likely (cf. Westermann) and may be supported by the fact that when it is omitted Yahweh's speech in 8:21 forms two lines in 3:3 rhythm:

l'-'sp lqll ^{c}wd 't-h'dmh b^{c}bwr h'dm
w^{e}l'-'sp ^{c}wd lhkwt 't-kl-ḥy k'šr ^{c}śyty

The lines are slightly prosy but this is not necessarily incompatible with an original verse form, later disturbed by the extra clause. A deliberate insertion of the clause makes the theologically minimalist interpretation unlikely.

Among those who construe the ky clause with lqll there is still no unanimity as to its significance. Petersen considers that the clause constitutes Yahweh's admission of his failure to have achieved his desired end of eliminating sin through the flood and his resolve to try a different way in the future. As such the verse represents the Yahwist's criticism of Yahweh for having resorted to a flood. Such criticism of Yahweh would however be without parallel elsewhere in J or in the whole OT, and while the lack of parallel does not of itself make the criticism impossible, a theologically congruent explanation, which does justice to the text and coheres with the theological emphases of J elsewhere, is to be preferred.

That the ky clause is of deep theological significance is made likely by the fact that it is in one of the divine soliloquies in Genesis, the divine soliloquies in Genesis being consistently revealing of the essence of the Yahwist's theological understanding (cf. MacKenzie). Such a theological significance is developed by Westermann who shows how 8:21 provides the Yahwist's theological interpretation of the preceding judgments in both Gen. 3 and Gen. 6, but especially the latter, in terms of Yahweh being a God who not only punishes man's sin but also patiently bears with it. Instead of actions of judgment and mercy being attributed to different gods, as in Mesopotamian versions of the story, the Yahwist strikingly shows how both these attributes are to be found in one and the same God.

> Im Unterschied zu der polytheistischen Darstellung, in der hinter dieser Wandlung des Entschlusses ein Streit der Götter steht, ist die Wandlung in der israelitischen Darstellung allein in dem Einen begründet. Es gibt keine Macht, die diese Zusage ins Wanken bringen könnte.[2]

Once one has seen the possible significance of the ky clause of 8:21 as a paradox, then an interpretation such as Westermann's must be preferable to interpretations which deny its significance or its paradoxical character. Westermann's interpretation is differently nuanced to that proposed on the basis of Ex. 34:9 for he is concerned to understand the Yahwistic moulding of the story against the Mesopotamian background. Nonetheless there is no significant difference, and his exegesis confirms the interpretation of the clause already proposed.

Chapter 3

EX. 32-34 AS A CULT LEGEND

It is time now to turn from the appreciative study of the text and to approach it analytically, putting questions of an historical-critical nature. It has already been argued that the understanding of the final form of the text must constitute the starting-point for this study. But it will be worthwhile to specify more precisely the nature of the task that lies ahead.

It has been seen that Ex. 32-34 is, in a real sense, a unity. Our task now is to account for that unity and to question how deeply it penetrates the material. Is it the case that there was an ancient tradition containing a sequence from sin and judgment, through intercession, to renewal and that this ultimately accounts for the unity? Or is it the case that originally diverse traditions have been creatively combined and moulded to make the present story? And if so, how far can one reconstruct the process by which this took place?

The present mode of investigation will differ from that generally adopted. For in place of the customary assumption of a compilation of diverse fragments, the heuristic assumption underlying the study will be that of unity. That is, the unity of the material in the course of its development and composition will be assumed until rendered unlikely, rather than vice versa.

Unity will be an heuristic assumption, not an inviolable datum. That is, it is important that one's heuristic assumption should not be subtly transformed into a controlling prejudice, whereby the unity of Ex. 32-34 at the various levels of the tradition becomes less a factor to be analyzed than a case to be demonstrated. The balance becomes particularly hard to maintain when the issue of the possible dependence of theological veracity upon historical content is introduced, for then one has a particular motive for wanting to discover at least a basic coherence in the tradition, such as could reflect a genuine historical sequence. Although ultimately the question of historicity must be put to Ex. 32-34, and the theological implications of the answer assessed, for the present the matter will be left in abeyance, for space does not permit a sufficient resolution of the preliminary literary and traditio-historical issues to make the drawing of historical conclusions possible. Historical questions will only be touched on insofar as they affect the assumptions of traditio-historical arguments.

The discussion even of literary and traditio-historical arguments will be selective.[1] It must be stressed that the following discussion is intended as a demonstration of the kind of difference that the exegetical method here proposed makes. It will be representative rather than exhaustive, though it will seek to touch on all the central and most difficult analytical problems confronting the modern interpreter of Ex. 32-34. Since there is such a mass of existing critical analyses, much of the argument will necessarily be somewhat negative, suggesting weaknesses in these analyses with less emphasis on alternative proposals for reconstruction. Some suggestions will be made, however, indicating the direction which further work might most profitably take.

The first step in the discussion must be an examination of the literary genre of Ex. 32-34. For it is difficult to penetrate the origins and development of a text until one has a reasonable understanding of what type of material it is and what sort of results one should expect to find. In the inevitably hypothetical penetration behind a text where the interpretation of evidence becomes harder to control, one's pre-understanding of the sort of answer one expects to find will play a significant, and sometimes decisive, role in one's evaluation. One's pre-understanding, however, will itself arise out of the text and the one will influence the other in circles of successive approximation.

In much of the following discussion reference will be to the whole JE Sinai pericope, Ex. 19-24, 32-34, since modern debate has usually dealt with these chapters together; indeed rather more with 19-24 than with 32-34. Detailed analysis, however, will be directed primarily to chs. 32-34, in keeping with the limitations of this study.

INTRODUCTORY SURVEY OF THE CULT LEGEND HYPOTHESIS

In its present form the text of Ex. 19ff. purports to be a narrative tradition concerning events at Sinai. Uncertainty as to the precise nature of this tradition and the extent of its historicity does not affect its basic nature as a narrative tradition. The question raised here is whether the text always was some such narrative tradition even in its earliest stages or whether it was originally something quite different.

The most widespread assessment of the genre of the Sinai material is that it is a "cult legend". Various other terms are also used, such as "festival legend" or "liturgical tradition",[2] but no significant difference in meaning is intended. For clarity the term "cult legend" will be adhered to in this discussion.

The two seminal[3] works for establishing the genre as cult legend are those of S. Mowinckel and G. von Rad,[4] and to these reference must briefly be made.

Mowinckel's analysis of the chapters concentrated on the presence in them of rituals and ceremonial practices similar to those recounted elsewhere in the OT, especially in the psalms. Using the method of form criticism and searching for the Sitz im Leben of these elements common to both Sinai and the psalms, Mowinckel reconstructed the contents of a cultic festival, that of the New Year (seen also as the feast of enthronement and of covenant renewal). In the light of this Mowinckel designated the Sinai pericope as follows:

> Ce que J et E rapportent comme récit des événements du Sinai n'est autre chose que la description d'une fête cultuelle célébrée à une époque plus récente, plus précisément dans le temple de Jérusalem.[5]

Mowinckel's analysis of the narrative is developed and modified by von Rad.[6] Von Rad criticizes the designation of the Sinai narrative as a "description" of a cultic ceremony on the grounds that there could be no obvious purpose in producing such a descriptive account. Nor is it the case that the narrative is such a description, even a free poetic one, or a late transposition of the constituent elements of the ceremony into literary terms. Rather the Sinai narrative is prior to the cult and normative for it; because the narrative provides the authority for a particular cultic occasion, it is the cult legend of that occasion. The legend preceded the cult and gave the cult its shape in the first place, though there was also subsequently a reciprocal influence of the cult upon the formation of the legend.

The pattern of the festival which is reflected in Ex. 19ff. can be reconstructed as follows:

1. Exhortation (Ex. 19:4-6) with an historical account of the Sinai events (Ex. 19ff.).

2. Proclamation of the law (Decalogue and Book of the Covenant).
3. Promise of blessing (Ex. 23:20ff.).
4. Ratification of the covenant (Ex. 24).

The fact that this same pattern can be discerned in Deuteronomy and also, less clearly, in Pss. 50 and 81, confirms the correctness of this analysis of the Exodus material.

Von Rad then proceeds to trace the origins and development of this covenant festival, which he locates in the autumn feast of Tabernacles at Shechem. He offers no further discussion of the origins and development of the Sinai narrative beyond some general observations about the process of transition from tradition to literature.[7] While von Rad differs from Mowinckel in tracing the origins of the festival reflected in Ex. 19ff. to the pre-monarchical period, he does not address the question of what in the Sinai narrative is original and constitutive, and what reflects the later influence of the cult.

These gaps have been largely filled by subsequent literature. Although Noth's treatment[8] is disappointingly brief, a thorough analysis has been provided by Beyerlin.[9] The most recent substantial work in the area, that of Halbe,[10] again confirms a cultic Sitz im Leben, even though the suggested location at Shechem is queried. While such later discussions have added detail to von Rad's analysis, his basic thesis has not been questioned but taken as established.

DEFINITION OF TERMINOLOGY

Before one can offer any assessment of this understanding of the Sinai narrative as a "cult legend", it is imperative carefully to define the meaning of the terms "cult" and "legend" so that it is clear what is being asserted.

i) Legend

The word "legend" can convey significantly different meanings and has been used ambiguously and inconsistently in much recent literature.[11] Broadly, one can find three main usages of the term. First, a legend can be an unhistorical, or largely unhistorical, story set in an historical context, perhaps reflecting original historical events which have since disappeared beneath later developments; such developments tend to accrue in "snowball" fashion. The Epic of Gilgamesh or the Arthurian stories could come under this heading.[12] Secondly, a legend can be "a virtue embodied in a deed".[13] The classic example of this is medieval hagiography where the saint will act in such a way as to provide a perfect example of some particular moral virtue, and the story is told to edify and to inspire.[14] Thirdly, a legend can be the account of the founding of a shrine or the beginning of a ritual custom, which is read at that particular shrine or on the occasion of the ritual custom. This is a technical usage, introduced by form critics.[15]

It is in the third of these senses that the term is used by von Rad. Hals observes that the form-critical designation of legend in this sense is basically unrelated to literary form.[16] That is, one of a number of possible literary types could constitute the narrative for the particular day or occasion. The narrative could be either entirely mythological or entirely historical, or somewhere in between. For the function of being read at a particular sanctuary does not prescribe the genre or content of what is being read - beyond the fact that it must relate to the sanctuary in question. If the Sinai narrative was read out at a festival of covenant renewal at Shechem, Gilgal, or Jerusalem, this would not of itself reveal anything about the nature of the narrative.

It is of course possible to designate the narrative as legendary in the first of the senses outlined above on the grounds that "the event is wrapped in mystery, and we are even in the dark about its historical background and context",[17] and because almost all the present narrative represents later elaborations. But such a conclusion must be based on historical and literary arguments, which are quite independent of the designation as legend in the third sense.

It is important clearly to distinguish these two different senses of legend. It is possible to hold that a narrative is legendary in both these senses together, but the use of the same word with two different significations is likely to lead to confusion. Von Rad's discussion uses the term consistently in its form-critical sense, although when he refers to the legend as being moulded and formed by the cult it is difficult not to import notions of legend in the "snowball" sense. A clear confusion can be seen in the treatment of M. Newman who says of the J and E covenant traditions that

> they both can be called "legends" because in their present form they not only reflect the original event but also have

> absorbed other elements which were not part of the event.[18]

This usage of "legend" corresponds to the first of the three defined meanings. Yet Newman goes on to write,

> Each tradition developed while used as the cult legend of a covenant ceremony. In the period nearer the event it would probably have reflected the event more accurately. The covenant event was re-enacted in the cult, and the cult legend both described and perpetuated the cult ceremony. Undoubtedly the legend was recited as part of the ceremony. Over a period of time new rites were introduced and new theological emphases developed, and these new elements were absorbed by the cult legend.[19]

Newman seems unaware that he is using "legend" in two different senses. Presumably his position is that the legend, in the sense of official legitimating narrative, is also a legend in the sense of an agglomeration of substantially unhistorical traditions. Such a position is only loosely connected with any implications of the term "legend". It arises rather from an understanding of the cult as involving a dramatic re-enactment of the event recounted in the legend in which past and present are merged together in the cultic "now"; as a result subsequent realizations of the event were not distinguished from the original event and it was seen as legitimate to tell the latter in terms of the former. The concept of "legend" in these two different senses together can thus be justified if the notion of the cult which it presupposes is correct, although the terminology is so confusing that it would be preferable to drop the term "legend" altogether.

ii) Cult

Mowinckel has defined "cult" thus:

> Cult or ritual may be defined as the socially established and regulated holy acts and words in which the encounter and communion of the Deity with the congregation is established, developed, and brought to its ultimate goal. In other words: a relation in which a religion becomes a vitalizing function as a communion of God and congregation, and of the members of the congregation amongst themselves.[20]

Eichrodt, following G. Quell, takes the term "cult" (or "cultus") to mean

> the expression of religious experience in concrete external actions performed within the congregation or community, preferably by officially appointed exponents and in set forms.[21]

Both these definitions lay stress on the communal and institutional nature of the cult, and with such a definition there is no difficulty. When "cult" is used without further qualification in the subsequent discussion, this will be the meaning intended.

It is possible, however, to offer a different sort of definition of the same term. Mowinckel writes:

> The cult is not only by its origin, but in all places and at all times, drama. The cult is sacred art. But at the same time it is sacred reality, not merely an acted drama or a play, but a real drama and one that manifests reality, a drama which realizes the dramatic event with real power, a reality from which real forces emanate, in other words it is a sacrament. The cult of primitive man is this, and nothing less ... The basic idea is this: that through the dramatic, "symbolic" presentation, realization and reanimation of the particular event this event is actually and really repeated; it repeats itself, happens all over again and exercises afresh the same mighty, redemptive effect that it exercised for our salvation on the first occasion at the dawn of time or in the distant past.[22]

The first pair of definitions of cult presents a more static conception than the latter one; that is, they are concerned primarily with the institution of worship, whereas the definition of cult as drama emphasizes the actual practice and inner meaning of worship. There is no absolute distinction between these two different meanings, and sometimes in practice it may be unnecessary to distinguish between them. Yet the difference is significant. For it is to cult in the sense of the actual practice of worship that one can most meaningfully refer in terms of its entailing dramatic involvement and reenactment. A legend authorizing the institution of worship or the fact of ritual at some particular cultic place is authorizing something unchanging which it is hard to conceive of as constantly moulding its authorizing legend. That is, it says *why* rather than *how* worship is carried on at a particular place. When, however, a legend is used in the context of a specific form of worship, as a part of an actual ceremony (authorizing the "how" rather than the "why"), then the inherently dynamic nature of worship could more easily be conceived of as moulding a narrative which was used in the course of that worship. This would mean that a legend authorizing a sanctuary would have an inherent stability which would not necessarily be shared by a legend used as a part of the ceremony at that sanctuary. Jdg. 17-18 as the cult legend of Dan would be a legend in the former sense. The Sinai pericope is envisaged as a cult legend in the latter sense. It would seem therefore that "cult" in the term "cult legend" as applied to the Sinai material, when the term is intended to designate the literary form and not merely the function of the material, must mean the actual practice of worship in its dramatic and symbolic sense.

A few words must be said on this dramatic and creative understanding of Israel's worship, particularly in the strong form in which it is set out by Mowinckel; although any substantial discussion lies beyond our present scope.

First, the dramatic concept of the cult, especially as Mowinckel develops it, derives mainly from phenomenology of religion in general and from the world of Mesopotamia in particular, and has been applied to Israel largely by analogy. In the realm of religious practices and the meaning attributed to them, such a comparative approach must be used with extreme caution. While the religion of Israel must be understood within its ancient Near Eastern environment, it is methodologically proper that one should attempt to comprehend Israelite religion first on its own terms, as a particular coherent religious system, before adducing transcultural parallels and applying them heuristically.[23]

Secondly, the fact is that we know regrettably little about the practices characteristic of Israel's festivals, or the meaning that these practices had for the worshippers. We know something about the practice of sacrifice, though little about its meaning, something about hymnody, and something about the nature of homiletic. But beyond this we are constrained to hypothesize. One may indeed offer an hypothesis about a type of worship which would have incorporated a "cult legend" in such a way as to mould and transform it and then apply the hypothesis heuristically to the final form of the legend in question. But the tentative and speculative nature of such an undertaking should not be forgotten.

iii) Cultic

In addition to the potential ambiguity of the noun "cult", the adjective "cultic"[24] has a range of possible meanings which can lead to considerable confusion. First, "cultic" can denote a practice which belongs exclusively to the cult (the institution of formal worship). For example, it is difficult to conceive of a priestly benediction, such as in Num. 6:23-26, being pronounced outside the cult, outside public worship. Secondly, a practice may be cultic if it is characteristic of the cult, and primarily belongs there, but is not necessarily confined to it; for example, sacrifice. Thirdly, "cultic" may denote a practice which belongs to the fundamental nature of religious belief and practice, and which originates prior to and outside of the cult, though it is subsequently taken into the cult and plays an important role there; for example, prayer. Fourthly, "cultic" may be used loosely to mean "having some role in the cult" without reference to the origins of the practice inside of outside the cult, or to whether its presence in the cult is normal or abnormal. Fifthly, "cultic" may be used loosely as virtually synonymous with "religious".

It is obviously important in certain contexts carefully to distinguish these different meanings of "cultic". Unfortunately, discussions of Ex. 19ff. have not always done so. Beyerlin, for example, points to the act of obeisance in Ex. 34:8 as evidence of a cultic background for the material:[25] "It is self-evident that this is not a distinctive, individual reaction", for elsewhere a "firm connection" can be seen between Israel's reverent obeisance and Yahweh's "cultic epiphany" (e.g. Ex. 33:10, Ps. 99:1,5,9, 132:7). This would only be self-evident if prostration belonged exclusively, or perhaps even primarily, to the realm of the cult. Since, however, prostration, like prayer, was a fundamental ancient Near Eastern religious act, and so can only be "cultic" in the third, fourth or fifth sense specified above, it provides in itself no evidence of a "cultic background" where the practice is referred to and any relation to the formal cult could only be inferred from the surrounding context in each individual case. The fact that an action appears sometimes in the realm of the cult in no way entails that it must always do so.

Apart from difficulties of definition, there are also difficulties over the applicability of the terms "cult" and "cultic"; that is, it may be unclear whether a term or practice genuinely belongs to the cult, or whether proposed links are purely accidental. F.-E. Wilms, for example, argues that the use of the term "to go up" (*^{c}lh*) in Ex. 34:2 (cf. Ex. 19:3,24, 24:1,9, 32:30) is significant for the cultic milieu of the passage, because elsewhere in the OT the word is the technical term for going up to a sanctuary.[26] Such a suggestion takes no account of the obvious fact that the use of the word may have been determined by the writer's need to portray Moses physically ascending Mt. Sinai. What else *could* he say but that Moses "went up", for which *^{c}lh* is the natural Hebrew verb? When the word can be naturally explained in this way it is illegitimate to deduce a "cultic milieu" from the term.

It is true that Beyerlin and Wilms have other weightier evidence which they adduce to show the links of the Sinai pericope with the cult. The arguments discussed above were adduced secondarily, as part of a total cumulative case, to support a position already reached on other grounds, and their lack of validity need not disturb the general position. But such question-begging arguments, where the central terms "legend", "cult" and "cultic" have not been carefully defined but used equivocally, are unfortunately not uncommon in discussions of the Sinai material. A fresh examination, with more careful use of terms, is in order.

THE USE OF FORM CRITICISM

Before turning to discuss specific features which are adduced as evidence for the cult as the *Sitz im Leben* of the Sinai pericope, it will be useful to consider the more general principles upon which this understanding of the material has been based.

The difficulty of establishing a sound method and approach is considerable. H.-J. Kraus has written,

> The "cultic legend" presents us with special difficulties. Reliable criteria are still lacking in this field - and it is not likely that they will ever emerge. When, for example, it is stated that the Sinai pericope was a "festival legend", this immediately raises the question what the actual relationship between the epic account and the cultic event was. It is too easy to avoid answering this question by asserting that there was a mutual interaction.[27]

And G.E. Wright, in a discussion of the relationship between cult and history, observes,

> Involved are procedural assumptions which determine conclusions, but which in themselves cannot be tested except as the question of cult and history is studied in a later period where the evidence can be more adequately controlled.[28]

The critical approach upon which most analysis of the Sinai pericope as cult legend has been based is form criticism. Some brief comments on the nature and scope of form criticism are therefore in order.[29]

The basic assumption of form criticism is that ancient Near Eastern man was influenced in his speech and literary composition by custom and convention; and these customs and conventions correspond to certain regularly recurring events in life. As a generalization this is quite acceptable. But as a universally binding principle it may become questionable. On the one hand it may leave insufficient room for individuality and innovation. On the other hand it can easily oversimplify the relationship between literary forms and the daily institutions which, in some way, correspond to them. Both of these points require amplification.

First, the emphasis upon custom and convention means that an inevitable weakness in the form-critical approach is that it has a tendency to find general and typical patterns at the expense of the individual and the unique.[30] It is argued that the Sinai pericope reflects a regular festival in Israel because of similarities between it and aspects of the later worship in Israel's cult. If, however, one imagines for the sake of argument that a tradition told of an encounter at Sinai between Yahweh and certain forerunners of the later people of Israel, an encounter unique in nature[31] and significance, and that this involved a theophany, a revelation of the will of Yahweh, and a commitment by the people to Yahweh, and that this experience became the basis for subsequent encounters between Yahweh and Israel, similar in some respects to, but not identical with, the initial experience - it must be asked how far a standard form-critical approach would be able to give an adequate analysis of such a unique and constitutive tradition. To say that such a tradition could not be described except in the light of similar subsequent events would be to beg the question. To say that such a tradition has not been described except in the light of similar subsequent cultic events also begs the question. For such a position could only be established on the basis, <u>not</u> of similarities between the Sinai tradition and later cultic practices - for such, *ex hypothesi*, are to be expected - but on the basis of elements in the Sinai narrative which could not reasonably be attributed to an experience at the mountain in the desert, but which plausibly would fit in a ceremony at a sanctuary in Canaan. Whether there actually are such elements in the Sinai narrative will be examined below. The point here is simply that the emphasis on the typical and the representative can (though of course does not necessarily) lead to a circular argument.

The second main difficulty with the form-critical approach inheres in the notion of a *Sitz im Leben*. B.O. Long has shown that this term is potentially vague and ambiguous.[32] Although it has been assumed that a particular literary genre can be shown to belong to one particular setting, Long argues that one must distinguish between original and transferred settings and that in practice diversity and plurality are more frequent than a single original setting in society. The relation of content to setting may vary and the same thematic content be used on distinct ritual occasions. Further,

> a given genre of literature may be completely at home in a variety of settings ... Here the field data stand in sharp contrast to a deeply held form critical assumption that every literary type has its definitive, essential setting, without which it ceases to be what it is.[33]

These considerations do not evacuate the notion of a *Sitz im Leben* of all usefulness, but they do show a need for greater flexibility and caution in the use of it, and

> especially, OT scholars should realize that factors influencing the match of genre and setting are often external to content and literary style and that reconstructions based almost wholly on internal literary arguments are likely to be seriously flawed from the outset.[34]

Given the need for a cautious and flexible use of form criticism, it will be appropriate to reconsider two passages whose standard analysis rests largely upon a form-critical approach. These are the divine pronouncements in 33:19, 34:6f., and the legal corpus in 34:11-26.

ANALYSIS OF EX. 33:19, 34:6f.

The pronouncements in 33:19, 34:6f. are classified by Eissfeldt as "solemn cult sayings" which "had their setting in particular public festivals for the whole people or the whole cult-community".[35] Weiser classifies the verses as "epiphany-formulas" recited by a priest "when the people came together for regularly recurring cultic purposes at the sanctuary of the covenant".[36] The argument appears to be that these sayings have a form which can be seen to correspond to that found in other similar sayings elsewhere in the OT, and that this form had its Sitz im Leben in the cult.

It may be observed, first, that there is some difficulty in classifying these two sayings as being of the same form. They have in common that they are both divine pronouncements, but the similarity between them is one of content,[37] in that they both reveal Yahweh as being gracious and merciful. They differ from one another in shape (form) and differ both in shape and content from other divine pronouncements such as Ex. 20:2//Deut. 5:6, or the oft-repeated "I am Yahweh" in Lev. 17-26.[38]

Secondly the fact that some divine pronouncements may originate in the cult does not entail that all do. There is great diversity of form and content in divine pronouncements recorded in the OT. Since, moreover, the OT has many traditions of Yahweh appearing and speaking outside the sphere of the cult, the relationship of a divine pronouncement to a cultic setting is complex. Are there clear criteria of either form or content which distinguish a saying which originates in the cult from a saying which originates in a narrative tradition?

It may also be asked how far it is justifiable to take a saying such as 33:19 as an independent saying, separable from the rest of Yahweh's speech. Although it is possible to set the words out as an independent pronouncement,[39] it is clear that what makes the words remarkable is their solemn and emphatic content, which is most naturally expressed in a formal parallelism. The assumption of the original independence of such a saying usually postulates a certain looseness of the saying in its present context,[40] so that the saying could be secondarily introduced. If exegesis reveals intimate links between the saying and its narrative context, the assumption of original independence becomes more problematic. It must be asked how far both the form and content of 33:19, 34:6f. may be influenced by literary and contextual considerations. In general terms theophanies are always serious occasions.[41] But Ex. 32-34 presents the particularly grave context of Israel's sin against Yahweh and their danger of total destruction; their forgiveness and restoration is no light matter but possible only through a revelation of the very being of God as a God who is gracious and merciful. How else could the tradition convey this adequately except by presenting these words as a solemn divine pronouncement?

Since the form of 34:6f. is more like that of an independent ritual pronouncement than is the case with 33:19, a few extra comments on it are in place.

First, there is disagreement over what kind of cult saying it is, whether it is spoken to God or by God (that is, by his representative). J. Scharbert interprets the verses as a liturgical prayer or "Bekenntnisformel" since the use of the third person singular rather than the first person, as is customary in revelatory formulae, is deemed awkward, and out of the present context the words are naturally taken as a vocative prayer formula.[42] Eissfeldt and Weiser, on the other hand, interpret the words not as a prayer but as a pronouncement by the priest in lieu of God.[43] For them, apparently, the third person formulation presents no problem. There is, therefore, no "obvious" use of the formula in the regular cult of Israel. But such disagreement is perhaps inevitable when a saying is interpreted in an hypothetical context, and does not show that the words are not a pronouncement in the cult of some sort.

Secondly, although it is obviously possible to interpret 34:6f. in isolation from its present context - numerous discussions have done so - the exegesis showed strikingly the aptness of the wording to the present context; so much so that it may be correct to conclude that the wording was in fact designed for the context. But if the saying is thus, at least to some extent, context-dependent, then there are particular problems in offering an interpretation in isolation of that context.

The likely influence of the present context on the formulation of 34:6f. still does not show that its contents could not, in some form, have had a prior history in the cult. One also has to account for the numerous other passages in the OT where parts of the formula of 34:6f. recur.[44] Many of these passages, most notably those in the psalms, are unquestionably cultic in the sense of originating in, and being used in, the formal worship of Israel.

What is at issue here, and indeed lies at the heart of the cult legend analysis, is the hazily-defined relationship between cult and narrative tradition. If the contents of 34:6f. originated in the cult but have been transposed into the literary context of the Sinai tradition, how is this process to be envisaged?[45] The hypothesis that the tradition of Ex. 32-34 existed in a form roughly resembling that which it has at present, but without 33:19, 34:6f., which were only added into the tradition at a comparatively late stage of development is untenable when the literary and theological development of Ex. 32-34 as a whole is considered. The verses are integral and constitute the high-point upon which the surrounding narrative is dependent and up to which it leads; 33:19 and 34:6f. must be regarded as primary to the tradition. If this is so, and yet it is maintained that the verses had their origin in the cult, then the whole Sinai tradition of Ex. 32-34 must have been built up around them as a special creation to give these pronouncements a new existence in a narrative setting. This creation could have utilized existing elements of tradition, but they could not previously have existed in anything like their present shape. Some such extremely complex development of the tradition must be envisaged, given the centrality of 33:19, 34:6f. to it. And some form of such complexity often is envisaged, though with less weight attached to the significance of 33:19, 34:6f. But while this is possible, one must ask whether it is either necessary or even likely as an account of the material.

A development in the opposite direction, from narrative tradition to use in the cult, presents less difficulty. A tradition as important as Ex. 32-34 for what it says about the character of God and the nature of Israel would naturally be taken up in the worship of Israel. All the other OT uses of the elements in 34:6f. can be understood as derivative from, and explicitly recalling, the supreme instance of God's self-revelation. For what would be more natural than to utilize the tradition and to call upon Yahweh as being of the character which he himself had revealed to Moses?[46] The originality of the formula to the narrative tradition is in no way incompatible with its frequent usage thereafter in the cult. The adoption of a tradition of fundamental importance into the context of worship is not only a pattern of development readily understandable in itself, but also can be paralleled elsewhere - not least in the history of the Christian Church.[47]

Some compromise on the relation of the narrative tradition to the cult is also possible. That is, the formula of 34:6f. may have originated within the Sinai tradition and been incorporated into the cult prior to its present literary formulation, but its present formulation could reflect the cultic usage. Such a development is readily conceivable and has an obvious parallel in the tradition of the eucharistic words of Jesus. There are, however, two difficulties with this. The first is the lack of clear evidence in its favour (general considerations apart). There are no parallel accounts of 34:6f., as there are of the eucharistic words of Jesus, to prove diversity of wording in the tradition and indicate some such development. None of the passages related to Ex. 34:6f. can be shown to be parallel to it, rather than dependent upon it (or even prior to it), and so show evidence of diverse cultic usage of the original tradition. Secondly, the influence that can most easily be argued to have shaped the wording of 34:6f. is the context of the Sinai tradition. Nonetheless, neither of these factors decisively rules out influence from the cult upon the wording of the saying.

In sum, these brief reflections suggest that the imagined development of Ex. 34:6f. from cult to narrative tradition is less likely than the development from narrative tradition to use in the cult. Within this development some reciprocal influence of the cult upon the formulation of the saying cannot be discounted. But such influence, if it did take place, would be a secondary development and would be far from showing that the cult was the original setting for the formula as a whole. Although further work is necessary, it may be suggested that to view the cult as the Sitz im Leben for 34:6f., or 33:19, is a less likely hypothesis than that they were originally a part of the narrative tradition in which they now stand.

ANALYSIS OF EX. 34:11-26

It is generally held that the laws of 34:11-26[48] reflect a cultic Sitz im Leben, that is, they reflect a rite of proclamation of laws at a ceremony of covenant renewal. The form-critical arguments used to support this take more than one form.

One argument is that one can discern in Ex. 34, as in Ex. 19/20, a covenant-treaty structure parallel to other ancient Near Eastern vassal treaties, especially those of the Hittites. W. Beyerlin,[49] for example, following G.E. Mendenhall,[50] presents an interpretation of the Sinai pericope along these lines.

The debate about the relevance and significance of vassal treaty forms has been extensive, but as it has been well summarized already,[51] a few comments here will suffice.

First, the real interest in the debate has tended to be less the explication of the text of Exodus than the larger historical questions of the antiquity of the Mosaic covenant and the connection of the Exodus and Sinai traditions. As such, there has been perhaps insufficient interest in interpreting the text of Exodus in its own right.

Secondly, it has become clear that the covenant-treaty form is present neither in Ex. 19/20 nor in Ex. 34. So many elements are missing that, despite some constructive insights, the parallel as a whole ceases to be helpful. As J. Barr already wrote in the early days of the debate, the appeal to Hittite treaties

> seems ... only to pick out points which might belong to any treaty supported by sacral sanctions, and not to explain more for the covenant in Israel than at most the form of certain more developed statements of it.[52]

The application of treaty patterns to the Sinai pericope has in fact tended to squeeze the text into a general mould at the cost of its individual particularities. As an heuristic tool, therefore, the treaty form has fulfilled its function and may now be laid aside.

The covenant-treaty argument is one particular form of the more general supposition that 34:11-26 reflects a cultic Sitz im Leben, and its inadequacy does not affect the more general position. It is this latter that must now be considered. Unfortunately, a thorough discussion lies beyond our present scope. Suffice it to say that form-critical and traditio-historical accounts of the development of legal complexes are influenced largely by one's historical understanding of the practice of ancient law-giving. And we have little knowledge of the practice of law-giving in Israel, on account of the OT's ascription of all authoritative law to Moses at Sinai. Apart from internal analysis and comparison of legal codes, there is little evidence to root a corpus of laws in a particular period or setting. Although the early settlement period seems to be widely favoured now for 34:11-26 (with varying degrees of secondary expansion), the wide variety of suggested dates, ranging from pre-Mosaic to post-exilic,[53] highlights the nature of the problem.

For the present, we will simply focus on one consideration that has received little attention in discussions of 34:11-26, that is the close relation of the section to its narrative context. This contextual approach has received little attention[54] partly because the originally independent existence of the laws has been assumed, and partly because most interest has focussed on the questions of whether or not a decalogue can be reconstructed from these verses and of how they relate as a parallel to the decalogue of Ex. 20. Despite the assertion that this section was introduced into the text of J without any reference to the narrative context,[55] it is clear that the opposite is the case. The exegesis has shown that the overall tenor of 34:11-26 is fully in harmony with the concerns of 32-34. In detail, the dependence of 34:17, and perhaps also 34:14, upon ch. 32 is striking.

Given the considerable links between 34:11-26 and the context of 32-34, how is one to interpret this? There are two possibilities. The first is to hold that while the laws are appropriate to the narrative in certain respects, they do not as a whole arise out of the narrative situation, and their original independence, followed by secondary incorporation into the Sinai tradition, is to be maintained. Secondly, one could argue that the laws were compiled specifically for their present context, largely out of other laws already contained within the tradition (i.e. Ex. 20-23).

Before one can choose between these some further clarification is required. In the first place, given that legal and paraenetic material are different literary types from narrative, one must ask what sort of correspondence of content one could reasonably expect to find between the two different genres if they were composed together. Clearly it would not be the same as that between two interrelated narrative episodes.[56] Neither paraenesis nor laws could be expected to show frequent verbal links to the narrative; a similar thematic concern would be most important.

A body of laws can be connected with its narrative context in a variety of ways. One may consider the relationship of Num. 15 to Num. 13-14. Here there is a real relation of the laws to the preceding narrative, seen in the concern for the promised land, jeopardized but reaffirmed (15:2), and for the event of the whole people being involved in sin (15:26).[57] Nonetheless, the thematic interest of ch. 15 bears no integral connection to the context and the present links may be seen as a redactional reordering of the material. The content of Ex. 34:11-26 is far more closely connected to its context than is the case with Num. 15.

It must also be asked whether alternative hypothetical contexts for the laws would explain their peculiarities more effectively than their present context. One would have to imagine a situation in which (a) the strong warnings against unfaithfulness were appropriate, (b) the cultic emphasis of the laws was appropriate, and (c) the specific wording of an individual unit such as 34:17 could be accounted for. The context of a festival in Canaan in, for example, the pre-monarchical period could account for the first two - though hardly better than the tradition of Ex. 32ff. - while for the third point one would have to confess ignorance of the point of the prohibition,[58] or offer a speculative account of the prohibition of different types of idolatry in Israel's history.[59] And even if 34:17 be discounted as a secondary addition when the laws were introduced into their present context, there is no other detail in any other law which gains explicit point through the postulation of such an alternative setting. In other words, a setting for the laws at a regular festival seems to explain them no better than their present narrative context.

To suggest that the laws of 34:11ff. were assembled for their context does not mean that they had no prior existence.[60] For they are explicitly a recapitulation of laws already given - particularly Ex. 23:12,14ff. (13:12f.) but presupposing also the first two (and fourth) commandments of the decalogue. The laws as an explicit response to the cultic sin of Ex. 32 can be understood as follows. First, a general homiletic warning against unfaithfulness (34:11-16) developing the warnings of 23:23ff., and then a repetition of the cultic laws already given (23:14ff.), the particular selection of laws being determined less by the situation of Ex. 32 than by the fact that they were the main cultic laws contained at an earlier point in the Sinai tradition, and the repetition of such laws was seen as appropriate after Israel's cultic sin. Apart from the presence of the laws of 13:12f., the major difference of content between 23:14ff. and 34:17ff.[61] is 34:17, which explicitly harks back to Ex. 32. Such a congruence between these laws and their context at least puts a question mark against the hypothesis that these laws were originally an independent collection and, if they were, that they reflect the regular cult of Israel.

Much work on the question, and in particular a probing of the sociological assumptions of setting the laws in the regular cult, remains to be done. The above arguments are an attempt not to resolve the question but to set it in a new light.

THE PROBLEM OF RELIGIOUS LANGUAGE

It is time now to turn to arguments about the Sinai pericope as a whole reflecting the regular cult of Israel. To do this rightly, one further methodological discussion is in order. This is to do with the nature of religious language. For parts of the text have frequently been interpreted in a way that is insensitive to the type of language being used.[62]

The attempt to describe an encounter with God will necessarily strain the resources of language and will necessitate the use of metaphor, imagery and paradox by the writer in the attempt to convey his meaning. This means, for example, that when the writer uses the language of volcanic or storm phenomena, as in Ex. 19, he may have little intention of trying accurately to describe such, still less of actually giving an account of a volcanic eruption or a thunderstorm. His aim rather is to convey the awesomeness of the coming of Yahweh to his people, and for the ancient man there were no phenomena more awful than the volcano and thunderstorm. The writer could hardly express his meaning without such language, and such language is primarily evocative and only secondarily, if at all, descriptive. The account, therefore, is not such as to allow us to reconstruct "what really happened". Indeed to attempt to do such is to misunderstand the writer's use of language. As Buber puts it, when writing of Ex. 19,

> Every attempt to penetrate to some factual process which is concealed behind the awe-inspiring picture is quite in vain. We are no longer in a position to replace that immense image by actual data.[63]

Yet numerous modern treatments take little cognizance of this aspect of religious language. Noth, for example, assumes that Ex. 19 shows that Sinai was an active volcano and attempts to locate it.[64] Von Rad, in a discussion of Ex. 33:18ff., interprets the passage as having been originally a cult aetiology which justified a theophany ritual:

> The congregation would call upon Yahweh, Yahweh would pass by and declare his name and attributes, and the

congregation would prostrate themselves.[65]

Von Rad adds in a footnote, "It is difficult to say how we ought to imagine the cultic process by which Yahweh 'passed by'", but offers a tentative suggestion of a ritual of the carrying past of cultic emblems. But surely the question is not how but whether we should attempt to imagine this cultic process. I. Barbour has argued for interpreting certain religious language "seriously but not literally",[66] and he writes, "An additional safeguard against literalism is provided by the sense of awe and mystery associated with religious experience".[67] Yet it is difficult to see how the evocation of awe and mystery, so clearly central in 33:18ff., receives sufficient recognition by von Rad. If one takes the language of 33:18ff. seriously, but not literally, it is doubtful whether it constitutes the sort of material from which von Rad's type of reconstruction could justifiably be attempted.

EVIDENCE FOR THE INFLUENCE OF ISRAEL'S CULT UPON THE SINAI PERICOPE

It is in the light of such considerations about religious language that one should assess the significance of those features in Ex. 19ff. which are supposed to reflect the influence of Israel's cult. Beyerlin, who provides a thoroughgoing "cultic" interpretation of the Sinai pericope, lists the following significant features:[68]

1. Purificatory rites (19:10-11a, 14-15a, 15b) reflecting the preparation for worship and the epiphany of Yahweh in the festal cult.
2. Cloud of smoke (19:9,16,18). This has its basis in an incense rite, cf. Lev. 16:2,12,13, Is. 6:4, 1 Kg. 8:10.
3. The trumpet blast (19:13b,16,19, 20:18), which corresponds to the blowing of the trumpet at the cultic theophany.
4. Proclamation of name of Yahweh (33:19, 34:6f.). This reflects the practice of invoking the divine name to "actualize" the theophany.
5. The act of obeisance (33:10; 34:8).
6. Eating of a covenant meal (24:9-11).
7. Rite of sprinkling blood of sacrificial victims on people and altar (24:3ff.).
8. Proclamation of covenant law (20:2-17, 34:10-26).
9. The fixing of a time and place for Yahweh's epiphany

(19:10f., 32:2,4, 19:12-13a, 20-24, 34:3).
10. Appointment and role of a covenant mediator (20:18-21, cf. 19:9).

The value of these indications varies. It has already been argued above that an action like obeisance (no. 5) is not "cultic" in any significant sense. Moreover, many of these features (1,5,6,7,9,10) can be understood without difficulty to be part of an actual Sinai tradition. Assuming that there were early traditions of an encounter with God at Sinai, it is hard to conceive what these traditions could have contained, if not some such practices as these. Any tradition of an encounter with Yahweh would necessarily be expressed in these "cultic" terms.

Features 4 and 8 have already been discussed, and they likewise constitute an integral part of the Sinai tradition and fit at least as well in that tradition, as a Sinai tradition, as they would elsewhere; indeed one might claim on the basis of the exegesis that they fit better here than elsewhere.

The cloud and smoke (they can be distinguished) need not be a problem, for it is hardly justifiable to separate the references to them from the other storm and volcanic phenomena (thunder and lightning, fire and quaking), the purpose of which is to evoke awe at Yahweh. The origins of such language are in actual storms and volcanoes and the effect they have on people, not in clouds of incense, and the function of the imagery is more emotive than referential. Given a tradition of an awesome encounter with Yahweh at Sinai, the language is appropriate and explicable in terms of the tradition.

The trumpet blast is the one feature which cannot so readily be accounted for purely in terms of a Sinai tradition. Newman, for example, writes,

> If the tradition is viewed simply as an account of the experience at Sinai, the loud trumpet blast with the thunders, lightnings, and thick cloud is most perplexing. Who, one might ask, was blowing the trumpet on the top of the mountain? Was it the Lord? But if the legend is associated with the cult, the trumpet can be understood as a cultic instrument which was blown in connection with a later covenant ceremony and was absorbed into the legend.[69]

It is possible that the trumpet references do show that the

theophany has to some extent been written up in a way that reflects the later cultic practices of Israel. If so, it would not follow that any of the other details in the narrative should also be explained thus nor that the narrative as a whole reflects a cultic Sitz im Leben. Moreover, this may be something peculiar to Ex. 19, a chapter with several distinctive characteristics not shared by the rest of the Sinai pericope. The trumpet references do not recur outside the chapter, and need show no more than that the recounting of Ex. 19 has been partially influenced by the experiences of Israel's cult.

Even so, however, the interpretation of the trumpet references needs further investigation. How are they to be understood? If they are interpreted literally, then the question of who blew the trumpet can be asked. To say that God himself sounded the trumpet is not as implausible as Newman implies; cf. Zech. 9:14. Nonetheless, such an answer fits awkwardly with the narrative.

Various non-literal interpretations have therefore been advanced. Cassuto, for example, says,

> It [the sound of a horn] signifies the strong wind that blows violently through the gorges between the mountains, rending the air with a great noise like the sound of a horn.[70]

This seems a somewhat rationalist explanation.[71] G. Friedrich argues that "the sound of horns probably denotes the inexpressible voice of God" and points to Ex. 19:19 for the trumpet and God's voice as parallel.[72] This also hardly does justice to the context where the trumpet is a distinct sound which precedes and accompanies God's speech.

The unsatisfactory nature of these interpretations shows that the problem is not eased but exacerbated by posing it in terms of a literal or non-literal interpretation. The awkwardness of answering the question "Who blew the trumpet?" suggests that this is an inappropriate question to ask, and this is significant for the genre of the material. Two things become clear. First, the trumpet references cannot be taken in isolation from the storm and volcanic phenomena; they are all of a piece. Secondly, the trumpet references are, like the rest of the narrative, evocative rather than referential. They are included in the theophany account because of the profound and emotive effect that a solemn trumpet blast can have on a hearer. If this is so, and one may not use such language to reconstruct events at Sinai, then it will also be an illegitimate use of the material to attempt to reconstruct or discern aspects of the regular cult of Israel from it.

It may still be asked why the trumpet blast was considered an appropriate element of the theophany and whether this does not still, in some way, reflect the regular cultic experiences of Israel. That the use of the trumpet does reflect some prior experience of its significance is likely. But though this experience may have been in the regular cult of Israel in Canaan it cannot be restricted to it. The trumpet was common in the ancient Near East, well attested in the third and second millennia.[73] The sound of the trumpet may well have been a common element in man's encounter with the divine throughout the ancient Near East. The use, therefore, of the trumpet as a significant symbol in Ex. 19 may reflect the regular cult of Israel, but it need not. The question must be decided in the context of one's overall understanding of the nature of the Sinai tradition, not because no satisfactory account of the trumpet can be given in different terms.

To conclude, it can be said that none of the "cultic" features of the Sinai pericope requires an explanation in terms of the regular cult of Israel. And even if some elements of the regular cult may have influenced part of the description in Exodus, this is far from showing that the cult was the Sitz im Leben for the content. An alternative explanation of the same data, that they not only are but always were part of a narrative tradition attempting to relate an encounter with God at Sinai offers a coherent and comprehensive understanding. This does not mean that this alternative is correct. But on the principle of Occam's razor, that for purposes of explanation things not known to exist should not, unless it is absolutely necessary, be postulated as existing, the comparative simplicity, yet comprehensiveness, of the hypothesis gives it a prima facie claim to acceptance. The alternative hypothesis, which requires a long and complex development and transformation of the material in question, not only does not explain the text any more fully but also postulates a large number of factors which are at best invisible and at worst illusory.

CONCLUSION

The argument of this chapter has been to present a cumulative case in favour of the Sinai material as a narrative tradition concerning Sinai rather than as a "cult legend", in the sort of sense in which that term has been commonly understood. There are perhaps six main elements in the argument.

1) There has been confusion in the use of the terms "legend" and "cult" in such a way as to be misleading.
2) A form-critical analysis has sometimes been used in such a way as to beg the question of the nature of the tradition.
3) An originally independent existence in the cult for some of the most "cultic" elements in the narrative is not necessarily the most likely explanation.
4) The adoption of a narrative tradition for use in the cult is a process at least as likely to underlie Ex. 32-34 as a postulated historicization of cultic rituals.
5) Too literalist an approach to the problem of religious language has resulted in illegitimate inferences being based on the material.
6) The cult legend hypothesis does not in fact explain any elements in the text which cannot equally be explained by the acceptance of the tradition as genuinely a Sinai tradition.

If these points are accepted, then serious doubts are cast upon the analysis of the Sinai pericope as a cult legend.

Admittedly these arguments do not disprove the cult legend hypothesis. But that is largely because in this sort of problem the arguments are not such as to admit of proof rather than probability. It is also difficult to discuss an issue when many of the arguments advanced are somewhat intangible. This is particularly the case when one attempts to interact with von Rad and Noth, the two most influential scholars in recent pentateuchal studies. Both maintain that there was a long and complex cultic tradition-history underlying the Sinai pericope, but neither offers much argument as to why this should be the case. Rather they take for granted that it must have been, this assumption being based on their larger understanding of the early history of Israel and the growth of pentateuchal traditions. But whatever may be the case elsewhere in the Pentateuch, that should not be allowed to prejudge the assessment of the Sinai material. Such difficulties attend the analysis of Ex. 32-34 as a cult legend that it becomes a difficult hypothesis to maintain. A reasonable alternative is to hold that the material is, and was from the start, a narrative tradition telling of Israel's encounter with Yahweh at Mt. Sinai.

Chapter 4

EX. 32-34 AS LEGEND

It has been argued that Ex. 32-34 is a genuine Sinai tradition. It remains to examine further what kind of tradition it is. This is important for its own sake, to further our overall appreciation of the nature of the tradition. It will also bear upon the question of how far it may be proper to see the narrative as possibly preserving genuinely historical tradition.

THE MOSES TRADITIONS AS LEGEND

The discussion will be approached by asking whether the Sinai material may aptly be designated as a legend - legend in the general sense of a largely unhistorical story set in an historical context (Sage).[1]

The view that many of the early narratives of the OT are legend rather than history was systematically developed in the early years of the 20th century, most notably by H. Gunkel and H. Gressmann in the context of a "history of religions" approach to the OT.[2] While Gunkel directed his attention primarily towards Genesis,[3] Gressmann produced a comprehensive interpretation of the Moses stories in Mose und seine Zeit. Since then "legend" has continued to play an important role in the analysis of early OT traditions.[4] As such it has made the quest for historical events underlying the traditions a somewhat nebulous undertaking, even though the last thorough interpretation of the Moses stories as saga,[5] M. Buber's Moses, was comparatively optimistic about the historical content of the traditions.

The use of "legend" to designate Israel's early traditions has not been unchallenged. In particular, in those areas where the biblical theology movement with its emphasis on the centrality of history was strong the use of the term "legend", while not explicitly denied,[6] receded into the background. But that movement failed to provide a sufficiently coherent and comprehensive approach of its own.[7]

A strong restatement of the legendary nature of Israel's early traditions, with a corresponding denial of their historical value, is to be found in the recent Israelite and Judaean History in which T.L. Thompson and D. Irvin contribute the discussion of the Joseph and Moses narratives.[8] Thompson argues for the non-historical nature of the Moses traditions partly because of the poverty of historical and archaeological evidence, but more fundamentally because of the nature of the traditions as "heroic tales":

> The "heroic tale" as a narrative type is markedly ahistorical both in structure and development.[9]

If the literary type is that of heroic tale, and the heroic tale is a genre that shows no genuine historiographical interest, then there simply does not exist the kind of material from which historical reconstruction could be undertaken:

> The problem is not simply that the narratives lack historicity, but rather that the pentateuchal narratives are impervious and irrelevant to questions about the historicity of events or figures of the past. Nothing more historically concrete about the historical Moses and Yahweh can be known than about the historical Tammuz and Ishtar; nor is our knowledge about the wandering in the wilderness qualitatively different from what we know of Odysseus' journey.[10]

Irvin treats the Moses stories as comparable with other ancient Near Eastern material which she classifies as "fiction" or "folktale".[11] Her primary concern is not historical but literary, seeking to gain insight into the function and meaning of traditional motifs in their respective contexts. But she too concludes by referring to the question of history and affirming that the literary form of the narratives is such that one cannot assume that any sort of historical events underlie them.[12]

Such an extreme denial of historicity does not represent a scholarly consensus. Nonetheless the approach to the problem, by which determination of possible historical worth should follow upon analyzing the literary type and intention of the material, is surely correct. It is therefore to the question of literary type that we must give further attention.

A PRELIMINARY CLARIFICATION

The problems and issues at stake are manifold. If any clarification is to emerge, certain potential sources of confusion must be dealt with at the outset.

First, it is dangerous to generalize. Thompson, for example, not only treats the Joseph and Moses narratives together as the same kind of material with no regard for their differences,[13] but also he allows for no differences within the Moses narratives. Irvin likewise seems to assume that the characteristics discovered in the early chapters of Exodus determine the genre of the remainder of the Moses narratives. But different narratives and traditions should be studied in their own right. The Sinai narrative is in many ways distinct from other Moses narratives and its genre should not be subsumed under that of other narratives.

Secondly, there is much diverse usage, with resultant confusion, of terminology. Terms like "legend", "saga", "epic", "heroic tale", "folktale", etc., tend to be used with insufficient definition and differentiation.

Irvin deliberately eschews the discussion of terminology on the grounds that the modern distinctions of literary type

> were not known or adhered to in the periods from which our stories date, and modern application of these terms is apt to be somewhat arbitrary, because it is not clear which ancient characteristics deserve which modern labels.[14]

Both these points may readily be granted. Nonetheless the precise differentiation of genre can hardly be a matter of indifference. For weighty historical and traditio-historical conclusions are made to depend on the understanding of genre, and the different genres are not identical in their historical implications. Legends, for example, centre on real people set within historical time; and although an historical nucleus may be so overlaid as to be unrecoverable it may also be possible to gain definite historical knowledge from a legend.[15] Folktales, by contrast, although set within historical time, do not deal with real people and are characterized by trickery and ingenuity as central concerns;[16] on almost no reckoning of folktale would one be justified in treating a folktale as an historical source.

Thompson bases the ahistorical nature of the Moses traditions on the fact that they are "heroic tales". But C. Conroy[17] analyzes the characteristics of heroic literature and shows that neither the patriarchs nor Moses can be considered heroic figures in the technical sense. For the milieu of heroic literature is aristocratic, the content is to do with banquets and battles, and the purpose is primarily entertainment. Thompson uses the term in a comparatively loose sense, to designate a story which focusses on one chief character, irrespective of whether his stature and qualities are heroic in the technical sense. Such a usage of "heroic" may be legitimate. But it is hard to see why such a narrative should necessarily be ahistorical, since it does not entail the use of traditional themes and motifs in the way that technically heroic literature does. A heroic tale (in Thompson's sense) may indeed by ahistorical, but that must be decided on other grounds than the simple fact that it is "heroic".[18]

It is obviously beyond the scope of this study to offer any resolution to the terminological problem. Rather it will be assumed that the designation "legend" (Sage) in some sense would be generally agreed to be applicable to the Moses tradition and may at least be heuristically applied to the Sinai material. The discussion, however, will seek to focus on analyzing characteristics of the material rather than build a case upon debatable terminology.

ORAL LITERATURE

It would be helpful initially to broaden the scope of the debate. Rather than discuss the applicability of, and criteria for, the designation "legend", a prior question is to ask whether the literature is oral literature, in the sense of "literature which has come into existence in an oral culture or group without the use of writing".[19] Oral literature is a broader category than legend and subsumes it. On most understandings of legend, legendary material was originally composed and transmitted orally and it is in the course of constant retelling that the historical nucleus (if any) which originally gave rise to the legend is overlaid. If, therefore, it seems likely that the material was not oral, it would also be unlikely that the material is legendary. If it was most likely oral, it would not therefore follow that it is legendary, since the precise nature of the material would still need to be decided; though "legend" would be the most likely candidate for the majority of early OT narratives.

The possibility of oral tradition bears directly upon the question of historicity. Oral tradition tends to make the historical value of a tradition comparatively limited. Although oral tradition can preserve material accurately and unchanged, it can also change it beyond recognition. The problem of course in any given case is to know which, and it is uncertainty here that largely accounts for the diversity of views concerning the historical reliability of Israel's early traditions. It can hardly be denied, however, that a considerable degree of transformation is characteristic of oral tradition, and as such necessitates caution in historical assessment.[20]

Significant though the implications of oral tradition are, the chief difficulty is to show that any particular tradition does genuinely represent oral tradition. The problem of distinguishing oral from written literature is great, with no clear consensus as to the demarcation.[21] Such is the problematic nature of the distinction that arguments about any particular text will usually fall short of demonstrability. The argumentation must be cumulative and applied heuristically.

First, one is looking for oral characteristics in a written text. This obvious point in worth emphasizing. For although it is possible that the written text is simply a direct transcription of an oral tradition, the transposition into writing can introduce scribal characteristics and obscure oral characteristics in the tradition. Allowance must be made for the possible loss of oral characteristics; their absence from a written text does not preclude the possibility of their original presence. Equally, however, it is important not to argue from a presupposed idea of oral tradition to the position that oral features "must have" originally characterized a particular story, even though most significant traces are no longer present in the text.[22] Unless there remains a substantial amount of oral criteria in the written text,[23] then either the supposed oral original lies so far behind written recensions as to become of minor importance, or else it may be the case that the postulation of oral origins is simply incorrect.

The relation of oral to written tradition is variable.[24] Particularly difficult to assess is the possible "transitional" text, a text from a time when a living tradition of oral composition is giving way to literary composition and when aspects of both modes of composition would be incorporated into the text. Such a possibility would make criteria for distinguishing oral from written characteristics difficult to establish firmly.

Finally, at this general level of discussion, it must be stressed that arguments about the likelihood of oral tradition, especially in the context of biblical literature where there is little evidence other than the final form of the written text, will necessarily be closely connected to one's overall understanding of the nature of early Israel and its culture and the likely extent of the use of writing and literacy.[25] Such considerations played a notable role in the pioneering work of Gunkel, and constitute both the strength and the weakness of his work. They are a strength in the comprehensiveness of the picture that thereby emerges. They are a weakness in that if the general considerations become suspect, then so does the whole position that is built around them. S.M. Warner, for example, strongly criticizes the anthropological assumptions that played a prominent role in the first edition of Gunkel's Genesis commentary;[26] on the basis of these Gunkel argued that brevity and lack of sophistication were sure indicators of early and oral material. This position, however, seems to be quite unfounded,[27] a fact which raises serious questions about Gunkel's whole pattern of argument.

In the search for specific criteria to distinguish oral from written tradition, scholars have not infrequently employed A. Olrik's famous "epic laws".[28] These thirteen laws or principles designate broad characteristics of a type of literature which Olrik called "Sage" in its broadest sense. Insofar as the laws arise out of Olrik's wide experience of folk literature, they usefully convey the "feel" of a particular type of popular literature. It has been increasingly questioned, however, whether Olrik's laws do genuinely enable one to differentiate between oral and written literature.[29] There are perhaps four main criticisms of their use in this regard. First, Olrik worked mainly with European material, and this will not necessarily be representative of literature from different cultures. Secondly, the "laws" are not laws; they are generalizations which admit of many exceptions. Thirdly, many of the "laws" are principles valid in most literary compositions. Fourthly, it is unclear how to use the "laws" in the sense that it is left uncertain whether the presence of few or many of the specified characteristics is necessary for the narrative to qualify as belonging to the genre in question.

Certain of Olrik's principles are clearly applicable to Ex. 32-34. The Law of Two to a Scene can be seen in ch. 32: vv. 1-6, Aaron and the people; vv. 7-14, Yahweh and Moses; vv. 15-20, Moses and Joshua; vv. 21-24, Moses and Aaron; vv. 25-29, Moses and the Levites; vv. 30ff., Moses and Yahweh. The Law of Contrast can perhaps be seen in 32:21-24, 25-29. The Importance of Final Position is exemplified in the way the mediator Moses is the object of all attention in 34:29ff. Other principles are only partially applicable. The Logic of the Sage, for example, demands an internal validity and consistency in the story; and while there is a consistency in Ex. 32-34 it is a highly theological, even paradoxical, consistency, hardly the kind of logic characteristic of popular stories. The principle of Concentration on a Leading Character cannot really do justice to the fine balance between Moses and Yahweh throughout the narrative.[30]

This partial applicability of Olrik's laws is not without significance for the nature of the narrative, but could hardly be said without further ado to constitute evidence of oral tradition in Ex. 32-34.

D.M. Gunn argues for patterning in narrative as evidence of oral tradition.[31] The recurrence of stereotyped and conventional descriptions reflects that constant use of traditional material which is a marked characteristic of the oral story-teller. Whether such patterning in Hebrew narrative reflects oral or literary technique is unclear.[32] One of its drawbacks is that it is only applicable to parts of narrative tradition and not the whole,[33] and so really needs the support of other criteria as well.

Even if patterning be accepted as a valid indicator of oral tradition, its applicability to Ex. 32-34 is questionable. The chief problem here, of course, is the extremely limited compass of material under consideration, within which one would hardly expect to find such repetition as Gunn posits. Such patterning could only be discerned in the comparison of Ex. 32-34 with the larger context of Exodus, yet here the distinctiveness of Ex. 32-34 becomes evident. There are certain parallels to Ex. 32-34 elsewhere in Exodus, for example Ex. 10:28f., 17:1-7,[34] but insofar as the parallelism is deliberate it is likely, especially in 17:1-7, to be a literary reworking dependent on the Sinai tradition. The striking parallelism between Ex. 32-34 and Gen. 6-9 remains to be investigated, but in any case does not show that kind of stereotyped patterning which is the concern here.[35]

The attempt to find oral criteria in Ex. 32-34 is not, therefore, particularly fruitful. The tenor of the arguments thus far suggests the unlikelihood of oral tradition closely underlying the material. Such a suggestion is further supported by Culley's important observation that

> the phase of oral composition is appropriate to the smaller unit, the prose story, the individual poem, or possibly even a cycle of stories, but not to collections containing different kinds of material having different styles and language. Larger collections of mixed material would presuppose that the individual units had become fixed before being brought together.[36]

Although Ex. 32-34 is hardly a "larger collection" of material, the variety of its contents is notable. Only in ch. 32 is there continuous narrative (which is why Olrik's principles are most readily applicable there, rather than in 33-34). In 33:12ff., 34:11ff. the intercession and the laws are a different type of material with a different style from the surrounding narrative. Yet it has also become clear how closely interwoven these different types are with their narrative context. If they were independent units joined together still at the oral stage one would expect the arrangement to be somewhat loose, characterized by catchwords or thematic grouping. In fact the relationship between units is close, there are no catchwords,[37] and there is a coherent development of thought throughout. The tight linkage of the different types of material is a clear literary achievement. This still leaves the possibility that there were independent oral units joined by a literary process, but this must lie so far below the present text that it is doubtful whether it can still be intelligibly discerned. In conclusion, then, there are no clear indications of oral tradition underlying Ex. 32-34. This is not to deny the possibility of original oral tradition, but it is to question whether the hypothesis of oral origins is at all illuminating for the tradition as we now have it.

CRITERIA FOR LEGEND

If the case for oral tradition in Ex. 32-34 is tenuous, and if legend presupposes oral tradition, then one might simply conclude without further ado that the notion of Ex. 32-34 as legend is equally tenuous. But such is the difficulty in this kind of discussion of producing demonstrative arguments rather than only probabilities or possibilities that it will not be out of place to consider the question of legend afresh from a different angle.

Four: Exodus 32-34 as Legend

This different approach will be to list a number of criteria which are generally considered to be indicative of legendary material, and see how far Ex. 32-34 conforms to them. The list of criteria offered here is not intended to be exhaustive but representative, and will be based largely on the work of those scholars who have dealt specifically with the OT and are alert to its peculiarities.[38] Many scholars have indeed made much use of Olrik's Laws in this context, and if they are taken as indicative of a type of narrative without prejudice to the question of oral tradition then they may still be used with profit. But since Olrik's Laws are not orientated towards OT narrative, and since not all scholars make use of them, they will not occupy the forefront of the discussion.

The following six features are generally considered as indicative of legend. They are not listed in any order of precedence. First, oral tradition. Secondly, the presence of miracles. Thirdly, the presence of aetiological motifs. Fourthly, the use of traditional motifs. Fifthly, a typical dimension. Sixthly, the lack of a clear distinction between past event and subsequent experience and interpretation.

1) Oral tradition

This has already been discussed. This is not based on any one specific trait but represents rather an overall assessment of the nature of the material. Although it has featured prominently in discussions since Gunkel, its significance for Ex. 32-34 would appear to be small.

The fact of oral tradition is sometimes connected with anonymity of authorship, this anonymity reflecting "the anonymous totality of the tribes and their several clans at those times when they were gathered together, that is, preeminently on cultic occasions".[39] Not only, however, is it the case that anonymity does not require corporate and oral authorship as opposed to individual and scribal, but also anonymity is so widespread in ancient literature that it cannot function as a distinguishing characteristic of legend.

2) Miracles

The presence of miracle is one of the most widely agreed characteristics of legend and other non-historical narrative. To say this is not, of course, to prejudge whether or not miracles actually occur, for such an issue cannot be decided on literary grounds; nor can it be said that miracles appear only in the context of legend. The point is simply that it is characteristic of a particular type of story to attract to itself accounts of miraculous happenings.

There are indeed many miracles in the narratives of Exodus and Numbers. This makes their absence from the Sinai pericope the more striking. The longest unit of narrative action, Ex. 32, is entirely unmiraculous. The theophany of Ex. 33-34 is extra-ordinary but is hardly a miracle in the customary sense; in content, presentation and result it is quite distinctive, and its ethos is not that of the legendary miracle. There is the fact that God writes upon the tablets (34:28b), and also the descent of Moses with the shining face (34:29ff.), but these cannot be considered determinative for the narrative as a whole.

3) Aetiology

Aetiology may be indicative of legend when the aetiology is a primary factor in the tradition and not a secondary addition to it, as is often the case in the OT.[40] There is, however, little that is indisputably aetiological in Ex. 32-34. The approach of Beyerlin, who argues for aetiologies throughout the narrative, raises acutely the problem of criteria. There is no formula such as "to this day". Although, for example, Beyerlin argues that the words "from Horeb onwards" (mēhar ḥôrēb) are indicative of the function of 33:3b-6 as aetiological of a later ceremony at Shechem, the words in fact function as part of the parallel between Israel and the Egyptians.[41]

There is no shortage of material in Ex. 32-34 which may be interpreted aetiologically. The golden calf may be considered aetiological for the establishment of Jeroboam's calves (or for the opposition to them); the incident of the Levites may be aetiological for later Levitical privilege; the role of Moses may be aetiological for subsequent cultic functionaries; and so on. But there is little formal indication of such concerns in the text. And while this does not rule out aetiological interest in the narrative, it does make it difficult to decide how far aetiology has genuinely controlled the development of the tradition. In general, the resolution of such issues must be subsequent to one's detailed historical and traditio-historical study of the material and cannot be decided in advance on literary grounds.

There is a sense in which the tradition of Ex. 32-34, as a Sinai tradition, functions aetiologically. It is because Yahweh revealed himself and made a covenant with Israel at Sinai that Israel subsequently knows itself as the people of Yahweh and worships him in the cult. In particular, it is because Yahweh first proclaimed his name as gracious that Israel can call upon him as such.[42] But to say this is to say no more than that Ex. 32-34 may function as a cult legend in the technical form-critical sense;[43] and since such a function is quite independent of literary type, it cannot be a factor in the determination of literary type, which is the present concern.

4) Traditional Motifs

A certain type of content is characteristic of legendary and other non-historical narrative. The standard work in this area is S. Thompson's Motif-Index of Folk Literature which is a massive compilation of the content and motifs of folklore (in the broadest sense of the term). The work needs to be used with care in that many of the motifs it contains, while present in folklore, are not peculiar to folklore and so are of limited value for identifying it.

In this context the distinctiveness of the Sinai pericope from the rest of Exodus again becomes apparent. J.G. Frazer, T.H. Gaster and D. Irvin,[44] all of whom cite abundant folkloristic parallels to the early chapters of Exodus, offer no such parallels to the narrative of Ex. 19-20, 24, 32-34. Ex. 32, with its continuous narrative action, might seem the most likely locus for traditional motifs. Yet Gressmann cites parallels only to the "book of life" (32:32f.), which is an incidental motif.[45]

Elements of Ex. 32-34 can be found in Thompson's Index, but the significance of these is unclear. The motifs of a bull-god[46] or a god assuming the form of a calf[47] reveal little about 32:1ff. Fratricide is a common folk motif,[48] and may be discerned in 32:29. It plays only a minor role, however, in the unit and does not constitute a genuine motif since it does not further the story in any way.[49] Perhaps the two most significant motifs are the taboo on seeing the deity[50] (cf. Ex. 33:20), and the "Holy man radiant"[51] (cf. Ex. 34:29ff.). Both of these, however, function in a strikingly theological way, and their distinctive ethos is not directly suggestive of traditional material.

5) Typical Significance

Von Rad argues that while history writing presents events in their isolated particularity, their historical contingency, legend presents people and events as types:

> Whatever tradition we select - the story of Cain, the

> betrayal of Sarah, the manna, Balaam, or the Blessing of Moses (Ex. 17) - it is perfectly clear that, while they refer us to the realm of history, yet, in spite of all the concreteness of their presentation, there is always at the same time a certain typical significance. Correspondingly, the men and women involved in the event are also to a large extent types, in that the ways in which they act are not to be regarded as having occurred only once: what makes them important is precisely their more general validity. They therefore possess a coefficient of present-day relevance which the documentary presentation of history lacks. There is no doubt that certain traditions set out to relate an event which occurred only once, yet give it the form of one which occurred over and over again.[52]

The perception that certain OT traditions have a typical significance is important. It is presumably this that is intended by reference to the "poetic" quality of such traditions. As Koch puts it,

> The knowledge that a biblical story is legendary does not detract from its significance. Sagas are reality poeticized.[53]

Nonetheless, it is again striking how little Ex. 32-34 conforms to such a criterion. First, typical narratives tend to have a certain "spacious" quality about them - there are only one or two characters, all unnecessary detail falls out, there is an unhurried feel in the action of the narrative. In Ex. 32-34, by contrast, the content and action is too dense; the scenes shift too quickly, the feel of the narrative is too urgent to convey much typical or poetic quality.

Secondly, there is a specificity about much of Ex. 32-34 which deprives it of typical significance. One may compare Moses' intercession in 33:12ff. with the "Blessing of Moses" (Ex. 17:8ff.). The latter indeed presents an archetypal picture, but how different is the agonized intensity of 33:12ff., centring on the specific problem of the restoration of God's shrine in the midst of sinful Israel. Nowhere in Ex. 32-34, except perhaps 34:29ff., is Moses a typical figure. The particularity of the promise to him in distinction from the people of Israel (32:10), the harsh role of judgment (32:19f., 25ff.), the urgency of the intercessions (32:11ff., 30ff., 33:12ff.) and the unique mediation between Yahweh and Israel are not such as one can easily identify with. There is exemplary significance, but that is a different matter. Ex. 32-34 does present a paradigmatic account of sin and forgiveness and the dependence of Israel upon the mercy of God,[54] and the use of the generalizing expression "stiff-necked people" is perhaps deliberately intended to generalize the significance and application of the narrative. But again this is quite different from a typical depiction of either people or events.

Thirdly, Ex. 32-34 is different from most typical narratives in that its basic presupposition is the particularity and exclusiveness of Mosaic Yahwism. It is notable that those traditions are most typical in character where the theology of the Mosaic covenant is least in evidence. This is particularly so in the patriarchal traditions where the absence of any exclusiveness is a significant aspect of the "everyman" character of the stories.[55] Ex. 32-34 presupposes throughout a religious exclusiveness, a unique phenomenon in the history of religion,[56] and the need for obedience to the moral and ritual laws of the decalogue. Such concerns are quite different in ethos from the typical or poetic.

6) The Lack of Distinction between Past and Present

The narrator of legend does not distinguish present and past in a strictly historical way. Rather, as von Rad puts it,

> the narrator - historical considerations notwithstanding - reports the events as he himself conceives them as having happened ... The event is naïvely placed within the horizon of the narrator's own faith, and he is of a later generation ... Saga is quite unable to safeguard its original content from later alterations. On the contrary, it is a ready vessel for new contents, it adapts itself to new possibilities of interpretation, and in the process it often leaves its original subject far behind.[57]

With such legends it is unhelpful to distinguish between an "authentic" historical kernel and a fictional overlay; for subsequent interpretations and experiences are also historical and bear witness to God's continual dealings with his people.[58]

The concept involved in this criterion is readily comprehensible. The difficulty is to know how and where it is genuinely applicable. For to recognize elements of a tradition as anachronistic presupposes a good knowledge of the respective periods in question so that one can be reasonably sure what is appropriate to each. With early OT traditions this puts one in a somewhat paradoxical position. Our chief, and sometimes our only, source of information for Israel's early history is Israel's early traditions.[59] And yet it is on the basis of these traditions, which are considered to present an inaccurate historical picture, that one can apparently acquire a competent knowledge of the periods in question. The logic of this position should not be pushed too far. A careful attention to peculiarities in texts and comparison between different texts can lead to likely reconstructions. Nonetheless, the tentative and hypothetical nature of the task is apparent and allows for widely divergent reconstructions. The problem is well illustrated by the diversity of views on the questions of what kind of monotheism, if any, is attributable to Moses and whether the religious and ethical teaching of the decalogue can be accepted as having existed as early in Israel's history as the time of Moses.

It follows from this that it will be a scholar's general understanding of early Israel in its ancient Near Eastern context that will play a major role in the assessment of whether and to what extent a tradition contains anachronistic and unhistorical elements. This obviously introduces major issues that lie beyond our present purview. Suffice it to say at present that there is nothing patently anachronistic in Ex. 32-34 that could not fit in its supposed historical context.[60] If this contention is correct, then the present criterion for distinguishing legend becomes difficult to apply fruitfully to Ex. 32-34.

SUMMARY AND CONCLUSION

The above rapid review of criteria for legend applied to Ex. 32-34 produces an interesting conclusion - that there is remarkably little in Ex. 32-34 that would qualify the material for the designation "legend". Obviously the discussion has hardly been exhaustive and is more in the nature of a few preliminary soundings. Nonetheless, sufficient has been said to justify drawing a conclusion in at least tentative terms. For the discussion has enabled the distinctiveness of the chapters to come more clearly into focus. Some may indeed feel that the discussion has been to some extent labouring the obvious. For it may be at least in part because of a recognition of the distinctiveness of the chapters that the special designation of cult legend has been so widely adopted. If, however, the designation of cult legend (in a sense which denotes the literary type of the narrative) is considered doubtful, it is appropriate to consider alternatives, especially when the term "legend" has been applied so freely to the Moses traditions.

What significance may one attach to the conclusion that the characteristics of legend are largely lacking in Ex. 32-34? A few suggestions may be made. First, although discussion of legend tends to focus on the possible historical value of the content of legend, the chief value of the above discussion has been the illumination of aspects of Ex. 32-34 which were not brought out by the exegesis. One's understanding of Moses' intercession in Ex. 33, for example, while based primarily upon the exegesis in context, is furthered by appreciating how different it is in ethos from a story like Ex. 17:8ff.

Secondly, although the discussion has argued the inadequacy of the terms "cult legend" and "legend", it is not part of the present purpose to replace these by some alternative designation of any degree of precision. For any precise and specific designation would probably have to be a rather baroque and ungainly term, coined for the purpose. As such it would be of limited value. A term such as "theological story" would be possible, but is inherently so vague that it could comprise a wide variety of different types of narrative. Besides, the term has already been used by Westermann, in his discussion of types of narrative in Genesis,[61] with a specific meaning; that is, a story which is effectively narrative theology, whereby some old tradition has been transformed into a vehicle for presenting theological questions and statements. And since it is uncertain, or at least unproved, that such a process underlies Ex. 32-34 (the theological shaping of the material is unquestioned, but there is more than one way of explaining it), it would only confuse matters to use a term with potentially misleading, or question-begging, implications. For the present, it will be sufficient to acquiesce in using the general term "story". Not, indeed, in a wholly undifferentiated sense, for many peculiarities of the narrative have emerged in our discussion. The important thing is so to read the story that one becomes aware of its characteristics, even if one lacks any precise term for classifying it.

Thirdly, there is the bearing of literary genre upon the determining of historicity. It has been seen that Ex. 32-34 generally lacks certain characteristics that would tend to disqualify it from being historical in intent or content. But it would be premature to conclude that the narrative therefore is historical, at least in intention whether or not in actual fact. For the bearing of the literary and theological dimensions of the story upon its possible historical intent has not yet been sufficiently examined. In terms of the discussion thus far it would be appropriate to leave open the question of historical intent. The nature of the material, as thus far perceived, is still open to the possibility of genuine historical concern in the material, but could not be said to require it, nor to be incompatible with its absence.

In any case, discussions of literary genre are only a preliminary to the task of historical study proper. The advancing of any historical conclusions must be based upon specifically historical arguments. It is appropriate, therefore, to turn again from literary considerations to consider further some of the historically-orientated questions that may be put to Ex. 32-34.

Chapter 5

SELECTIVE CRITICAL ANALYSIS OF EX. 32-34

In this final section we shall consider some of the most important problems that confront the interpreter as he seeks to discover the origins and development of Ex. 32-34 in the light of the final form of the text. Even if Ex. 32-34 does not owe its structure or major elements to the historicization of a regular cultic ritual, and even if it does not show clear signs of legendary development, its integrity as a narrative tradition may still be called in question on a variety of grounds. In particular, weighty source-critical and traditio-historical arguments have been adduced to show the composite nature of the material. The following, necessarily partial, examination of previous analytical work will seek to determine how far such arguments affect the essential plot of Ex. 32-34 and also how they bear on elements which are secondary to the central concern.

AN ANALYSIS OF EX. 34:1-28

There are two central issues in existing treatments of Ex. 32-34. One is the mainly literary question of Ex. 34 as a covenant renewal,[1] the other is the mainly traditio-historical question of the origins of the golden calf story in Ex. 32. Although distinct issues, they are inter-related. For if the people's apostasy was original to the tradition, then some renewal of the ruptured relationship would be required. If the covenant renewal was original, then something must have required such a renewal. Conversely, the denial that either element was original carries the natural corollary that the other element is likewise unlikely to be original. Given the inherent complementarity of the stories and the close literary and theological links between them in the present text, the heuristic assumption will be that the two stories do indeed belong together to the same tradition, unless good reason can be found to deny this.

First, Ex. 34 as a covenant renewal. It is widely agreed that Ex. 34 was originally the J account of an initial covenant making, parallel to the E version in Ex. 19-20; when the J and E Sinai narratives were combined, the J covenant was preserved but redactionally transformed into a covenant renewal.[2] Five principal considerations can be advanced in favour of this position.

First, the hypothesis is part of the larger documentary analysis of the Pentateuch, the Sinai pericope being considered a striking example of parallel J and E versions being preserved together, as can also be observed elsewhere.

Secondly, the specific references to renewal in vv. 1, 4, 9 can easily be recognized as secondary modifications. These references are:

v. 1. "like the first (kr'šnym) ..." to the end of the verse.
v. 4. "like the first".
v. 9. Every phrase in this verse harks back to some part of the preceding narrative, and so must be entirely secondary.

Thirdly, it may be argued that the chapter reads like an initial covenant making.

Fourthly, the laws of 34:11-26 have been seen as an alternative or parallel tradition to the decalogue of Ex. 20 (or even a J parallel to the E Book of the Covenant). This is usually supported by an appeal to the "ten words" in 34:28, understood as in some way designating the foregoing laws.

Fifthly, if the story of the golden calf is, on other grounds, considered as a late addition to the Sinai tradition, yet the covenant renewal presupposes it, then the renewal must also be a late addition.

These arguments are mainly to do with broad considerations of the role of Ex. 34 within the Sinai pericope. Commentators have indeed argued in detail particularly concerning vv. 5-7, 9-10, 27-28 that there is incoherence in these verses and that much is secondary. But the exegesis offered above[3] has shown that most of the difficulties felt in these verses are unfounded once the development of the narrative as a whole is appreciated. There is a smoothness and coherence which more likely suggests original unity than secondary modification. While the latter possibility can never be ruled out, the exegesis of Ex. 34 may well be taken to exemplify how a fresh perception of the final text can render unnecessary certain arguments for a complex prehistory.[4] Assuming therefore the substantial correctness of the exegesis, the present discussion will concentrate on the more general questions that may be raised.

1) There are several difficulties with the documentary analysis. First, there is the widespread questioning of the validity of the documentary hypothesis in the current scholarly debate. Secondly, even if the documentary hypothesis is deemed to be generally valid for the Pentateuch - and as yet no superior alternative hypothesis of similar comprehensiveness has been advanced - it would not follow that it was valid for the Sinai pericope which may well have a literary and traditio-historical background different from that of other pentateuchal material.

Thirdly, even if one granted the usual assumption that J and E both contained accounts of the Sinai tradition and that both of these were available to a redactor, the redactional combination could be understood in more than one way. The customary assumption that a redactor was only able to preserve a J covenant narrative by transforming it into a secondary renewal is not a necessary one. It would be possible for the redactor to have used solely J or solely E throughout, suppressing the other account. Either J or E could have included both an initial covenant-making and a subsequent renewal, and to use both would have been unnecessary. Alternatively, if Ex. 32-34 is considered characteristically J while Ex. 19-24 is characteristically E, it could be that a redactor, possessing two accounts each with a covenant initiation and renewal, took the covenant initiation from one source and the renewal from the other, so that both sources were represented. Either of these suppositions is consistent with an acceptance of J and E; independent J and E accounts of Sinai would not _ipso facto_ entail that covenant renewal was a secondary element. One needs to show not only that J and E documents or traditions are represented but that neither contained, or is likely to have contained, both a covenant initiation and a subsequent renewal. To the best of my knowledge, this point has not received satisfactory treatment.[5]

It may be remarked in passing that there are considerable difficulties attendant upon an analysis in terms of J and E even within Ex. 19, 20, 24. The appalling diversity of suggested source divisions[6] must raise questions about the nature of the undertaking. This is not to deny that the material may indeed be composite at both a source-critical and a traditio-historical level, but it is to ask whether the attempt to explain this in terms of independent and parallel J and E accounts is the most fruitful method of approach. And if a different approach were adopted, this would be a further reason to reconsider the need to postulate Ex. 34 as the J parallel to Ex. 20. But this cannot be pursued at present.

2) Noth asserts that the references to renewal in vv. 1, 4, 9 "are inserted only loosely" and "can easily be separated as secondary".[7] But in fact they fit naturally and smoothly within the development of the story and are not in themselves problematic. They only need to be understood as secondary when a decision has already been reached about the chapter on other grounds.

3) Childs argues that Ex. 34 reads like an initial covenant making.[8] The natural response is to ask, How else would one expect the account to appear? Unless one can plausibly demonstrate which significant differences could be expected to distinguish a covenant renewal from an initial making, this point lacks cogency.[9] In fact, one would naturally expect the two occasions to be similar. The difference between initiation and renewal would be made clear chiefly in two ways: through the overall context and through specific references. When the context of Ex. 32f. is discounted and the specific references in vv. 1, 4, 9 are considered secondary, it is hardly surprising that there may seem little indication of renewal in the chapter.

Having said this, however, one can point out that there are indeed various distinguishing characteristics of Ex. 34 that appear in the exegesis: the privacy of the theophany to the faithful mediator, as opposed to the publicity of Ex. 19; the particular stress upon the grace of Yahweh in 34:6,9 as the foundation for a renewed covenant, an emphasis unnecessary in Ex. 19-20 when the problem of Israel's sin had not been raised; the heightened emphasis upon faithfulness to Yahweh in 34:11-16; the cultic laws appropriate to Israel's cultic sin; the absence, after Israel's unfaithfulness, of any account of the people's response (such as in Ex. 24), appropriate to the emphasis upon the sovereign action of Yahweh towards an unfaithful people. In context, these are all important features of covenant renewal and would not read more naturally as an initial covenant making.

4) The next issue is the relationship of the laws in 34:11-26 to the Decalogue and the Book of the Covenant. The exegesis has made their function clear. The laws are a recapitulation of the earlier laws, selecting those relevant to the situation. While it

is possible to view the laws as an alternative to those given earlier, there is no need to do so. Now that the unhelpful antithesis between a ritual and ethical decalogue has long since been abandoned, and the particular emphasis of the laws of Ex. 34 can be fully explained by the context, there is little reason to set up the laws of Ex. 34 as themselves the original basis of a covenant. It has been suggested, moreover, in the exegesis that the attempt to find a decalogue in 34:11-26 on the basis of 34:28 rests upon a misinterpretation of that latter verse. Despite a certain initial plausibility in identifying the laws of vv. 11-26 with the covenant words of vv. 1, 28, this creates the double tension of v. 28 with both vv. 11-26 and v. 1. Since both difficulties are so smoothly solved by the exegesis proposed, it becomes doubtful whether one is still justified in postulating the displacement of material, a different decalogue, or conflicting traditions.[10] The laws of 34:11-26 provide insufficient reason to doubt the nature of the chapter as an original renewal.

5) Finally, there is the fact that Ex. 34 as covenant renewal presupposes the story of Ex. 32. It is, therefore, to an examination of the golden calf that we must now turn. Because the two stories are to a considerable extent interdependent, it is not only the case that if the calf story can be shown to be late and secondary, then doubts are cast upon Ex. 34 as a renewal.[11] For, equally, if there is good reason to suppose that Ex. 34 as a renewal is original, this constitutes an argument in favour of regarding the sin that caused the renewal, i.e. Ex. 32, as also original to the tradition.

Admittedly, if one abandons the generally held view that Ex. 34 contains an early tradition, one can see Ex. 34 as indeed written as a renewal by interpreting it as a deuteronomistic literary context created for the golden calf story.[12] But the general tenor of the arguments in this study would not support such a late date for the creation of Ex. 32-34 as a whole, given its importance within the traditions and worship of Israel which are dependent upon it.

AN ANALYSIS OF EX. 32:1-6

The examination of the story of the golden calf in Ex. 32 involves a complex of literary, historical, and traditio-historical issues.

Taken by itself the story is, at first sight, straightforward. There are no real literary unevennesses in 32:1-6 such as might suggest the presence of diverse traditions. Despite various arguments for literary disunity,[13] the narrative is in fact "clearly of one piece".[14] The central problem[15] is posed by asking what is the relationship of Ex. 32 to the story of Jeroboam's golden calves in 1 Kg. 12:26-32. There is a certain similarity of outline between the two stories and also some similarity of detail,[16] the most notable being the identical phrase, "This is your god, O Israel, who brought you up out of the land of Egypt"[17] in both Ex. 32:4,8 and 1 Kg. 12:28. That there is some relationship between the two narratives seems clear. But the literary relationship, not in itself complex, is generally considered as but a pointer to a complex traditio-historical development underlying Ex. 32.

The significance of the similarities between the two narratives, and in particular its bearing upon determining the relative priority of the two texts, constitutes the main problem at issue. The similarity cannot of itself resolve the question of priority either way. The relationship between the two narratives may be construed in a number of different ways. First, Ex. 32:1-6 in its present form may be the earlier narrative, the resemblances in 1 Kg. 12 being intended as deliberately reminiscent.[18] Secondly, while the basic substance of Ex. 32 may be early, its literary presentation reflects later polemic against Jeroboam.[19] Thirdly, the content and presentation of Ex. 32 may have been entirely created out of polemic against Jeroboam.[20] Fourthly, and most complex, a substantially different version of Ex. 32:1-6 may be original, a tradition originally favourable to both Aaron and the calf, and it was to such a favourable precedent that Jeroboam was appealing. 1 Kg. 12 is thus earlier than Ex. 32 in its present form, Ex. 32 being a major reworking of the older calf tradition as part of a polemic against the northern kingdom.[21] Finally, an alternative form of the preceding would be the more general thesis that in early Israel cultic calves were quite acceptable and that Jeroboam based himself upon such a tradition, the connection of a calf with Aaron (and Sinai), as well as the polemical presentation, being the retrojection of post-Jeroboam conflicts.[22]

It is one of these last three options, particularly the last two, that the substance of Ex. 32 is dependent upon the Jeroboam tradition but that both reflect some early calf tradition, now lost, that is most widely held today. Since Jeroboam's cultic actions can be dated with reasonable confidence to the penultimate decade of the tenth century, this would entail a terminus post quem for the Ex. 32 tradition of the end of the tenth century, and would make it a comparative latecomer into the narrative traditions of the Pentateuch.

It is necessary to examine Ex. 32 and its relation to 1 Kg. 12 de novo. To start with the most striking link between the two narratives, one must determine the significance of the sacral cry, 'ēlleh (hinnēh) 'elōhêkā yiśrā'ēl 'ašer heᶜelûkā mē'ereṣ miṣrāyim. ("This is [behold] your god, O Israel, who brought you up out of the land of Egypt"). It is customarily argued that the unusual plural form of the verb after 'elōhîm is appropriate to the context of 1 Kg. 12 where there is a plurality of calves but inappropriate to the single calf of Ex. 32. Therefore the reference in 1 Kg. 12 is original and that in Ex. 32 dependent upon it.

There are two difficulties with this. The first is that the plural verb is not in fact appropriate to the situation pictured in 1 Kg. 12. It is evident that Jeroboam was not trying to introduce some new polytheism into the northern kingdom, but rather a particular form of the worship of the one deity Yahweh. Only on a crassly materialistic understanding would a plurality of images be seen as entailing a plurality of gods; and one can hardly ascribe such an understanding to Jeroboam. Jeroboam was setting up two cult objects for the worship of one deity. The plural verb, when the one deity is subject, is not appropriate.

Secondly, it has been seen in the exegesis[23] that a plural verb after 'elōhîm can be employed by a writer wishing to convey a pagan understanding of God, which is best rendered in English by "god", and that this is the likely significance of the plural form in Ex. 32. This is also the likely significance of the verb in 1 Kg. 12:28 where, as in Ex. 32, the writer clearly disapproves. This means that in both Ex. 32 and 1 Kg. 12:28 the plural verb conveys the writer's theological interpretation of the incidents.

What of the appropriateness of the cry itself? The reference to the immediately preceding exodus fits well in the context of Ex. 32. Leaving aside the historical problems,[24] the literary presentation of Ex. 32 presupposes both that Yahweh has brought the Israelites to Sinai and that he will lead them away again. A sacral cry which identifies the calf with the God who leads the people is appropriate.

The sacral cry is less appropriate to the situation of Jeroboam because, strictly speaking, it would not be relevant to his aims. Jeroboam's general concern was to provide a rival to the Jerusalem temple, which specifically involved establishing a rival to the Jerusalem ark.[25] Since the ark was by then settled in the temple and may well have been seen less as a symbol of the God who moved around with and guided his people and more as signifying the one who protected the chosen city by his presence, an appeal to the exodus tradition seems slightly misplaced as not providing a theological equivalent to the significance of the ark.[26]

Given these considerations, the natural conclusion is that the sacral cry is original to Ex. 32 where the writer has modified it slightly to convey his interpretation of its significance. In 1 Kg. 12:28 the whole phrase represents the interpretative work of the redactor who wants to show how Jeroboam's act was no better than the notorious apostasy of Israel at Sinai.

Beyond the literary question, it remains to discuss the historical and traditio-historical problems concerning Ex. 32 and 1 Kg. 12. These are best approached by asking first why it was that Jeroboam chose to set up cultic calves, and secondly why this apparently drew no protest until the time of Hosea, approximately 170 years later. For if there was an ancient tradition of Israel's apostasy at Sinai, an apostasy centred on the worship of a calf, it is _prima facie_ remarkable that Jeroboam should have chosen a known symbol of apostasy to establish his cult of Yahweh, and still more remarkable that such committed Yahwists as Elijah, Elisha, Jehu (2 Kg. 10:28-31) and Amos[27] should, apparently, have registered no protest.

The clue to understanding Jeroboam's policy lies in the contemporary religious environment. The bull was the most widespread religious symbol in the religion of the Levant. Not only in Canaan, but also in Egypt, Ugarit and Mesopotamia the bull was _the_ symbol, par excellence, of male deity, and is abundantly attested in the literature and iconography of these areas. Jeroboam had to produce an effective rival to the Jerusalem temple. Within his kingdom he had many diverse elements, some only recently incorporated into Yahwism under David. For many such it is unlikely that their Yahwism was more than a veneer; their basic religious understanding would still have been largely in the terms of traditional Canaanite religion.[28] To win their allegiance, a presentation of Yahwism in terms of the religious symbols already familiar to them, would have seemed the obvious solution. Hence the calves of Bethel and Dan.

What significance would have attached to these calves? It is generally held[29] that the calf (bull) was intended as a throne or pedestal for the invisible deity above it.[30] This would provide an exact parallel to the ark (cf. Jer. 3:16f.) and correspond with numerous iconographic conceptions of the deity.[31] As Noth puts it,

> As the ancient Near East (in contrast to Egypt) knows no theriomorphic deities but only the association of beasts with deities pictured in human form whose companions and bearers they are, the "golden calves" of the royal sanctuaries of Jeroboam are also surely meant merely as pedestals for the God who is imagined to be standing invisibly upon them.[32]

The situation is not, however, so clear-cut. First, it is not the case that the ancient Near East knew no theriomorphic deities or, at least, deities that could be theriomorphically conceived.[33] Animals were seen to embody a deity's attributes such as strength, speed or fertility, and an animal image could be the object of worship.[34] Secondly, the texts of Ex. 32, 1 Kg. 12 (and also the bull references in Hosea[35]) give no hint that the calves were conceived of as pedestals. Of course silence does not exclude the possibility, and the portrayal of the calf as identified with the deity may simply represent the Tendenz of the writer. Nonetheless the absence of specific evidence should not be forgotten.

What should be clear is that it is dangerous to dogmatize or generalize about an issue such as the relationship of a deity to his cult object. Attempts to define the divine presence in the cult are notoriously difficult and controversial.[36] Some may have understood the calf as pedestal, others as an actual representation or materialization of the deity, and others might have had different conceptions or no coherent conception at all. Even if Jeroboam conceived of the calves as pedestals, it is doubtful whether the ordinary Israelite would have shared his understanding.[37]

What precedent, if any, within Israelite tradition would

Jeroboam have had? On this we do not have sufficient evidence for a definite answer. Bethel and Dan were certainly sanctuaries of ancient significance. Bethel is associated with the patriarch Jacob (Gen. 28:10-22), and Dan with the migration of the Danites (Jdg. 17-18). The account in Jdg. 17-18 is significant in that it shows that in pre-monarchical times Dan was an important cult centre which contained a cult object (pesel), and had a priesthood claiming Mosaic descent (18:30). Was Jeroboam therefore simply reviving the ancient traditions of Dan? Although it is often suggested that there was a bull-calf at Dan prior to Jeroboam,[38] we cannot be sure. Jdg. 17-18 does not say that Micah's image was a bull, and had there been a tradition of a bull-image such silence would be unlikely. In general terms the prestige of Bethel and Dan would have been important for Jeroboam, but such was the strength of bull symbolism in Canaanite religion that it is doubtful that Jeroboam needed any specific Yahwistic precedent. A history of religious pluralism within his territories would provide an appropriate context within which to introduce a new, but seemingly natural, form of the worship of Yahweh.

Leaving aside temporarily the question of why Jeroboam's calves were not opposed, since this question would in any case lead one back to Ex. 32, it is time to consider Ex. 32 in the light of what has already been said.

First, any ambiguity about the divine presence in Jeroboam's calves must equally be the case in Ex. 32. To reconstruct some clear original understanding of the calf in its relationship to Yahweh is not possible. The text's presentation of the calf as itself representing Yahweh may obscure its original significance, but is not necessarily tendentious. Either way, the issue is in fact of little importance.

Secondly, it has been debated whether the text is consistent in its portrayal of the nature of the people's sin. Childs sees the present text as depicting apostasy from Yahweh into polytheism, but argues that the prehistory of the text suggests that the original issue was syncretistic in character.[39] This seems to me to misrepresent the problem in that it does not sufficiently appreciate the particular perspective of the writer in Ex. 32. That is, for this writer (as also for the redactor of 1 Kg. 12:28) there is no essential difference between syncretism and apostasy. There is either legitimate worship of the true God or there is illegitimate worship of a false god. The intermediate possibility, illegitimate worship of the true God (i.e. syncretism, the incorporation into Yahwism of non-Yahwistic rites and practices) is not possible; illegitimate worship cannot, by definition, be worship of the true God. This is why although the present text of Ex. 32 clearly reveals the intention of the people as syncretistic, for the writer this is tantamount to total apostasy. The distinction between syncretism and fetishism or polytheism is alien to him. Such a perspective is basic not only to Ex. 32:1-6 but also to the whole of chs. 32-34.[40] The issue is not one of varying estimates of the calf, but of the particular perspective of Mosaic Yahwism.

It has been further questioned whether a calf tradition is intelligible as a Sinai tradition on the grounds that it presupposes the settlement in Canaan; polemic against a calf would not make sense outside the context of the struggle against Canaanite fertility religion. So widespread, however, was the calf as a religious symbol that a calf tradition, while of great relevance within Canaan, can hardly be localized or limited to Canaan. Rather than asking how a calf tradition could make sense outside Canaan, the different question may be put: "If the Israelites, even at Sinai, wished to express their Yahwistic faith in an image of the deity, what would be more natural than for them to choose a bull?"

The traditio-historical suggestion of an early calf tradition probably favourable to the calf and probably associated with either Bethel or Dan is hard to assess in the absence of firm evidence, either in Ex. 32 or elsewhere, that could be adduced in support. The suggestion depends entirely on a general understanding of early Israelite religion and tradition. There are, however, at least two serious difficulties with regarding Ex. 32 as originally the cult legend[41] of either Bethel of Dan.

First, Bethel and Dan already have cult legends recorded in Gen. 28, Jdg. 17-18. More than one cult legend, in the technical sense of the official story of the founding of a particular sanctuary, would be inappropriate for any shrine. Admittedly one could argue that Ex. 32 was the cult legend of the object at the shrine, as Num. 21:4-9 might be for the serpent in Jerusalem (cf. 2 Kg. 18:4), distinct from the cult legend for Jerusalem itself. But this meets a second difficulty.

From a form-critical perspective, Ex. 32 lacks the characteristics of a cult legend. The calf is localized not at Bethel or Dan but at Sinai, and, with the possible exception of Num. 21:4-9, no other cult legend for X is located at Y. The story is not linked to any sanctuary at Sinai; and there is little evidence of Sinai functioning as a religious centre in OT times, apart from inferences which may possibly be drawn from the journey of Elijah in 1 Kg. 19 or the wilderness itineraries, especially Num. 33:1-49.[42] There is no statement, even implicit, about continuity of religious practice from what was established in Ex. 32 to the writer's day. Indeed, such is impossible when the cult object created in the story is destroyed. But then Ex. 32 could only function as the aetiology of the idea or institution of calf worship, not the worship of some actual calf; and such a theoretical aetiology would have no exact parallel in the OT. One could of course argue that an earlier form of Ex. 32 contained the necessary characteristics. But such an hypothesis is hard to control inasmuch as it has no foundation in the text. The most relevant parallel, Num. 21:4-9, also argues against such a transformation of the text. We know that the serpent fell into disrepute (2 Kg. 18:4), yet no later polemic has been read back into Num. 21, which presents the serpent in a wholly favourable light. The hypothesis of Ex. 32 as a cult legend has, in short, little to commend it.

There remains the large issue of the use of images, and of opposition to them, within early Israelite religion. Even if Jeroboam's calves needed little Yahwistic precedent, it may still be asked why, if the second commandment, and Ex. 32 which presupposes it, is early, various images were sometimes used in early Israelite religion (Num. 21:4-9, 2 Kg. 18:4, Jdg. 8:24-27, 17f.) and there is no recorded protest or hostile action of Elijah, Elisha, Jehu or Amos against Jeroboam's calves.

It must be frankly admitted that there is no entirely satisfactory explanation of this. At the same time, alternative theories, according to which the prohibition of images was a comparatively late introduction, are also beset with difficulties.

Much of the problem lies in our uncertainty as to the meaning and scope of the prohibition of images; for this is hardly self-evident. It is likely that this uncertainty was also felt within early Israel. The singularity of this prohibition within the ancient world should not be overlooked. As von Rad puts it,

> Here becomes manifest something of the mystery of Israel, something of her nature as a stranger and a sojourner among the religions. Anyone who seriously devotes himself to a study of religions as they appear and to their worship of images can find absolutely no way of transition from them to Israel's prohibition of images.[43]

Given such an "unnatural" prohibition, it is hard to say how either the ordinary, or the theologically aware, Israelite would have comprehended it. Only once does the OT offer any explanation of the prohibition, in Deut. 4:9ff., and we cannot know either how ancient or how widespread the deuteronomic conception was. The scope of the prohibition is not self-evident in that no objection is made to the ark or the cherubim in the official cult of Yahweh. But why these and not others? The answer probably lies at least partly in the distinction between those images and rituals which are officially prescribed by Yahweh and so are legitimate, and those which are not prescribed and are therefore illegitimate.[44] But just as no single account can be given of the imagined relationship of the deity to a cult object such as a bull, so it is doubtful that any univocal understanding of the prohibition of images existed within Israel.

The singularity and the potential ambiguity of the prohibition may account for the chequered history of its observance. A history in which the commandment was constantly ignored, misunderstood or varyingly interpreted is readily comprehensible.

The major difficulties of theories which suggest a comparatively late introduction for the prohibition of images are twofold. First, there are legal texts which contain the prohibition and which are generally considered early, especially Ex. 34:17, Deut. 27:15. Secondly, and more significantly, such theories find it difficult to give a satisfactory account of how a commandment so out of keeping with general ancient Near Eastern religious practice was either introduced or accepted within Israel. If the commandment was not part of that initial creative movement which gave Yahwism a distinctive existence, then whence came it? It was clearly not the creation of Hosea, for his language (8:5f., 10:5, 13:2) in no way suggests a major theological innovation. Though the denunciation of bull worship is a significant concern within Hosea, its presentation is not one of the major themes of the prophecy, as would be natural with a substantive innovation. The bull references are all made en passant, and the tone of them is one of scorn -

> A workman made it; it is not God ... Men kiss calves!

Such bull worship is unworthy of the Israelite, who should know better. If Hosea presupposes[45] the commandment, and the OT gives no hint of anyone else prior to Hosea who might have been responsible, the least difficult solution may indeed be to attribute it to the beginnings of Mosaic Yahwism.

How then does one explain the lack of any ninth century opposition to Jeroboam's calves? Several factors must be taken into account here. First, there is a silence in our evidence for this period concerning almost all the patriarchal and Mosaic traditions; the prohibition of images and Ex. 32 should not be taken in isolation. And while the attempt is sometimes made to lower the date of the major pentateuchal traditions to near the time of the Exile,[46] this creates more problems than it solves in explaining the early history of Israel. Secondly, it is possible (although the argument is admittedly conjectural) that most traditions of Israel's origins which did exist at the time of the division of the kingdom were, initially at least, confined to the southern kingdom, the written account being available only in Jerusalem; in the northern kingdom they may have been largely unknown. The hypothesis of a selective account of early Israelite traditions current in the northern kingdom, such as the E document would represent, is not in itself unlikely but can only be used with caution. Thirdly, the records give no evidence of any approval of the calves. It is not unreasonable to surmise that disapproval was felt, without being felt as strongly as by the deuteronomistic redactor of Kings.

If, therefore, the Ex. 32 tradition with its condemnation of the calf was an ancient tradition antedating Jeroboam, Jeroboam's establishment of the calves and the lack of recorded opposition to him would not thereby be rendered unintelligible. Jeroboam's action can be seen as a plausible syncretism. The unfortunate precedent of Aaron could either be ignored, if the tradition was not widely known, or to some extent justified, depending upon the interpretation given to the prohibition of images, or ruled out as irrelevant, if a theologically crass interpretation was given to Aaron's calf while a theologically sophisticated interpretation was given to Jeroboam's. This brief discussion of a highly problematic area does not, of course, claim to have resolved all the problems. The above argument has sought to re-open, rather than resolve, the generally-discounted possibility of Ex. 32 as an ancient anti-calf tradition. The resultant picture is by no means free from difficulties (though greater or lesser problems confront all proposals), but does possess a reasonable overall coherence. And it would mean that the possibility of a tradition of apostasy and renewal in the early levels of Ex. 32-34 would require serious attention.

Arguments for the antiquity of the tradition are as such independent of the exegetical arguments for the coherence of the text. There is no inherent reason why a unified text should be early rather than late. Nonetheless there is still a certain relationship between the two concerns. For it was the exegetical study of Ex. 32:4 which prompted a reassessment of the relationship between it and 1 Kg. 12:28 and so led on to a discussion of the larger issues. And it is at least salutary to be reminded that proposals of a complex tradition history of pro- and anti-calf polemic underlying Ex. 32 have really no foundation in the present text. That does not mean that such proposals are necessarily wrong, given that one must take into account the larger historical issues. But it should urge caution in advocating such proposals, and at least allow an openness to an alternative way of understanding the tradition.

AN ANALYSIS OF EX. 33:7-11

The paragraph Ex. 33:7-11 is almost universally agreed to be an independent fragment of tradition, now only loosely connected to its present context by the common theme of the divine presence. As such it preserves an ancient, and probably historical, tradition of a tent of meeting much simpler than the elaborate structure of P. The following discussion will suggest a different understanding of the verses which will throw into sharp relief the problem of exegetical method and the difficulties of assessing the same material in terms both of literary unity and of underlying diversity.

Arguments concerning the origins of 33:7-11 are various, some based on features of the text, others on larger reconstructions of early traditions into which 33:7-11 as an independent unit can be seen to fit. The problem has little to do with the question of sources. From a literary perspective there is no real unevenness in the paragraph, despite occasional suggestions that diverse traditions have been combined.[47] Source-critically the unit is usually ascribed to E, but there are no clear criteria for this and disagreement has remained.[48]

The problem is best approached through looking at those elements in 33:7-11 which are held to be discordant with their context. The most notable of these is the use of the verbs in the imperfect throughout the section. This is usually taken to describe the habitual practice of Moses throughout the wilderness wanderings at every encampment that was set up.[49]

Such an interpretation is possible but it is not the only, nor even the "obvious", interpretation. In the exegesis it was suggested that the frequentative force of the imperfect on the one hand conveyed the impermanence of the arrangement - this tent was a temporary expedient periodically put up and taken down at Sinai, pending the restoration of God's presence "in the midst" of the people; and on the other hand that this is a stylistic device to slow the narrative and create a lull and a sense of transition prior to the intense intercession of Moses.

How does one weigh these alternative, and mutually exclusive, interpretations? Both entail difficulties. The suggestion of impermanence may be countered by appeal to the fact that the tent outside the camp was, on the contrary, a permanent institution, which is referred to in other contexts (Num. 11:16,24-26,30; 12:4; cf. Deut. 31:14f.).[50] If the imperfect verbs describe the habitual practice of Moses at every encampment, then the problem is not so much that they are incongruous but that they may entail a puzzling inconsistency on the part of a redactor. If the unit is indeed an ancient tradition incorporated without modification or addition by the redactor,[51] then there is no problem, granted the general congruity of the re-use of the tradition. But if it becomes clear that parts of the unit were composed for their present context, i.e. that at least some of the details of the unit are specifically made to fit in their larger context, then it becomes implausible to suppose that the redactor should have at the same time retained an obvious incongruity without making the appropriate minor adjustments. Both of these difficulties direct one to the larger questions of the interpretation of the unit, and cannot be decided in isolation.

The second main cause of debate is the reference to the tent "outside the camp". To argue on the basis of this alone that this is a different sort of tent which represents an alternative tradition to the P tent in the midst of the camp, would be wide of the mark. The contrast between the temporary tent outside (v. 7) the camp, because the people have forfeited Yahweh's presence in their midst (vv. 3,5, $b^e qirb^e k\bar{a}$) is one of the main points of the section. The arguments must appeal simultaneously to the other tent passages (Num. 11:16,24-26,30, 12:4) which, taken in conjunction with Ex. 33, show the existence of an ancient tradition of a tent of meeting, different from the P tent of Ex. 25-31, 35-40. This tent is much simpler than the complex structure of P. It is situated outside the camp, while the P tent is in the centre of the camp. This tent is served by one attendant, Joshua (an Ephraimite), as opposed to the exclusive service of the tribe of Levi (Num. 3:5-10). This tent is a prophetic institution, a place of intermittent divine revelation, as opposed to the cultic institution of P, a permanent sanctuary for God.[52] These cumulative references are taken to show that this tent was a permanent institution, and not a temporary second-best.

This argument is sometimes, though not necessarily, supported by a further argument to the effect that an early account of the ark, which would have been kept in the tent, was originally included before 33:7 but was later suppressed when the P account of the ark was included within the book.[53] Five arguments are adduced in favour of this. First, the abrupt transition from 33:6 to 33:7. Secondly, the ornaments stripped from the people (33:4-6) would have been used for this purpose. Thirdly, the indirect object lô (33:7) refers to the ark. Fourthly, JE elsewhere presupposes the ark (Num. 10:33ff.), yet has no account of its construction. Fifthly, there is the parallel account in Deut. 9-10, in which Moses makes the ark after his intercession and prior to his ascent up the mountain with two new tables of stone (Deut. 10:1-5).

The somewhat hypothetical nature of these arguments makes them difficult to assess, but there are good reasons for not adopting them. The exegesis shows that the transition from 33:6 to 33:7 is not abrupt, or at least not problematically so. The point of the stripping of the Israelites is to leave them despoiled as the Egyptians were. The stripping is an act of judgment and if any notion of constructing anything is implied, it is to remove those objects used for the calf to prevent any possible repetition - rather than to build the approved ark.

The interpretation of lô in 33:7 is unclear. Conceivably lô could be the object of w^e^nāṭāh, referring back to the tent, since later in the same verse lô is used as an object after w^e^qārā'. Nowhere else, however, is nth used with a dative object so this rendering is improbable. It is likely that lô is a dativus commodi, but it does not have to be an object such as the ark that is intended. It could be for a person - Moses, Joshua, or Yahweh or even Israel. Probably Moses himself is intended.

The exegesis has suggested that Ex. 32-34 as a whole presupposes instructions for the ark and tent which are forfeited and then restored; if the P directions to build and the actual building of the ark and tent within Ex. 25-31, 35-40 are secondary, then an earlier account both of instructions prior to Ex. 32-34 and of construction subsequently has been displaced. The appropriate locus for the lost account would not be between 33:6 and 33:7.

Fifthly, although the relationship of Deut. 9-10 to Ex. 32-34 is a topic requiring separate treatment, it is doubtful that the Deuteronomy passage, which is clearly a secondary homiletic recasting of earlier tradition, can be used as evidence to determine some originally different sequence of events in Ex. 32-34.

One further point is that the tent containing the ark would have been kept inside the camp, and any tent outside the camp would not contain the ark and must be distinguished from the tent that did.[54] In conclusion, the argument is essentially one from silence; and when there are positive reasons why the construction of the ark would be inappropriate at this point, then the hypothesis becomes unnecessary.

This still leaves the unquestionable references to a tent in Num. 11-12 to be accounted for; Ex. 33:7-11 should not be explained without some reference to these. If the relationship between these passages is to be explained satisfactorily, two points of principle must be clarified.

First, all accounts of the nature of the ancient pre-P tent derive their understanding almost entirely from Ex. 33:7-11. Num. 11-12 (and Deut. 31) add no new information about the tent but confirm certain details of the picture derived from 33:7-11, viz. that the tent was outside the camp and that the cloud descended at its entrance. If, however, the understanding of 33:7-11 was based on an exegesis which discounted its connections with its context, then the whole conception of the tent must be examined afresh in the light of the new perception of the text. The references in Num. 11-12 are basically silent witnesses which in themselves yield insufficient information to gain any clear understanding of the nature of the tent envisaged. They cannot be used to support an understanding of Ex. 33:7-11, which 33:7-11 itself no longer supports.

Secondly, it is correct method initially to interpret the tent references in Num. 11-12 in their own context, without cross-reference to Ex. 33. Too rapid an appeal to an apparent parallel may prevent sensitivity to the peculiar nuances of the text in question. If the references to the tent in Num. 11-12 are not read in the light of Ex. 33, then it becomes possible, and perhaps even desirable, to understand them differently. That is, it is at least questionable whether Num. 11-12 actually does envisage the tent as being outside the perimeter of the camp. A possible meaning of the text is that the tent is in the middle of the camp, constituting a separate holy area within it, and one is to imagine three concentric areas, tent - camp - outside the camp.[55] The verb yṣ' may be used for the transition either way between tent and camp. In 11:26, 12:4 it indicates the transition from camp to tent, while in 11:24 it apparently indicates movement from tent to camp (the tent presumably being the location of Moses' dialogue with Yahweh in the preceding verses, and the camp around the tent the place where the people were). The area outside the perimeter of the camp is mentioned only as the place where the quails fell and where Miriam went in her uncleanness. If this is correct, then appeal to Ex. 33:7-11 positively obscures the meaning of Num. 11-12. The parallel is apparent rather than actual.[56] This is quite independent of more general difficulties about the inherent unlikelihood of a sanctuary being situated in an exposed position outside the camp.[57]

It can, of course, be objected that such an interpretation of Num. 11-12, even if it accurately describes the present form of the text, fails to reckon with an underlying history of tradition. A traditio-historical development from an older story in which the tent was outside the perimeter of the camp cannot be discounted. But here the problem of approach becomes acute. If Ex. 33:7-11 and the tent references in Num. 11-12 are read in isolation from their present context but in conjunction with each other, then an early tradition of a tent of meeting outside the perimeter of the camp is the natural conclusion. If they are read as part of their context and independently (initially) of one another, then Num. 11-12 may, and Ex. 33:7-11 does, make the assumption that the tent of meeting properly belongs in the midst of the camp. On such an approach, the tent of Ex. 33:7-11 is indeed a temporary construction.[58] The tent presupposed in Num. 11-12 is not that of Ex. 33. It is that shrine which is a central concern of Ex. 32-34 as a whole and which, if not to be identified with the present tent of Ex. 25ff., would have been in the place where the present P account is and been displaced by it. How does one weigh traditio-historical arguments on behalf of an old tradition of a permanent tent outside the camp, arguments which took little account of the literary context of the relevant units, against a more literary approach which, while it certainly does not rule out the possibility of traditio-historical development, raises the question of how far such an hypothesis is necessary to explain the material?

In addition to these considerations about the relationship of Ex. 33:7-11 to Num. 11-12, it is necessary to examine those elements in Ex. 33:7-11 which were most likely composed for their present context. First, the emphasis on the tent as not only outside the camp (miḥûṣ lammaḥ^{a}neh, twice in v. 7) but far off from it (harḥēq min-hammaḥ^{a}neh, v. 7) is surely dependent upon the situation of the unit in its present context following on the denial of Yahweh's presence in the midst of the people (vv. 3,5).[59] Such an emphasis suggests a theological significance in the position of the tent, and would be harder to account for if the positioning of the tent is considered to be descriptive of what happened at successive encampments without implications of Yahweh's disfavour.

Secondly, it is probable that v. 11a was composed for its context. On the one hand there is the significance of Yahweh speaking with Moses "face to face" (pānîm 'el-pānîm). This is the first part of the profound treatment of the theme of man's approach to the presence of God, continued in vv. 14f.,20 with further uses of pānîm. In particular, vv. 11,20 belong together as the two poles of a paradox. On the other hand v. 11a is important for the larger structure of the narrative. It is not only that the favour shown here to Moses prepares the way for the bold and successful intercession which follows, though that is the case, but also 33:11 can be seen as the hinge of the whole narrative.[60] The pivotal significance of the faithful mediator is part of that fine divine-human balance which has been seen to be central to Ex. 32-34. In both these ways 33:11a fits so integrally into its context that it becomes a likely assumption that it was composed for it.

It is these compositional elements in vv. 7,11 that cast doubt on the hypothesis of vv. 7-11 as a unit incorporated without alteration into the larger tradition. But if it be accepted that some elements of vv. 7-11 presuppose their present context, then it must be asked why the frequentative verbs, if implying successive encampments in a way incongruous with the present context, should have been left unaltered. It does suggest an inconsistency on the part of the redactor. One might argue that the verbs originally implied successive encampments, but that the redactor saw that they could be re-interpreted, perhaps along the lines suggested in the exegesis, and thus they were retained. But it must be asked how far such an hypothesis is still necessary to explain the text.

The above discussion has not demonstrated that Ex. 33:7-11 did not have an independent existence prior to its inclusion in its present context. But it has shown that the arguments customarily adduced in favour of its independence are of limited cogency, and that the links between 33:7-11 and its context require a more careful explanation than they have yet received. Unlike the arguments concerning Ex. 34 as an original renewal which are, in my judgment, relatively clear-cut, one's verdict on the origins of 33:7-11 must, at the present time, be non liquet. But such a conclusion, in contrast to the customary assessment, does illustrate well the kind of difference that the exegetical approach here advocated makes.

AN ANALYSIS OF EX. 34:29-35

This is the one unit in Ex. 32-34 which has consistently been attributed to P. The basis for this is the presence of vocabulary characteristic of P, in particular "Aaron", "the leaders of the congregation" (hannᵉśi'îm bāᶜēdāh), and "the tables of the testimony" (luḥōt hāᶜēdut).[61] The presence of these terms raises many questions. Are they so characteristic of P that their occurrence in non-P material becomes unlikely? If so, do they indicate more than a secondary P reworking of an older tradition?[62] Even if the unit as a whole did derive from P, could it still have been composed for its context[63] - depending on how one understands the nature of P and P's relation to earlier tradition?

First, it may be noted that against these arguments from vocabulary, considerations of content suggest close connections between the unit and its context. In particular one may point out the use of qrn to recall the calf and to form an inclusio for chs. 32-34 as a whole, the further development of the pānîm motif, and the significance attached to Moses which so aptly concludes his unique mediatorial role throughout Ex. 32-34. If, as is customary, the unit is said originally to have followed the end of Ex. 31, none of these factors would retain their significance. This raises the problem of the criteria according to which source-critical analysis can best be carried out.

Secondly, the vocabulary evidence is of differing value. The reference to Aaron is the least significant. Although Aaron appears most frequently in P material, he is not restricted to it and already belongs to the non-P tradition of Ex. 32. The tablets are called lḥt h^{c}dt in 32:15, and although this could be a P gloss, it may more likely be that this is evidence for a pre-P tradition designating the tablets as ^{c}dt.[64] The use of ^{c}dh is the strongest argument, for this term is strongly characteristic of P and nowhere else in the Pentateuch is it to be found in non-P material.[65] Although one would be reluctant to base a source-critical argument essentially on one word, the presence of this distinctively P term must be given its due weight; although, again, one could argue that this is evidence for a pre-P tradition which referred to Israel as ^{c}dh.

The suggestion that the P terminology represents a secondary gloss raises problems. For while it is possible to conceive of the story with a slightly different wording, it is hard to see why, given such a story, it should be glossed in the suggested way when no clear point, theological or otherwise, is conveyed by it. One could take the terms as indicative of a more thoroughgoing rewriting of the tradition by P, but that would undermine the argument that the tradition as a whole does not feel characteristic of P.[66] There is no good reason, therefore, to separate the terminology under discussion from the rest of the unit.

These brief considerations leave one with two main options. One could minimize the significance of the terminological affinities to P and argue that the content shows the unit, in its present form, to stand close to the basic tradition of Ex. 32-34. Alternatively, the proposal that the unit stems from P but was composed for its present context would explain all the relevant data. The former of these is, in my judgment, the more likely.

Whatever the source-critical arguments concerning 34:29-35 may show, the real interest in most recent study has been in the traditio-historical investigation of possible earlier forms of the tradition, and it is these that must now be briefly considered. For the story is usually interpreted in the light of the widespread religio-historical evidence for priests' masks.[67] As such the passage was originally an aetiology for such a mask within the early cult of Israel. The fact that in the present text it is clearly a veil and not a mask that is envisaged and the veil functions differently from a priestly mask reflects the reinterpretation of the tradition according to later Yahwistic sentiment which no longer found the mask acceptable.

Such an hypothesis is difficult to assess largely because it is difficult to see what evidence would be allowed to falsify it; or, to put it differently, it is unclear what are the objective criteria which could serve as a control upon such hypothesizing. The hypothesis is built upon two general considerations. The first is an understanding of the early history of Israelite religion. The second is the significance of religio-historical parallels to OT practices from different cultures. These are both vast issues on which it is not possible here to offer more than two brief comments.

First, the nature of early Israelite religion is a subject about which we know all too little. Given the known religious pluralism of the premonarchical period, the question of the degree of religious distinctiveness and theological depth that may reasonably be ascribed to the earliest traditions of Mosaic Yahwism is difficult to answer. For the present it may simply be observed that the theology and content of Ex. 34:29-35 stands close to the theology and content of Ex. 32-34 as a whole. It would be dubious, therefore, to treat the question of 34:29-35 in isolation. Ex. 32-34 reflects a strong and distinctive Mosaic Yahwism throughout. And if it is plausible to view the substance of Ex. 32-34 as representing an early tradition, then the same may well be true of 34:29-35 as well. At the very least one should ask again whether it is necessary or even helpful to postulate the section as reflecting a practice found discordant in later Yahwism.

Secondly, the interpretation of religio-historical parallels is a complex matter. If one is to emerge successfully from the maze, the one fundamental principle that must be observed is that *apparent similarities should not be isolated from their cultural context*. An atomistic approach which finds trans-cultural similarities by interpreting individual practices independently of their cultural milieu is methodologically unsound.[68] This being so, the relevance of priestly masks to Ex. 34:29ff. is highly problematic. The assertion of a real parallel in 34:29ff. involves not only taking the verses out of their larger OT context but also discounting Yahwistic elements within the unit itself. It is difficult to see how this does other than to demonstrate what is initially assumed; that is, the argument is circular. The exegesis has suggested that part of the point of 34:29ff. may lie in the specific *contrast* to the idea of the deity's representative being masked. If such a meaning, reflecting the presupposition of Yahweh's close and personal revelation to men and *through* men, is a coherent element of Mosaic Yahwism as a whole, then it is hard to justify, even though one cannot disprove, the reversal of this meaning at a putative earlier stage of the tradition on the basis of certain transcultural resemblances.

There is always a tension and interplay between a scholar's overall understanding and the specific data of the text. It is surely not unfair to suggest that in most recent works on Ex. 34:29-35 general considerations have weighed more heavily than the actual phenomena of the text. May it not be appropriate that the perspectives of the present text be given a larger role in the formulation of hypotheses concerning origins - not to rule out traditio-historical development, but to control it?

The sections Ex. 33:7-11, 34:29-35 are not integral to the story of Ex. 32-34 in the same way as 32:1-6, 34:1-28, and the possibility of their being secondary additions need not affect the basic unity of the tradition of sin and renewal. The above discussion has sought to argue not so much that they are not secondary but rather that they are more deeply linked to the surrounding narrative than is generally appreciated and that analyses which have discounted these links stand in need of revision and restatement. Whether, and in what way, 33:7-11 and 34:29-35 are secondary to the tradition of 32-34 may at present be left open. The important point for present purposes is that the nature of the methodological issues at stake should have been further made clear.

BRIEF NOTES ON THREE SECTIONS

1) Ex. 32:25-29

Ex. 32:25-29 presents a fresh set of problems. It is generally considered secondary[69] for reasons not of vocabulary but of content, even though in itself it gives the impression of being an ancient tradition.

Within the context of Ex. 32-34 the episode presents no problems. It fits well, though a little loosely, in the account of the aftermath of Israel's sin. It presupposes some problem such as the apostasy which the calf represents. The seriousness of the Levites' execution is in keeping with the seriousness with which the sin of the calf is taken elsewhere in the narrative (cf. 32:7-10,30-33). Its central theme, that of total faithfulness to Yahweh, is likewise in keeping with the tenor of Ex. 32-34 as a whole, especially 34:11ff. The fact that the episode is not referred to again in the narrative is no difficulty. Subsidiary characters, including Aaron who after 32:25 only appears again in 34:30, are only mentioned when they are appropriate to the story. The storyteller naturally focusses attention on Moses and Yahweh as the central protagonists.

It is within a larger OT context that the story becomes problematic. Two particular difficulties may be singled out. First, the story stands in some tension with Deut. 33:8-11. Deut. 33:9 would seem to refer to the same episode as in Ex. 32, yet 33:8 locates this at Massah/Meribah, not Mt. Sinai. Secondly, there is a tension with the surrounding P material in Ex. 25-31, 35-40. In Ex. 28-29 Aaron and his sons are designated as priests and their ordination rite is described, and this is taken up again in Ex. 39:1-31,41, 40:12-15, Lev. 8-9. How does the ordination of the Levites relate to this? Both these difficulties are fundamentally aspects of the larger problem, one of the most complex in OT study, of the origins and development of priests and Levites. No decision about Ex. 32:25-29 can be reached in isolation of a treatment of this issue. And that lies far beyond the scope of this present study. Suffice it to say that there are considerable historical and traditio-historical difficulties with the story of Ex. 32:25-29 in its Sinai context such as make it a not unlikely candidate for being a secondary addition to the tradition.

2) Ex. 32:30-33:6

Little will be said about this section at the present time. As has been seen, the section is reasonably unified with the intercession of Moses leading to the departure of Israel from Sinai, yet still under Yahweh's disfavour.

The section plays an important role in the development of the narrative, for the restoration of Yahweh's presence "in the midst" of the people, here denied (33:3,5), is basic to 33:7-34:9. There are also two of the four occurrences of the "stiff-necked people" motif which is central to the theological meaning of the narrative as a whole. The content of the section is without question deeply rooted in the Sinai tradition.[70]

Nonetheless, the unity of the section seems slightly artificial, and it lacks that coherence which is characteristic of other units in Ex. 32-34, an exception which admits of no obvious explanation. What sort of development of the material is thereby indicated is unclear, and further study will be needed before serious proposals can be advanced.

3) Ex. 33:12-23

Three points may briefly be made about Ex. 33:12-23.

First, the exegesis has shown a coherence and development within the section such as makes it unclear whether it is necessary to postulate internal diversity at the source-critical level, in the sort of way that is often proposed.

Secondly, the section is linked to its context both in content and vocabulary. De Vaux's statement that "This text also has nothing to connect it with the context"[71] is hardly well founded. The major difficulty is the difference between the theophany foretold in 33:19,20-23 and the theophany recounted in 34:5ff. Nonetheless the verbal links between the two passages show that the writer of 34:5ff understood the passage as a fulfilment of the former; and the exegetical discussion suggested that the differences between the two accounts may in fact be explicable in terms of literary and theological considerations. Whether or not there is an underlying complexity at a traditio-historical level remains a difficult issue requiring futher consideration.

Thirdly, such are the links between 33:12ff and the situations as depicted in the surrounding context that it becomes questionable whether one should postulate some originally independent setting for the prayer. Muilenberg, for example, generalizes 33:12-17 into an "intercession of the covenant mediator", the passage being a liturgy used at amphictyonic centres in Canaan to celebrate the fact that Yahweh has accompanied the people into Canaan.[72] To maintain this, the development of 33:12-17 as outlined in the exegesis would need to a considerable extent to be set aside and reinterpreted. It may be more natural to suppose that the prayer is original to its present literary context.

THE REDACTION OF EX. 32-34

After this brief survey of some of the individual units of Ex. 32-34, which has attempted to set their problems in a fresh light, we will turn, even more briefly, to the question of redaction. The study thus far has suggested that a good case can be made for a tradition which contains both apostasy and renewal as underlying Ex. 32-34. The literary and theological coherence of the final text is not simply a reworking of discrete and fragmentary traditions, even though some elements may indeed be secondary, and no attempt has been made to discuss all difficulties. The following discussion will seek not to exhaust the question of redactional activity, but rather to focus on the redactional contribution that is both most clearly discernible and probably also the final level of redaction in that it presupposes the content of most of the rest of Ex. 32-34. Three elements stand out.

The first is Ex. 33:11a. Some reference to God speaking with Moses is demanded by the story. But the way in which this is expressed with the use of "face to face" introduces the theological development of pānîm in what follows. Whether the use of pānîm in either 33:14f. or 33:20 is also redactional is less clear in that both references are well-embedded in the tradition, and may have suggested to the redactor the paradoxical heightening of one of the theological issues at stake. Either way, the interest in the paradoxical nature of man's possible access to God which is indicated by 33:11a may reasonably be ascribed to a redactor.

Secondly, there is the paragraph 32:7-14. Although some original element of dialogue between Moses and Yahweh upon the mountain is demanded by the story,[73] the section in its present form is largely redactional. The exegesis showed that 32:7-14 contains, in nuce, many of the major theological themes more fully developed elsewhere in the narrative. Its present position, ending with the note of mercy in v. 14, provides the theological context in which the following narrative of judgment is to be read. For these reasons the section may be interpreted as a piece of narrative theology whereby the redactor eschews overt comment but offers a programmatic interpretation of the meaning of the narrative by developing some earlier tradition of Yahweh's discourse with Moses. The section also introduces the motif of a "stiff-necked people" (32:9),[74] and this constitutes the third redactional element.

The use of the "stiff-necked people" motif in 34:9 bears the mark of theological reflection on the meaning of the Sinai tradition in conjunction with the flood tradition. It focusses the theological significance already present, especially in 33:19, 34:6f. The intercession of Moses in 34:9 reads smoothly without the clause ky ᶜm-qšh-ᶜrp hw' and could have existed without it; the other elements of 34:9 reflect the concerns deeply embedded in ch. 33 and read naturally as part of the tradition.[75] The intercession provided a convenient locus for the interpretative phrase.

Which other uses of "stiff-necked people" are redactional is difficult to decide. The occurrence in 32:9 in a highly-redacted section is most likely part of the redaction. In 33:3,5 the phrase may be redactional or it may be original to the tradition. Further study of 32:30-33:6 may help clarify the point. That it is the usage of the phrase in 34:9 that makes it of significance within the tradition is, in any case, clear.

It is probable that these three redactional elements are all the work of one person. The theological perspective of 32:7-14 is akin to that of 34:9. And the author of the paradoxical treatment of the presence of God in 33:11 is easily identified with the author of the paradoxical treatment of the grace of God in 34:9.

The question then arises whether it is possible to locate or identify this theological redactor. One suggestion would be to locate him in deuteronomic (or deuteronomistic) circles. Linguistically, "stiff-necked people" can be described as a deuteronomic/deuteronomistic expression,[76] and some of the terminology of 32:7-14 has deuteronomic/deuteronomistic parallels.[77] More generally, also, there is much in Ex. 32-34 that is apparently deuteronomic. For example, there is the requirement of exclusive faithfulness to Yahweh; the role of Moses as mediator; the importance of the decalogue; the prohibition of images, especially the calf, which receives its major OT treatment in Deuteronomy and the deuteronomistic redaction of Kings; and the very mention of "covenant" (34:10,27,28) may be deemed deuteronomic. The deuteronomic affinity of much of the Sinai material has been extensively argued in recent times by Perlitt,[78] who has been followed by Schmid,[79] and Nicholson.[80]

There are serious difficulties, however, with such a setting for the redactor. On the general level there are concerns of Ex. 32-34 not reflected in Deuteronomy or deuteronomistic literature. The concern for the movable shrine of Yahweh's presence is not in Deuteronomy;[81] the clear deuteronomic distinction between the decalogue and all other legislation is lacking in Ex. 32-34; the fine divine-human balance of Ex. 32-34 is not paralleled in Deuteronomy where there is a more straightforward emphasis upon the sovereignty of Yahweh.

Further, whatever the precise relationship between Ex. 32-34 and Deut. 9:6-10:11, it is clear that they do not emerge from the same hand (or school). None of the central theological concerns of Ex. 32-34 is given any special significance in the deuteronomic rendering of the tradition, except the importance of Moses as intercessor. And Deut. 9-10 contains elements about which Ex. 32-34 is silent (e.g. Deut. 9:20).

Linguistically the situation is also unclear. Generally speaking, affinities with deuteronomic language, unless extensive and close, may indicate pre- or proto-deuteronomic tradition.[82] As for the central phrase ᶜm-qšh-ᶜrp, it in fact only occurs six times in the OT: four times in Ex. 32-34 and twice in the Deuteronomy passage (Deut. 9:6,13) which is explicitly a recapitulation of the older tradition. The influence of Exodus upon Deuteronomy, rather than the reverse, would be the natural deduction. There are, of course, occurrences of the verb qšh in conjunction with ᶜrp in deuteronomistic literature but they are neither extensive nor confined to that literature.[83] The phraseology is a general Hebrew, not a specifically deuteronomistic, idiom.

Perhaps the decisive argument against the deuteronomic identity of the redactor of Ex. 32-34 is the parallelism of the paradoxical kî clause in both Ex. 34:9 and Gen. 8:21 which one can hardly conceive of as not being from the same hand. Now the composition and redaction of the Flood narrative is a question which the recent studies of Anderson and Wenham have re-opened,[84] so that one cannot appeal to an analysis of that narrative with the confidence usually shown in the past. Nonetheless no one (to the best of my knowledge) has suggested a deuteronomic redaction of the Flood tradition or that Gen. 8:21, even with its interpretative kî clause, does not belong to the older levels of the tradition. Until the accepted understanding of Gen. 6:5, 8:21 is overthrown, it provides strong evidence for the non-deuteronomic identity of the Ex. 32-34 redactor. Since the redactor of Gen. 8:21 is held to be the Yahwist, this means that the redactor of Ex. 32-34 would be the Yahwist.

A word of clarification is in order here. Reference has been made to the current questioning of the nature, and existence, of the Yahwist, and the present study has argued the inadequacy of the customary J and E source analysis, at least in Ex. 32-34. In what sense, then, may one justifiably appeal to the Yahwist as redactor?

There is not space to enter into the debate about the Yahwist. All that we wish to suggest at present is that the final redaction of Ex. 32-34 is to be identified with that level of pentateuchal redaction which is generally considered to be the earliest and which is generally considered to be distinct from the deuteronomic redaction. Majority opinion would locate this redaction in either the tenth or the ninth century, and while we would incline to the former,[85] we cannot pursue the matter here. Even a ninth century final redaction would show a greater antiquity in the content of Ex. 32-34 than is often recognized.

CONCLUSION

Given the uncertain state of current pentateuchal criticism and the fact that Ex. 32-34 cannot be considered in complete isolation from other pentateuchal material, the analytical discussion of this chapter, in particular the attempt to locate the final redactor of Ex. 32-34, must be regarded as tentative. There are, moreover, numerous unanswered questions about the origins and development of Ex. 32-34 which we have not even attempted to discuss, and these remain as a task for further study. As already stated, the aim of this discussion has been to give a practical demonstration of the kind of approach to critical analysis which this study advocates. It is intended not to foreclose but to stimulate further study, and to suggest some lines along which that study might most profitably develop.

EPILOGUE

Our revels now are ended. But before we conclude it will be appropriate to add a few final comments to relate the findings of this study to one or two areas of current OT debate. Obviously the present argument has implications for many issues in the literature, traditions and history of Israel, but only two will be singled out.[1]

First, the problem of pentateuchal criticism. Although it is perilous to generalize conclusions based on a provisional reassessment of part of the Sinai material, certain indications emerge. On the one hand, little support is offered for a traditional documentary analysis. At least in Ex. 32-34, the major narrative section in the Sinai tradition, the hypothesis of an independent J and E, whether documents or traditions, has not been found heuristically useful. Insofar as it has seemed helpful to retain the designation "J", this is not to denote a literary source, but rather a theological redactor of substantially pre-existing tradition.

On the other hand, Rendtorff's arguments for independent blocks of tradition, as opposed to continuous threads, blocks which are linked by a secondary _Bearbeitung_, have not commended naturally themselves either. The significant links between Ex. 32-34 and Gen. 6-9, which seem more than a _Bearbeitung_, do not in themselves disturb his position, which could be modified accordingly. More serious are the implications of a literary approach in which allusion or silence is allowed to presuppose knowledge of other traditions. Since Rendtorff's approach depends considerably on arguments from silence and the supposition that connective links represent secondary _Bearbeitung_ it would be difficult (though not impossible) to adopt his approach in conjunction with the literary approach advocated.[2]

The problem is that a new comprehensive model or paradigm for pentateuchal traditions is required. The old documentary hypothesis used the model of historical documents and sources. Such a model has co-existed somewhat uneasily with the growing perception of different literary types and also an interest in tradition history. With a consistent approach to the material as literature, the documentary model becomes still less appropriate. Literary works do not employ sources in the same way as historical documents. Even when it is likely that a genuinely ancient source has been utilized, as in Ex. 32-34, its relation to the present text is such as to make it doubtful whether it can still be isolated and identified.

It is harder to specify the kind of model that would be appropriate. Clearly any model must take seriously the nature of much pentateuchal narrative as literature, and allow for the ways in which storytelling concerns may mould traditional and historical material. But if any new comprehensive model for pentateuchal traditions is to be proposed, there is much preliminary groundwork still to be done.

Secondly, the theology of Ex. 32-34 is important for the question of the relationship between the Mosaic and Davidic covenants. It is customary to pose an antithesis between these two covenant traditions, the Mosaic covenant being conditional while the Davidic is unconditional.[3] Yet Ex. 32-34 is the tradition, par excellence, which deals with the question of what happens after Israel is unfaithful to her covenant obligations. It presents a theology of the Mosaic covenant in which the covenant is renewed precisely because it depends upon the character of Yahweh as gracious and merciful and not on the people who continue to be stiff-necked and unrepentant. According to our present text, the Mosaic covenant, as the Davidic, rests ultimately upon the faithfulness of Yahweh and as such can hardly be less enduring.[4]

This is not, of course, to assert an identical theology for both covenants. Much difference of emphasis remains. The Davidic covenant rests upon the explicit word of Yahweh in a way that the Mosaic covenant does not; the Mosaic covenant stresses the moral obligations of the recipient in a way that the Davidic covenant does not; and the Mosaic covenant is given through a mediator in a way which the Davidic covenant is not. The point is that in both the ultimate continuation of the covenant, even when the recipient has acted in such a way as to forfeit it, is ensured because it depends upon the faithfulness of Yahweh, his revealed character or his word of promise. As such, there is a deep theological continuity between the two covenants.

It would be illuminating to see whether such a theology of the Mosaic covenant can be discerned in the later prophetic preaching. There is much in Hosea that suggests a similar theological perspective, and perhaps it is to be found in

Jeremiah and Ezekiel also. T. Raitt, for example, in his study of Jeremiah and Ezekiel,[5] makes much of the shift after the judgment of exile to a proclamation of salvation in which God's forgiveness is unconditional and does not specify repentance or moral transformation as a necessary precondition or accompaniment. This he says to be discontinuous with earlier covenant theology and without precedent in the OT. Yet in fact Ex. 32-34 contains precisely such a theology of the Mosaic covenant, and Jeremiah and Ezekiel may have been explicitly taking their stand within the ancient tradition. Amidst all the rich diversity of OT theology, there is also profound continuity.

Notes to Introduction

1. *VT* 28 (1978), p. 381.
2. M. Noth, *The History of Israel*; J. Bright, *A History of Israel*; R. de Vaux, *The Early History of Israel*; S. Herrmann, *A History of Israel in Old Testament Times*; J.H. Hayes, J.M. Miller (ed.), *Israelite and Judaean History*; N. Gottwald, *The Tribes of Yahweh*.
3. W. Eichrodt, *Theology of the Old Testament*: G. von Rad, *Old Testament Theology*; W. Zimmerli, *Old Testament Theology in Outline*; R.E. Clements, *Old Testament Theology*.
4. *Moses*, p. 149.
5. *Exodus*, p. 243.
6. *A History of Pentateuchal Traditions*, p. 31, n. 115.
7. "The Intercession of the Covenant Mediator, Exodus 33:1a,12-17", p. 162.
8. *History I*, p. 399.
9. *The Elusive Presence*, p. 158, n. 63.
10. *Tribes*, p. 113.
11. *Exodus*, pp. 557f.
12. F.-E. Wilms, *Das Jahwistische Bundesbuch in Exodus 34*; J. Halbe, *Das Privilegrecht Jahwes, Ex. 34.10-26*; E. Zenger, *Die Sinaitheophanie*.

Notes to Chapter One
METHOD IN NARRATIVE INTERPRETATION

1. See, for example, R. Rendtorff, *Problem*; H.H. Schmid, *Der sogenannte Jahwist*; *JSOT* 3 (1977) contains articles discussing the implications of Rendtorff's and Schmid's proposals.
2. See, for example, D.A. Knight, *Rediscovering the Traditions of Israel*; J. van Seters, *Abraham in History and Tradition*, esp. pp. 139ff.; R. Polzin, "Martin Noth's 'A History of Pentateuchal Traditions'"; S.M. Warner, "Primitive Saga Men"; W. McKane, *Studies in the Patriarchal Narratives*, pp. 105ff., esp. p. 194. The problem is complicated by the lack of agreement as to the nature of tradition history. Rendtorff's conception, whereby different stages of the tradition can still be seen in the literary sources, is significantly different from that of Noth.

3. See, for example, T.L. Thompson, The Historicity of the Patriarchal Narratives; J.H. Hayes, J.M. Miller (ed.), Israelite and Judaean History, pp. 70ff.
4. J.H. Hayes, An Introduction to Old Testament Study (1979), pp. 194ff. offers a brief survey of current issues in pentateuchal study.
5. The tension between source criticism and traditio-historical criticism is particularly acute; cf. Rendtorff, Problem.
6. The term "historical-critical method" is a convenient shorthand for a wide variety of analytical approaches which share certain general characteristics. Such a use of the term has been popularized particularly through the work of Brevard Childs.
7. It is appreciated that expressions such as "the final form of the text" can raise problems both on the text-critical level of establishing what the text actually is, and with respect to establishing the final level of redaction and relating this to subsequent glosses. Nonetheless, the difficulty is not of significance for the discussion. For in general the notion of the final or received text is perfectly clear. And when a concern for the final text is compared to the investigation of its prehistory, again the intention is clear. The fact that difficulties may arise in the treatment of specific problematic texts need not detain us at this point.
8. Cf. the influential work of T. Kuhn, The Structure of Scientific Revolutions. Although Kuhn's thesis is directed towards the sciences and cannot be transferred simpliciter to the arts, its suggestive qualities have gained it a widespread currency.
9. Cf. D. Robertson, "The Bible as Literature", p. 548; J.D. Crossan, "Perspectives and Methods in Contemporary Biblical Criticism", p. 40.
10. Childs' fullest exposition of his approach is in his Introduction to the Old Testament as Scripture; cf., most recently, "On Reading the Elijah Narratives" (1980), and in particular, "Response to Reviewers of Introduction to the Old Testament as Scripture" (1980).
11. The Theme of the Pentateuch; "Story and Poem: The Old Testament as Literature and as Scripture".
12. From Moses to Patmos.
13. Theology as Narration.
14. "Exodus 3:14: History, Philology and Theology".
15. "From Analysis to Synthesis: The Interpretation of Genesis

1-11".

16. P. 1.

17. "Interpreting the New Testament Today", p. 4.

18. A useful introduction to Ricoeur's work, with bibliography, is provided by the articles in Semeia 4 (1975).

19. The designation "history-like" was suggested by Frei (Eclipse, p. 10) and a wider use for it has been advocated: cf. J. Barr, "Story and History in Biblical Theology", J.J. Collins, "The 'Historical Character' of the Old Testament in Recent Biblical Theology".

20. The Business of Criticism, p. 99.

21. Ibid., p. 27.

22. "Literary Criticism", p. 63. My italics.

23. Theory of Literature, p. 73.

24. P. ix.

25. P. 9.

26. "From Analysis to Synthesis", p. 26.

27. Ibid., p. 27.

28. "Exodus 3:14", p. 319.

29. Ibid., pp. 320f.

30. Regrettably, considerations of space preclude consideration of structuralism and its rapidly burgeoning literature. As a general comment, however, it may be said that although structuralists eschew the historical-critical approach, their own methods tend to raise not entirely dissimilar problems. That is, insofar as their primary interest is to discern the "deep" structures of a work and the ways in which the structures of the mind are reflected in it, there is a similar tendency to discount the work as meaningful in itself and to reduce the text to being a means to the end of discovering meaning elsewhere than in what the words actually say.

31. See esp. Introduction, passim.

32. Cf. "The Sensus Literalis of Scripture", pp. 90f.

33. "Exodus 3:14", p. 319.

34. Cf. the premonitions of J. Barr, The Bible in the Modern World, p. 65; idem, "Childs' Introduction to the Old Testament as Scripture", p. 15.

35. An exception may lie in the early chapters of Deuteronomy in their relationship to the narrative traditions of Exodus and Numbers. The deuteronomic formulation of tradition presents peculiar problems of its own which need not be considered here.

36. W. Beyerlin, Origins and History of the Oldest Sinaitic

Traditions; E. Zenger, Die Sinaitheophanie; F.-E. Wilms, Das Jahwistische Bundesbuch in Exodus 34; E.W. Nicholson, Exodus and Sinai in History and Tradition; J. Halbe, Das Privilegrecht Jahwes; cf. also E. Otto, Das Mazzotfest in Gilgal, pp. 199ff.; D.J. McCarthy, Treaty and Covenant,[2] pp. 243ff.; H. Valentin, Aaron, pp. 205ff.

37. At the very least these scholars have too quickly assumed that the fragmentary nature of the chapters has been conclusively demonstrated without bothering to verify for themselves whether or not this actually is so.

38. K. Koch, for example, describes the task of the source critic thus: "The literary critic ... approaches the text with, so to say, a dissecting knife in his hand, looks out particularly for breaks in continuity, or missing links in the train of thought" (Growth, p. 69).

39. Storytelling, pp. 144-149.

40. Ibid., p. 146.

41. The Practice of History, pp. 103f.

42. "From Analysis to Synthesis".

43. "The Coherence of the Flood Narrative".

44. See above, p. 6, n. 2, for a brief bibliography on the nature and practice of tradition history.

45. This is not the understanding of tradition history held by Rendtorff, but it is that which is widely held, most influentially by Noth.

46. Cf. McKane, Studies, p. 194; J. Barton, Review of D.A. Knight (ed.), Tradition and Theology in the OT, p. 242.

47. Cf. the strictures of van Seters, Abraham, pp. 139ff., esp. p. 142.

48. A useful brief bibliography is provided by S. Bar-Efrat, "Analysis of Structure in Biblical Narrative", p. 154, n. 1. One may note also, S. McEvenue, The Narrative Style of the Priestly Writer; D. Irvin, Mytharion.

49. "The Joseph Story and Pentateuchal Criticism", p. 528. Some other scholars are also rejecting traditional source criticism in their assessment of the Joseph story; cf. G.W. Coats, From Canaan to Egypt; H. Donner, Die literarische Gestalt des alttestamentlichen Josephgeschichte.

50. See the convenient discussion in C.R. North, "Pentateuchal Criticism".

51. Cited in P. Hazard, The European Mind 1680-1715, pp. 225f.

52. "From Analysis to Synthesis", p. 35.

53. Gen. 7:17 does not use the verb gbr but rather rbh. Arguably it enhances the effect to start the account with the less dramatic word rbh and then to replace it, in two stages, by the more forceful gbr. Thus in v. 17 the waters increased (rbh); in v. 18 they prevailed (gbr) and increased (rbh) greatly (m'd); then, v. 19, the waters prevailed (gbr) exceedingly greatly (m'd m'd), until finally, v. 20, they prevailed (gbr) over the mountains, fifteen cubits deep.
54. Noth, Exodus, p. 257; Childs, Exodus, p. 595.
55. See the exegesis for a justification of this.
56. Licht, Storytelling, pp. 103-105, discusses aesthetic and dramatic considerations which may also influence the use of speech-introducing formulae. One may also compare the use of wk[c]nt in Aramaic.
57. Introduction to the Old Testament, p. 91.
58. HPT, pp. 21f.
59. Exegese, p. 51. In n. 6 Richter lists other scholarly references to the importance of the doublet criterion.
60. Ibid., pp. 54f.
61. Noth (HPT, p. 23) comments that "What is very clear in the Abraham tradition can be confirmed in a less striking way in the entire old Pentateuchal tradition", but offers no further discussion. Three examples would be generally cited, Ex. 16//Num. 11:4-35; Ex. 17:1-7//Num. 20:1-13; Ex. 20//Ex. 34:11-26.
62. Such J elements as are discerned in Ex. 19 are usually combined with the narrative of Ex. 34:1ff.
63. See the exegesis, pp. 84f, for a justification of this.
64. See further the discussion, p. 160.
65. A. Olrik, "Epic Laws of Folk Narrative", p. 137.
66. Cf. Caird, Language and Imagery, pp. 117-121, for the Hebraic predilection for parataxis, the juxtaposition of apparently contradictory usages of a word.
67. See p. 200, n. 79 for references for such a suggestion.
68. OT Theology I, pp. 234-241.
69. Ibid., p. 237.
70. See e.g. Clements, God and Temple, pp. 37, 136.
71. OT Theology I, p. 239, n. 115.
72. Cf. Licht, Storytelling, pp. 14ff.
73. Cf. below, p. 119, for further discussion of the term, and also the general discussion in ch. 4.
74. M. Buber, for example, is considerably more optimistic about the historical worth of the Moses traditions (Moses, esp.

pp. 13-19) than is, say, K. Koch in his reflections on the nature of early Israelite traditions (Growth, pp. 148-158). See further below, pp. 141f.

75. Le Décalogue, p. 120.

76. "Form-Critical Problem", pp. 20ff.

77. Ibid., p. 68.

78. Cf. the thirteenth of Olrik's Epic Laws, "Concentration on a Leading Character".

79. Cf. the seventh of Olrik's Laws, "The Importance of Final Position".

80. This hierarchy is not, of course, a rigid rule but a general guideline which in practice will admit of much variation.

81. Cf. pp. 32f.

82. Storytelling, p. 146.

83. Ibid.

84. See below, pp. 157ff.

85. See below, pp. 171ff, esp. p. 175.

Notes to Chapter Two
AN EXEGESIS OF EXODUS 32-34

1. Only in 19:5 and 24:8, and perhaps 24:7, is any technical or formal designation given to this relationship, where the term berit is used.

2. The Inspired Word, p. 245.

3. The reference in Ex. 16:34 which presupposes the ark is anachronistic or anticipatory of a later situation.

4. Cf. the recent theology of S. Terrien, The Elusive Presence, which is arranged around this theme.

5. Since the present task is to interpret the text in its final form, the question of the origins of Ex. 25-31 (35-40) cannot be raised here. It will, however, become clear that even if the present form of Ex. 25-31 is late, some other, earlier account of a movable shrine of Yahweh is an important presupposition for understanding Ex. 32-34.

The argument that Yahweh's accompaniment of Israel in a shrine is a major concern of Ex. 32-34 will be one of the most novel features of this exegesis. Recent works on Yahweh's presence with, and accompaniment of, Israel in the early period make comparatively little reference to Ex. 32-34 and none to a shrine there; cf. e.g. H.D. Preuss, "... ich will mit dir sein!"; T.W. Mann, Divine Presence and Guidance in Israelite Traditions; Terrien, The Elusive Presence.

6. This does not mean that in v. 5 one should follow the Syriac and read wayyirā' (so NEB) rather than wayyar' of MT.
7. The orgiastic nature of the worship has been questioned by J.M. Sasson, "The Worship of the Golden Calf". Sasson argues that the worship was "an orderly ritual" following known practices. On the basis of parallels in other cultures he argues that ṣḥq (Pi.), usually considered to have sexual connotations on the basis of Gen. 26:8, 39:14, simply means "ritual sporting" before a deity, and that mḥlt (Ex. 32:19) means probably "antiphonal singing, a double group of performers which includes females and musical accompaniment, and ritual sporting". While it is possible that these terms are in fact neutral in implication, their use in this context where the writer disapproves of the worship (cf. v. 25) would suggest that the traditional interpretation is to be preferred. If the people cast off restraint in the presence of an image which was the symbol of fertility, the implications are obvious.
8. The Hebrew ᶜgl is traditionally rendered "calf". It is generally agreed that in fact "bull" or "young bull" would be more strictly accurate; cf. Ps. 106:19f. where, in reference to this incident, ᶜgl and šwr are used in parallelism. For convenience, however, the traditional rendering will be maintained here.

The question of whether the calf was a free-standing object, and if so of what size, or whether it was a standard on a pole (cf. Eissfeldt, "Lade und Stierbild"), is of little relevance to the exegesis, but will be discussed later (below, p. 221 n.29).
9. The technical problem concerning the construction of the calf need not be dealt with here. A concise statement of the issues, with basic bibliography, is provided by Childs, Exodus, 555f.
10. The verbs in 32:6a are plural in the MT. In the LXX, however, they are singular, indicating Aaron alone as subject. The reason for this variation is perhaps the later emphasis upon Aaron as priest which suggested that he alone, and not the people generally, should offer sacrifices. There is no reason to prefer the LXX reading to that of the MT.
11. Cf. M. Aberbach, L. Smolar, "The Golden Calf Episode in Postbiblical Literature".
12. Except perhaps in the sense of Ex. 7:1.
13. Cf. below, pp. 108f.
14. For a discussion of whether or not the bull was intended as a pedestal for the deity, and how precisely it was seen to

embody the divine presence, see below, pp. 165.

15. Admittedly the verbal parallel is not exact in that 20:2 uses hwṣy' whereas 32:1,4 uses h^{c}lh. Whether one may discern any systematic distinction between the two words is an open question. The attempt by J. Wijngaards, "hwṣy' and h^{c}lh, A Twofold Approach to the Exodus", to show distinct meanings and origins for the two formulae depends on an atomistic approach which treats them in isolation from their context and other motifs.

16. For a discussion of the varying implications of '^{e}lōhîm with plural verb or predicate, see esp. H. Donner, "Hier sind deine Götter, Israel!"; also GK § 145 i, S.R. Driver, Deuteronomy, 65.

17. For the bearings of 1 Kg. 12:28 upon Ex. 32, see below, pp. 163f.

18. Cf. Childs, Exodus, 562f.

19. On the possible use of the introductory formula as a device necessitated by the absence of punctuation or paragraphs, cf. above, p. 30.

20. Cf. Childs, Exodus, 563, 567.

21. Cf. W. Michaelis, "hodos", 51ff.; contra Koch, "derek", 283, who interprets derek in 32:8 as signifying the course of salvation history, a difficult meaning in context.

22. This assumes that Ex. 20:3 represents the first commandment, with 20:2 as preamble, and 20:4 is distinct as a second commandment and not part of the same commandment as 20:3.

23. Cf. below, pp. 166f.

24. Cf. S. Kaufman, "The Structure of the Deuteronomic Law", esp. 121, 145.

25. Cf. W. Zimmerli, "Das zweite Gebot", for the close connection between the first two commandments entailed by the expansion of the second commandment in Ex. 20:4-6.

26. The omission of v. 9 in the LXX is discussed below, p. 224 n.74.

27. In 32:8 one Heb. MS, LXX and Vulgate read ṣiwwîtām rather than ṣiwwîtim of MT. This repointing would fit well with v. 7, and Ehrlich, Randglossen I, 391, observes that the first person singular in defective script is extremely rare. On the other hand the decalogue is distinctively presented as the direct address of God both in Deuteronomy and in Ex. 20 (cf. Nicholson, "The Decalogue as the Direct Address of God") - which supports the MT. The parallel in Deut. 9:12 does not help

as the same problems apply there. One cannot be sure which pointing is original, nor does it matter greatly.

28. Cf. Num. 14:11; also Ex. 32:1, "This Moses".

29. This has been disputed. Even Calvin considered the suggestion "too subtle" (Harmony, III, 338). There are other passages in 32-34 where the use of the suffix is not significant (e.g. 33:1, 34:10).

30. Cf. Childs, Exodus, 567f.

31. An appeal on these terms is of course characteristic of many other intercessions in the OT. But this in no way detracts from its significance in the present context.

32. The reading in Sam. Pent. and LXX is an accommodation to the more usual formula. The use of "Israel" in a prayer of particular significance is also found in 1 Kg. 18:36, where it "emphasizes God's national role" (Childs, "Elijah Narratives", 133).

33. Moses, 8f.

34. The Yahwist, 158. Cf. also G.A.F. Knight, Theology as Narration, ix-x.

35. "Moses versus Amalek", 37ff.

36. Ibid., 41.

37. Ibid., 40. Cf. idem, "History and Theology in the Sea Tradition".

38. This is true not only of the text in its present form but also, with only slightly varying emphases, in the reconstructed J and P accounts.

39. Exodus, 559, 563.

40. Exodus, 249; cf. Coats, Rebellion in the Wilderness, 188.

41. P. 45.

42. The decision as to what constitutes a separate word is problematic. Here prepositions and particles are taken as separate words, even when joined by a maqqeph.

43. Although the speaker in v. 18 is not specified, contextual considerations make it likely that the speaker is Moses and not Joshua.

44. The interpretative crux of v. 18 need not be discussed here. Since, however, the exegesis is of interest, an excursus is appended at the end of the chapter, pp. 111f.

45. The puzzling sequence of verbs in v. 20 - how can gold be burnt? - is best understood through a comparison with the Ugaritic text 1.6 II:31-37. (The numbering is that of M. Dietrich, O. Loretz, J. Sanmartin, Die keilalphabetischen Texte aus Ugarit. For an English translation see ANET^3, 140, or J.

Gibson, Canaanite Myths and Legends, 77). When Anath kills Mot the verbs appear in the sequence of burn, grind, scatter, and seem to be a literary idiom for expressing thoroughness of destruction. It is possible that there are also overtones of a fertility ritual. Cf. S. Loewenstamm, "The Making and Destruction of the Golden Calf"; F.C. Fensham, "The Burning of the Golden Calf and Ugarit".

46. The superficial similarity of 32:20 to the ordeal in Num. 5:11ff. has frequently been noted. The ritual in Num. 5 does not, however, greatly illuminate the significance of the action in the present context where the concern is to administer punishment rather than determine guilt.

47. Exodus, 570.

48. Ibid.

49. Cf. Gressmann, Mose, 202.

50. Cf. H. Ringgren, "'āch", 190.

51. There is less evidence for bn being used in an extended sense than there is for 'ḥ. One may at least note its use for a subordinate within a prescribed relationship, cf. 2 Kg. 16:7; also Arad Ostraca 21, 40 (Lemaire, Inscriptions Hébraïques, 186, 207).

52. It is of course possible that the tradition-history of the story may account for its inner tensions. But the present task is to explain the text as far as possible in its own right without recourse to questions of its history until a second stage, unless no satisfactory sense can be made of the final form of the text.

53. "The King's Loyal Opposition", passim.

54. Cf. Cassuto, Exodus, 421.

55. An alternative reading in the Sam. Pent. is prw^c, as in v. 25.

56. It is probably unnecessary therefore to emend br^ch in v. 17 to pr^c, even should it be correct to adopt pr^c in v. 22 (contra Ehrlich, Randglossen, 393, Gressmann, Mose, 200).

57. It is unnecessary to find the idea of vicarious suffering in v. 32.

58. On this question, see J.J. Stamm, Erlösen und Vergeben im AT, and recently T. Raitt, Theology of Exile, 185ff.

59. On the problems raised by this sort of language, cf. below pp. 61f.

60. Childs shows that on syntactical grounds one cannot translate the words by "for what they did with the calf that Aaron made" (Exodus, 557).

61. Cf. Noth, Exodus, 254, "a sincere and lasting repentance".

62. The full significance of this motif will become apparent at 34:9.
63. There is a slight verbal variation in that the 2nd plural, 'tm, is used instead of the 2nd singular, 'th. Since the rest of the verse reverts to the 2nd singular, there is no significance in the use of the plural pronoun, which has been put in the plural under the influence of the plural substantive immediately preceding.
64. "Angel" is not a wholly satisfactory rendering of ml'k as it is difficult to escape overtones of later angelology. It is doubtful, however, whether a more neutral term like "messenger" would escape being misleading in a different way. And so, with reservations, "angel" will be retained.
65. Exodus, 588.
66. Cf. above, p. 33.
67. See below, pp. 91f.
68. For 'hl mw^{c}d cf. Ex. 27:21; 28:43; 29:4,10,11,30,32,42; 30:16,18,20,36; 31:7.
69. The LXX reading, tēn skēnēn autou, shows that this was the LXX interpretation. The reading is most likely an attempt to explicate an ambiguity rather than evidence for an alternative textual tradition.
70. Cf. Buber, Moses, 153, 215, n. 193.
71. See below, p. 173.
72. For the use of the definite article with indefinite sense see GK § 126, q,r,s.
73. Contra e.g. Driver, Exodus, 359, Childs, Exodus, 584.
74. See further below, pp. 171ff.
75. See further below, pp. 171ff.
76. See also below, p. 72 and also p. 91.
77. V. 11, enôpios enôpiôi: v. 20 ou dunēsēi idein mou to prosôpon.
78. So Targums Onkelos, Jonathan ben Uzziel and Neofiti I. On the interpretation of Ex. 33:11 in the LXX and Targums, cf. M.R. D'Angelo, Moses in the Letter to the Hebrews, 101ff.
79. So e.g. J.E. Huesman, "Exodus", 65; W. Zimmerli, OT Theology in Outline, 74; A.W. Jenks, The Elohist, 53.
80. There are particular text-critical problems in this section as the LXX diverges from the MT at numerous and significant points. This is a subject for study in its own right, and for the present only a few brief comments will be made. A useful review of the issue is provided by D.P. Niles, The Name of God, 147, n. 1.

The following conclusions emerge from a comparison of the

MT and LXX:

i) The MT in itself present no problems. There is no crux which the LXX helps resolve.

ii) The subtle development of the intercession in the MT (see exegesis below) is lost in the LXX.

iii) No single motive for the LXX divergences is discernible. The LXX readings are sometimes less and sometimes more anthropomorphic.

iv) The LXX both simplifies and interprets the MT.

For these reasons the MT will be accepted as the basis for exegesis.

81. So e.g. Noth, Exodus, 257; R. Clements, God and Temple, 27; J. Muilenburg, "Intercession", 173f.

82. Beyerlin, Origins, 101.

83. For a discussion, see Beyerlin, ibid., 102.

84. The treatment of man's possible access to God in 33:11, 20-23 is indeed concerned with a metaphysical problem, but of a different kind, and it is not the theme of primary importance in the narrative.

85. Terrien comments on this verse, "A mode of psychological communion is thereby implied, for the phrase carries no hint of the later priestly motif of the column of fire or of the cloud which journeyed in the wilderness ahead of the people (Exod. 13:21f., etc.)" (Elusive Presence, 140). Unfortunately he does not raise the possibility that some concrete manifestation other than the fire and cloud might be envisaged.

86. Cf. above, p. 63 for the dangers of Yahweh's shrine.

87. For the significance of 34:9, see below, pp. 89ff.

88. It has been suggested that there are structural parallels between Ex. 33:1-34:10 and Gen. 15:7-21. See D.P. Niles, The Name of God, 142ff., 155, who develops arguments of Seebass, Lohfink, and B.W. Anderson. In fact the similarities are no more than one would expect from two accounts of Yahweh's gracious dealings with a chosen individual. The present exegesis shows the tenor and development of Ex. 33-34 to be fundamentally different from that of Gen. 15.

89. So e.g. D.N. Freedman, "The Name of the God of Moses", 153: "scholars resort to desperate measures to secure continuity".

90. Exodus, 594.

91. "Intercession", 168, 173.

92. N.M. Waldman, "God's Ways", 67, n. 2, notes the stylistic use of chiastic patterns in 33:12ff. Whether there is deliberate

chiasm is unclear, but that there are recurrent and interlocking motifs in no strictly logical progression is evident.

93. It is sometimes suggested that these words originally referred to Hobab, cf. Num. 10:29ff.

94. The theme of Num. 10:29-32 is not Israel's need of a guide, but whether or not Hobab will share in Israel's "good". The possibility of Hobab serving as eyes is introduced only secondarily into Moses' request, giving Hobab a reason to stay by virtue of his sense of being needed and valued by the Israelites, as Moses deferentially puts it.

Moreover, the juxtaposition of the ark passage in 10:33-36 with the preceding verses (both usually ascribed to the same source, either J or JE) suggests that, to one writer at least, any human guidance and help was not incompatible with, and was certainly not a substitute for, divine guidance.

95. C.J. Labuschagne, "The emphasizing particle *gam* and its connotations", 200, suggests that *gam* in Ex. 33:17 functions as a particle of emphasis. The exegesis indicates that the customary meaning "also" should be retained.

96. It may also be possible to detect the presence of a word play between *^{c}im* and *^{c}am*; cf. Waldman, "God's Ways", 68, n. 2.

97. Cf. Muilenburg, "Intercession", 177. Waldmann, "God's Ways", 68, n. 3, offers several Mesopotamian parallels. A more general discussion of the issues is provided by H.H. Rowley, *The Biblical Doctrine of Election*. Unfortunately Rowley does not discuss either the present passage or Gen. 6:8 (see below).

98. Cf. E.A. Speiser, *Genesis*, LXVII; W. Zimmerli, "*Charis*", 380.

99. E.g. Gen. 18:3, 30:27, 50:4, Num. 32:5, 1 Sam. 27:5, 2 Sam. 16:4, Esth. 5:8, 7:3, 8:5.

100. 1 Sam. 20:29; and with striking paradox in Num. 11:15.

101. 1 Sam. 1:18.

102. E.g. 1 Sam. 16:22, 20:3, 2 Sam. 14:22, Ruth 2:10,13.

103. Gen. 32:6 (ET 32:5), 33:8, 1 Sam. 25:8, 1 Kg. 11:19, Ruth 2:2.

104. Gen. 19:19; perhaps also Jdg. 6:17, which is akin to Ex. 33:13.

105. See further below, p. 91f.

106. "*Charis*", 380.

107. Cf. A. Laurentin, "*W^{ec}attah-Kai nun*", 171.

108. Cf. Muilenburg, "Intercession", 176; G.A.F. Knight, *Theology as Narration*, 195.

109. It is possible that the word should be pointed in the singular, cf. GK § 91k. A plural is supported by the Samaritan text, but the Syriac has a singular. The LXX and Vulgate present a different wording in the request. Since derek in the singular (as applied to God) tends to refer to the way of life God approves of, this is less appropriate in context than the plural.
110. Cf. Deut. 32:4, Is. 55:8f., 58:18. One may also compare Ps. 103:7, "He made known his ways (drkyw) to Moses ...". Although the parallel to "ways" is "deeds" (ᶜlylwtyw), the general context, esp. v. 8, echoes Ex. 33-34 and indicates an interpretation of "ways" in terms of God's gracious character.
111. For a survey of recent research on 2 Sam. 7, see T.N.D. Mettinger, King and Messiah, 48ff. Mettinger's own analysis of vv. 18ff. is that vv. 18-22a, 27-29 form a pre-deuteronomistic unity, while vv. 22b-26 are a deuteronomistic expansion.
112. Cf. Noth, Exodus, 257; Childs, Exodus, 594.
113. Theology, II, 38, n. 1.
114. It has been suggested that wahᵃniḥōtî should be emended to wahinḥētî, "and I will lead you" (Ehrlich, Randglossen, 405; Eichrodt, Theology II, 38, n. 1). The change is unnecessary, and is at odds with the context where divine leadership is not the issue. The idea of giving rest is hardly "impossible in the context" (so Ehrlich), since nwḥ is used elsewhere of God giving rest in the promised land (cf. Deut. 3:30, 12:10, Josh. 1:13,15, etc.), and is an appropriate word of assurance.
115. On pānîm, see A.R. Johnson, "Aspects of the use of the term Pānîm in the Old Testament"; Eichrodt, Theology II, 35-39.
116. Cf. G.B. Caird, Language and Imagery, 103ff., for a discussion of different types of deliberate ambiguity.
117. The text here is uncertain. One should probably follow LXX, Pesh., Vulg. in reading bᵉqirbām (so S.R. Driver, Notes, 322). The parallel to Ex. 33 would then be even closer.
118. Cf. Deut. 4:37, Is. 63:9, Lam. 4:16; perhaps also Ex. 20:3 // Deut. 5:7, Ps. 21:10.
119. Above, p. 68.
120. Ex. 25ff. uses the term pnym only in connection with Yahweh's presence in the tabernacle in the case of the shewbread, or bread of the Presence (25:30 lḥm pnym). Such a passing reference to the shewbread probably presupposes the notion of the divine pnym in the sanctuary which need not be elaborated since the expression "to see/appear before the face

of Yahweh" is already used as a standard expression for visiting a sanctuary in what are possibly the earliest texts relating to the subject, Ex. 23:15,17, 34:20,23; cf. Noth, *Exodus*, 192.
121. Noth (*Exodus*, 257) comments that "It is not said how the 'presence', the side of the divine being presented to men which gives a particularly direct representation of this being is to manifest itself ...", and suggests that "Perhaps the thought here is of the worship of Yahweh in the cult at the sanctuaries of Israel, to which men go to 'see' the divine 'face'". This suggestion, however, ignores the important detail of God's presence "on the move", which must envisage a portable and not a fixed sanctuary.
122. For the use of *plh*, "to be distinct", cf. Ex. 8:18, 9:4, 11:7.
123. Below, pp. 105f.
124. It is interesting to compare Ps. 27 where the psalmist seeks God in the sanctuary. The psalm is reminiscent of Ex. 33 and draws on similar terminology. One may note the following parallelism:

v. 8	*'t pnyk yhwh 'bqš*	cf. Ex. 33:11,14,15,20,23.
v. 11	*hwrny yhwh drkk*	cf. Ex. 33:13.
v. 13	*lr'wt bṭwb yhwh*	cf. Ex. 33:19.
v. 4	*lḥzwt bn^{c}m-yhwh*	cf. Ex. 33:18,22.

V. 4 is put last for two reasons. First, the change in tone between vv. 1-6 and vv. 7ff. has made the literary unity of the psalm a matter of debate. Secondly, there is no exact parallel to *n^{c}m* in Ex. 33. Von Rad, however, comments that *n^{c}m* is "more or less synonymous with the 'glory of Yahweh' (*kbd yhwh*)", ("'Righteousness' and 'Life'", 257f.). *N^{c}m* is a rare word whose precise meaning is difficult to ascertain, but von Rad's suggestion is not implausible and enhances the parallelism to Ex. 33.
125. It is difficult to be sure how far the request to see Yahweh's glory points to a desire for a visible manifestation of Yahweh as such. For it is always characteristic of the glory to be hidden in the cloud, and both the cloud and the glory are visible phenomena. One would necessarily refer to the glory in terms of seeing it, whereas in v. 13 Moses asks that God's "ways" be made known to him, since the divine "ways" are more naturally referred to in terms of knowledge rather than vision.
126. Cf. Hos. 3:5, Jer. 31:12,14, Ps. 27:13.
127. On this formula, see D.P. Niles, *The Name of God*, 52ff., 123ff.

128. Gressmann, *Mose*, 225.
129. On this formula, see S.R. Driver, *Notes*, 185f.; *idem*, *Exodus*, 352f.; D.N. Freedman, "The Name of the God of Moses", 153f.; J.R. Lundbom, "God's Use of the *Idem per Idem* to Terminate Debate".
130. Freedman, *ibid*.
131. *Notes*, 186.
132. "Name of God", 154; *contra* e.g. Gressmann, *Mose*, 229, who characterizes the saying as showing "absolute Willkür".
133. Cf. the implications of its usage in Ex. 4:13, 1 Sam. 23:13, 2 Sam. 15:20, 2 Kg. 8:1.
134. Cf. Lundbom, *op. cit.*
135. On Ex. 3:14, see most recently B.J. Beitzel, "Exodus 3:14", who argues against finding any etymological interest in the passage.
136. On the problem of interpreting this formula, cf. above, p. 30.
137. "Theophany and Anthropomorphism in the OT", 36.
138. Cf. Barr, *ibid*., 32.
139. *Exodus*, 596.
140. Cf. Gen. 32:30, Deut. 4:33, 5:24,26, Jdg. 6:22f., 13:22, Is. 6:5.
141. In 33:20 there is perhaps also an echo of Ex. 10:28f. There Pharaoh says to Moses, "Never see my face (i.e. come into my presence) again; for in the day that you see my face you shall die". Pharaoh, in claiming that to see his face means death, pretends to be God and so becomes the archetype of human hybris. Ex. 33 presents, by contrast, the true God whose face may indeed not be seen but who nonetheless graciously does allow some access to his servants.
142. For recent discussions of Gen. 16:13, see H.C. White, "The Initiation Legend of Ishmael", 285f.; C. Westermann, *Genesis 12-50*, 296f.; T. Booij, "Hagar's Words in Gen. 16:13b".

A literal rendering of the MT of Gen. 16:13b would be, "For she said, Have I even here (lit. hither) seen after him that sees me?" or "... seen the back of him that sees me?" In the first case *'ḥry* "after" is used in a spatial rather than temporal sense, somewhat reminiscent of Ex. 33:23. The alternative, construing *'ḥry* as a substantive, would make the parallel to Ex. 33:23 close indeed.

The interpretation is, however, problematic. First, the text is possibly corrupt. The chief difficulty is with *hᵃlōm* which means "hither" rather than "here" and this fits awkwardly. If one emends this, as often suggested, to 'elōhîm then, with or without further emendations, there are two consequences: 'lhym, and not 'ḥry as a substantive, must be the object of r'yty; and 'ḥry as an adverb must have a temporal rather than a spatial significance. This would rob the parallel with Ex. 33:23 of its force.

Secondly, the context of Gen. 16:7-16 bears no resemblance to Ex. 33. Gen. 16:7-12 lays no stress on any marvellous apparition of Yahweh's angel, who is treated in a matter-of-fact way. It is therefore not clear how far the play on seeing (r'h), present in both MT and most emendations, conveys the nuance of physical sight or an interest in theophany as such. God's "seeing" seems to mean his providential caring for Hagar, while Hagar's "seeing" seems to refer to her gradually-dawning awareness of the nature of the person who spoke to her. There is thus no connection with the explicit theophany of Ex. 33.

143. For hiding one's face, cf. Deut. 31:17, Is. 53:3, Ps. 13:1, Job 13:24, etc. For turning one's back, cf. Jer. 2:27, 32:33, 2 Chr. 29:6.

144. Cf. Ex. 26:12, 1 Kg. 7:25, Ezek. 8:16.

145. Cf. M. Haran, "Nature of the "'Ohel Mo^c edh", 57.

146. See below, p. 86.

147. There are interesting links between 33:18-23 and Ex. 17:1-7, the murmuring at Massah and Meribah. The reference to the rock "at Horeb" (17:6) has occasioned much discussion. Geographically it is difficult, unless it designates Horeb as a large district, and it is usually deleted as a gloss. But why should anyone have so glossed the story? "At Horeb" may be a redactional note of typological rather than geographical significance, seeking to point parallels between the rock at Massah and that at Sinai. Interestingly, at Massah Yahweh stands before Moses on the rock (17:6), as Moses stands before Yahweh (33:21, 34:2). Moses passes (^c br) before the people (17:5), as Yahweh passes (^c br) before Moses (33:19,22). The concern of the people in 17:7 is said to be whether or not Yahweh is in their midst (bqrb), even though this is nowhere explicit in the preceding narrative. It may be a deliberate echo of Ex. 33, esp. 33:3,5, cf. 34:9a. At a different level there is the fact that Deut. 33:8f., which appears to refer to the same incident as Ex. 32:25-29, locates this incident in the testing at Massah and Meribah (cf. Ex. 17:7). Since the OT identifies Meribah with Kadesh (Num. 20:1,13,14, 27:14, Deut. 32:51), this

could point to a possible confluence of Kadesh and Sinai traditions, possibly the patterning of other traditions in the light of the centrally important Sinai narrative.

Since, however, the present concern is exegetical rather than traditio-historical, and since such similarities as there are between Ex. 33 and Ex. 17 are more likely to be of significance in interpreting the latter rather than the former, this question cannot be further pursued at this point.

148. See further below, pp. 101ff.

149. The problem of the composite nature of Ex. 19 is not of importance. Both J and E versions, however they are reconstructed, portray a similar public character of the theophany.

150. Cf. I Sam. 3:10, *wyb' yhwh wytyṣb*.

151. Cf. Niles, *Name of God*, 126f. One may also note Num. 14:17f. which refers back to Ex. 34:6f. and interprets Yahweh as the subject of *wyqr'*.

152. Above, p. 83.

153. For a recent discussion of the formula in v. 7b$^{\alpha}$ *wnqh l' ynqh*, see J. Piper, "An Interpretation of Ex. 33:19", 212. Piper's interpretation of 33:19, 34:6f. is similar to that advanced here.

154. *The Meaning of Hesed in the Hebrew Bible*, 119.

155. There is no need to emend *ûn^{e}ḥaltānû* to *ûn^{e}ḥîtānû* as proposed by Dillmann and Beer (*ad loc.*), following an original suggestion by Ewald.

156. Cf. Mann, *Divine Presence and Guidance*, 158, who calls this a "curiously repeated request".

157. It is not possible to survey more broadly the usage of *kî*. For recent discussions, see J. Muilenburg, "The Linguistic and Rhetorical Usages of the Particle *ky* in the OT"; T.C. Vriezen, "Einige Notizen zur Übersetzung des Bindeworts KI".

Much interesting debate on the meaning of *kî* among medieval Jewish commentators arose out of the dictum of the Talmudic sage Resh Lakish that *kî* has four meanings (B. Gittin, 90a). This too lies beyond our present purview.

158. All the early versions imply a causative sense. Among medieval commentators Ibn Ezra specifically argued for a causative, as opposed to concessive, meaning here.

159. See *BDB*, 473, col. 2; Vriezen, "Einige Notizen", 267ff.

160. *Ibid.*, 270ff.; cf. E. Zenger, *Die Sinaitheophanie*, 250, n. 123.

161. Above, pp. 60f.

162. The recent debate on the interpretation of Gen. 8:21, while important, need not detain us here. It is outlined and

assessed in excursus 2.
163. See the bibliography cited in excursus 2.
164. Buber, Moses, 89.
165. For the structure of the flood narrative, see B.W. Anderson, "From Analysis to Synthesis"; G.J. Wenham, "Coherence".
166. See Anderson, ibid., 36, 38; Wenham, ibid., 339f.
167. See above, pp. 70f.
168. For a possible further parallelism between Noah and Moses in Ex. 1-2, see J.S. Ackerman, "Literary Context", 91.
169. Cf. J. Halbe, Das Privilegrecht Jahwes, 283.
170. There is no reason to suppose that any theological significance, such as in 32:7-14, is intended in the use of the suffix here.
171. The use of bqrb here is perhaps a purely literary echo of the previous use of bqrb. It is unlikely that there is any substantive implication, such as that Israel will be distinctive in the midst of other people because Yahweh is in the midst of them.
172. For npl'wt cf. Ex. 3:20, Josh. 3:5, Jer. 21:2, Ps. 78:32, 105:2, etc. For nwr' cf. Deut. 10:21, 2 Sam. 7:23, Ps. 65:5 (66:3,5). The two words are combined in Ps. 106:22 and, differently, in Ex. 15:11c.
173. Admittedly not much can be built on this use of ᶜm for in e.g. Deut. 10:21 't is used in a way similar to ᶜm here to denote things done on Israel's behalf.
174. K.-H. Bernhardt, "bārā'", 248.
175. See further below, pp. 131ff. For recent detailed treatments, see E. Otto, Das Mazzotfest, 199ff.; F.-E. Wilms, Bundesbuch, 137ff.; and esp. J. Halbe, Privilegrecht, passim.
176. Above, p. 37.
177. Exodus, 364.
178. Cf. above, p. 49.
179. On the significance of Yahweh's name being "jealous", cf. above, p. 79.
180. The plural in the LXX is an accommodation to the customary formulation.
181. Such a pattern of principle and application is evident elsewhere in the OT, notably in Deuteronomy.
182. Cf. Childs, Exodus, 614.
183. The particular selection is to be seen as largely a recapitulation of those laws already contained in the Sinai narrative, esp. 23:14ff. See further below, pp. 131ff.

184. When taken in isolation from its context, this verbal change has appeared puzzling, and has often been taken as evidence for different stages of development of Israelite opposition to images. The interpretation in context casts doubts upon the validity of certain such reconstructions. On the prohibition of images in Israel, see below, pp. 164ff.
185. Cf. R. de Vaux, *Studies in Old Testament Sacrifice*, 52ff.
186. P.C. Craigie, "Deuteronomy and Ugaritic Studies", 156-159; J.C.L. Gibson, *Canaanite Myths and Legends*, 29f., 123; M. Haran, "Seething a Kid in its Mother's Milk".
187. An interesting modern parallel is given by N. Glueck, *The Other Side of the Jordan*, 9. But one should also note Haran's sceptical comment on Glueck's experience ("Seething", 31, n. 24)!
188. Cf. above, p. 45.
189. So Buber, *Moses*, 139; cf. Knight, *Theology as Narration*, 203.
190. A history of modern study of Ex. 34 is conveniently provided by Wilms, *Bundesbuch*, 15-135; see also Halbe, *Privilegrecht*, 13ff. The comprehensive documentation provided there makes it unnecessary to list the adherents of the various viewpoints cited in the present brief discussion.
191. So Childs, *Exodus*, 608. Interestingly, Perlitt, who argues for 34:1-28 as a deuteronomic composition in its entirety and does not find a decalogue anywhere in vv. 11-26, sees "the ten words" as a secondary deuteronomistic gloss of no special significance (*Bundestheologie*, 229f.).
192. It may also be noted that there is no omission or displacement of the words in the MSS tradition. This would at least rule out their being a very late gloss.
193. See the table in Wilms, *Bundesbuch*, 200-205. The question of secondary expansion of the laws does not affect the basic point.
194. So e.g. Beyerlin, *Origins*, 77ff.
195. Cf. the comments and citations of Perlitt, *Bundestheologie*, 223. The table in Wilms, *Bundesbuch*, 200ff., well illustrates the diversity of reconstructions.
196. See Halbe, *Privilegrecht*, 23, n. 65, for reference to one or two such doubts.
197. The proposal that it was Yahweh who wrote on the tablets is not novel; see e.g. Keil & Delitzsch, Dillmann, Hertz, Beer, and Childs, *ad loc*. But the argument has tended simply to appeal to 34:1 without detailed consideration of the related

issue of the relationship between v. 28b and v. 27 and the laws of vv. 11-26.

It is also possible that the verb wyktb could be interpreted in an impersonal sense ("and there was written"), thereby intending a more oblique reference to Yahweh.

198. Prof. E.W. Nicholson has suggested to me that the uniqueness of the decalogue resides not only in its being spoken by God (cf. his "Decalogue as Direct Address"), but also in its being written by him; the speaking and the writing belong together. If this is so, it would further support the contention that in v. 28b the writer need not actually specify Yahweh as writing the ten words, on the grounds that he takes for granted that it is only Yahweh who would write the ten words.

199. The writer need not describe the tablets more fully because that was already done in 32:15f. and it is assumed that these renewed tablets are similar. There is of course the difference that the former tablets are said to have been themselves God's handiwork, while with the new tablets only the writing is God's. But no special significance attaches to this in the narrative. At most there may be a tacit suggestion that Israel's sin has forfeited something of unique value and that the covenant renewal does not simply restore the status quo ante. One may compare the discussion in the next three paragraphs about the significance of the renewal being "with you and with Israel".

200. The word occurs only here, in vv. 33,34,35.

201. Noth, Exodus, 267.

202. Conjectures about the teraphim having been some kind of mask are precarious.

203. Cf. K. Jaroš, "Des Mose 'strahlende Haut'", 275ff.

204. Below, pp. 177ff.

205. The verb qrn appears only in Ex. 34:29,30,35 (Qal) and Ps. 69:32 (Hiph. ptc.). Since the Hiph. meaning in Ps. 69 is "bring forth horns" it is natural to interpret the Qal as "have horns". The noun in the OT always means "horn". Even the apparent exception in Hab. 3:4 is probably no exception after all, cf. Jaros, op. cit., 277. Linguistically, therefore, the evidence in favour of the verb meaning "to be horned" is overwhelming.

206. This meaning is already present in the LXX, dedoxastai hē opsis.

207. J.P. Brown, "The Sacrificial Cult and its Critique in Greek and Hebrew (I)", 171.

208. J.M. Sasson sees in Ex. 34:29-35 a fragment of old pagan

worship of Sin, a moon god represented by a bull, here symbolized by Moses who is now confronted by the new deity YHWH who gives orders and henceforth asserts his dominance ("Bovine Symbolism in the Exodus Narrative", 387). One cannot but feel that this is a classic example of such misunderstanding.
209. The transition from Yahweh's revelation on Sinai to his revelation in the tent has been prepared for by the subtle change to the frequentative imperfect in 34:34f.
210. Childs, *Introduction*, 175.

Notes to Excursus One

1. For recent discussions, see F. Andersen, "A lexicographical note on Exodus 32:18"; R. Edelmann, "To ^{c}*nwt* Exodus 32:18"; R. Whybray, "^{c}*nwt* in Exodus 32:18"; H. Valentin, *Aaron*, 212f.
2. So e.g. Dillmann, *Exodus und Leviticus*, 340; Driver, *Exodus*, 353.
3. So Edelmann, *op. cit.*; Whybray, *op. cit.*
4. Cf. LXX, *phōnēn exarchontōn oinou.*
5. Gressmann, *Mose*, 202.
6. Andersen, *op.-cit.*, 111.
7. Andersen, *ibid.*
8. Valentin, *op. cit.*, 213.
9. Valentin, *ibid.*
10. *Loc. cit.*
11. *Loc. cit.*
12. *Exodus,* 111.
13. Cf. the play on *pr^{c}/br^{c}h* (above, p. 56); also the development of *pnym* in the narrative; and the subtle development of motifs in 33:12ff.
14. Edelmann, *loc.cit.*

Notes to Excursus Two

1. Among the numerous treatments, the following may be noted: R. Rendtorff, "Genesis 8:21 und die Urgeschichte des Jahwisten"; W.M. Clark, "The Flood and the Structure of the Pre-patriarchal History", 204-209; O. Steck, "Genesis 12:1-3 und die Urgeschichte des Jahwisten"; D.L. Petersen, "The Yahwist on the Flood"; R.A.F. Mackenzie, "The Divine Soliloquies in Genesis"; D.J.A. Clines, *Theme,* 70-72. Among the commentaries, G. von Rad, *Genesis*^{2}; U. Cassuto, *Commentary*

on Genesis II; B. Vawter, On Genesis; C. Westermann, Genesis 1-11.
2. Westermann, op. cit., 612.

Notes to Chapter Three
EXODUS 32-34 AS A CULT LEGEND

1. Among the numerous interesting issues which must be shelved, but which it is hoped will be discussed in the future, three may be singled out for mention. First, the relationship of Ex. 32-34 to Ex. 19-24 may be fruitfully re-examined in the light of the numerous instances where the exegesis has suggested that chs. 32-34 presuppose the general content, and sometimes the precise wording, of chs. 19-24. Secondly, the exegesis has suggested links between Ex. 32-34 and Ex. 25-31 closer than hitherto appreciated. Suffice it at present to say that if the present form of Ex. 25-31 is late, some earlier account of at least the ark and some kind of sacred tent must be presupposed. This is similar to the frequently-made suggestion that some earlier (JE) account of the ark was displaced by the later and more developed P account. Thirdly, it has been shown that there are striking parallels in language, structure and theology between Ex. 32-34 and Gen. 6-9. The linkage of these two stories in the tradition provides the basis for an important traditio-historical and redactional study. That too remains a task for the future.
2. Cf. Noth, HPT, 142; Eichrodt, "Covenant and Law", 308; P.F. Ellis, The Yahwist, 87.
3. J. Halbe calls their work "epoch making" (Privilegrecht, 325).
4. S. Mowinckel, Le Décalogue, 113ff.; G. von Rad, "The Form-Critical Problem of the Hexateuch", esp. 20-26.
5. Décalogue, 120.
6. See also above, p. 36.
7. "Problem", 48ff.
8. HPT, 59-62, 141-145.
9. Origins and History of the Oldest Sinaitic Traditions.
10. Das Privilegrecht Jahwes.
11. For a survey of recent usages with constructive clarification, see R.M. Hals, "Legend: A Case-Study in OT Form-Critical Terminology".
12. The German term for this is "Sage".
13. Cf. A. Jolles, Einfache Formen, 23-61.

14. The German term for this is "Legende".
15. The German term for this is "Kult(us)sage".
16. "Legend", 171.
17. Noth, History, 128.
18. The People of the Covenant, 54.
19. Ibid.
20. The Psalms in Israel's Worship, I, 15.
21. Theology I, 98.
22. Psalmenstudien II, 21, cited by H.-J. Kraus, Worship in Israel, 9.
23. For an important discussion of the methodological problem, see S. Talmon, "The 'Comparative Method' in Biblical Interpretation". Another significant treatment, which illustrates the practical consequences of the approach proposed, is M. Noth, "God, King and Nation in the OT".
24. The same is true of the term "cult" in the phrase "cult legend". Although a substantive, it is adjectival in force.
25. Oldest Sinaitic Traditions, 138.
26. Bundesbuch, 139.
27. Worship, 23.
28. "Cult and History", 14.
29. The standard account of form criticism is Koch, Growth; see also J.H. Hayes (ed.), Old Testament Form Criticism. For an important critical appraisal, see R. Knierim, "Old Testament Form Criticism Reconsidered"; also B.O. Long, "Recent Field Studies in Oral Literature and the Question of Sitz im Leben"; idem, "Recent Field Studies in Oral Literature and their Bearing on OT Criticism"; M.J. Buss, "The Idea of Sitz im Leben"; D.A. Knight, "The Understanding of 'Sitz im Leben' in Form Criticism".
30. Cf. the criticisms of J. Muilenburg, "Form Criticism and Beyond", 5. Richter (Exegese, 72ff.) attempts to meet the objection by distinguishing between Form and Gattung: "Damit bezieht sich hier 'Form' auf einen Einzeltext, 'Gattung' auf einen Texttypus" (74). Although this obviates some difficulties, it raises the new problem of the relationship between "Form" and "Gattung". That is, the problem of the relation between the general and the particular is redefined rather than solved.
31. This naturally does not mean that there are not similarities between this experience and other encounters with Yahweh, within or outside the cult, but that the overall course and impact of the encounter is without subsequent parallel.
32. See esp. "Recent Field Studies ... Sitz im Leben".

33. Ibid., 41.
34. Ibid., 44.
35. Introduction, 73.
36. Introduction, 51.
37. The relationship between form and content has always been an unresolved tension in form criticism; cf. J.A. Wilcoxen, "Narrative", 88.
38. On these sayings, see W. Zimmerli, "Ich bin Jahwe". Unfortunately Zimmerli makes no reference to Ex. 33:19, 34:6f. in his discussion.
39. Cf. Eissfeldt, Introduction, 73.
40. See further below, p. 130.
41. For a general treatment of the topic, see J. Jeremias, Theophanie. Jeremias offers a useful survey of all the relevant OT material, but the value of much of his argumentation and conclusions depends largely on the assessment of the form-critical and traditio-historical approach which underlies them. He does clearly show, however, the difference between the Sinai theophany and other OT theophanies (105ff.), although having shown the origins of the latter independently of the former he offers no comparable discussion as to the origins of the former. His criticisms of the cult as the Sitz im Leben for theophany (118ff.) are also relevant to the present discussion.
42. "Formgeschichte und Exegese von Ex. 34: 6f.", esp. 131f.
43. Loc. cit. (nn. 34, 35).
44. See the listing and discussion of these passages in Scharbert, loc. cit.; R.C. Dentan, "The Literary Affinities of Ex. 34:6f.".
45. Although von Rad frequently asserts that such a transposition (and transformation) has taken place (e.g. "Form-Critical Problem", 68; Theology I, 39), it is unfortunate that he offers no detailed account of how this should be understood to have taken place.
46. See above, p. 77, for the significance of the unparalleled usage of the qr' bšm formula with Yahweh as subject.
47. Cf. above, pp. 125f, for G.E. Wright's comment on the importance of using a control which can be tested.
48. For present purposes the difference between the paraenetic vv. 11-16 and the laws of vv. 17-26 is of no significance.
49. Oldest Sinaitic Traditions, esp. 51ff., 63f., 145ff. Cf. also Halbe, Privilegrecht, 43ff.
50. "Covenant Forms in Israelite Tradition".

51. See D.J. McCarthy, Old Testament Covenant: A Survey of Current Opinions; idem., Treaty and Covenant[2]; E.W. Nicholson, Exodus and Sinai in History and Tradition; B. Childs, Exodus, 344ff.
52. "Covenant", 184.
53. See the history of research in Wilms, Bundesbuch, 15-135.
54. Of all the scholars discussed in Wilms' history of research only H.L. Strack, cited on Bundesbuch, 29, argued that the context was the determining factor for the content of 34:11ff.
55. So J.A. Soggin, "Ancient Israelite Poetry and Ancient 'Codes' of Law, and the Sources 'J' and 'E' of the Pentateuch", 191: "There is no difficulty in ascertaining that there is a lack of connection between the narrative sections of [J] and Ex. 34:10-25 [sic]".
56. It is a weakness of Soggin's discussion (ibid.) that he does not raise the question of what kind of connection between different types of material might reasonably be expected.
57. Cf. Childs, Introduction, 198.
58. So Noth, Exodus, 263.
59. So e.g. Mowinckel, Le Décalogue, 63ff. See most recently Halbe, Privilegrecht, 215ff., for a restrained account, but an account still in these terms.

If a cultic context subsequent to Jeroboam were suggested, then it would be possible to interpret 34:17 in terms of Jeroboam's calves. A decision on this issue will depend largely on one's view of the relationship of Ex. 32 to 1 Kg. 12:26ff., for a discussion of which see below, pp. 161ff.
60. The possibility of a pre-Israelite existence for some of the laws is neither affirmed nor denied. The issue is not the originality of the laws but how they became a part of the tradition of Ex. 32-34.
61. The present argument does not attempt to account for the differences in order and wording between the sets of laws. The hypothesis that they were originally independent collections, or else two recensions of one collection, could explain the differences in general terms, but still leaves one in the dark as to specific reasons for detailed differences. In any case, the question of the internal development of the legal complexes and their interrelationship in detail is distinct from that of their general relationship and incorporation into their present context.
62. For a general discussion of the nature of religious language, see I. Barbour, Myths, Models and Paradigms. For a

discussion related specifically to the use of language in the Bible, see G.B. Caird, *The Language and Imagery of the Bible*.

63. *Moses*, 111.

64. *History*, 131; cf. *HPT*, 204, n. 553. Admittedly Noth does allow that "it is just possible that among the tribes wandering about in southern and eastern Palestine volcanic manifestations which were well known in north-western Arabia were traditionally thought of as phenomena accompanying theophanies, and that they were mentioned even when the theophany occurred in a place with no volcanoes". But even this recognition, together with Noth's most cautious discussion of the issue in *Exodus*, 157, 160, does not sufficiently come to terms with the question of what type of language it is that is under consideration.

65. "'Righteousness' and 'Life'", 258.

66. *Myths*, 50.

67. *Ibid.*

68. For a convenient summary of Beyerlin's argument, see E.W. Nicholson, *Exodus and Sinai*, 43f.

69. *People of the Covenant*, 52.

70. *Exodus*, 231.

71. Although there are instances in Greek literature of the trumpet as the sound of thunder, e.g. Iliad 21. 388, *amphi de salpinxen megas ouranos*, such an idiom is unparalleled anywhere in the OT, let alone Ex. 19 where the trumpet blast does not function in a naturalistic way. Similar considerations apply to the proposal of J. Koenig ("La Localisation du Sinai", 17) that the trumpet blast attempts to describe an aspect of a volcanic eruption. The apparent parallel in Dio Cassius' account of Vesuvius, *kai salpingōn tis boē ēkoueto*, provides no real parallel to the function of the trumpet blast in Ex. 19.

72. "*Salpinx*", 80.

73. Cf. G. Friedrich, *ibid.*, 73.

Notes to Chapter Four
EXODUS 32-34 AS LEGEND

1. Cf. above, p. 119.

2. See also J.G. Frazer, *Folklore in the Old Testament* (3 vols.).

3. See esp. the introduction to the first edition of the Genesis commentary which was published separately and recently re-issued in translation, *The Legends of Genesis* (1964).

4. See the discussions in all the standard Introductions.
5. For Buber's understanding of the term, see Moses, 13-19. The term "saga" appears to be synonymous with "legend" as a rendering of the German Sage.
6. See e.g. Albright's introduction to the re-issue of The Legends of Genesis, vii-xii.
7. For a survey and analysis of the biblical theology movement, see B.S. Childs, Biblical Theology in Crisis.
8. Pp. 149-212. N. Gottwald's Tribes of Yahweh likewise attaches little historical value to the Moses traditions (e.g. p. 32). His distinctive and comprehensive approach cannot be treated here, but it may be questioned whether his comments at least on the Sinai tradition (cf. above, p. 12) do not show an insufficient appreciation of the nature of the material.
9. History, 173.
10. Ibid., 177.
11. Ibid., 182.
12. Ibid., 210.
13. Cf. the criticisms of J.B. Geyer, "The Joseph and Moses Narratives: Folk-Tale and History", 55.
14. History, 184.
15. So especially Buber; cf. above, p. 141.
16. Cf. G.S. Kirk, Myth, 38.
17. "Hebrew Epic: Historical Notes and Critical Reflections", 19-22.
18. Although it might be objected to this argument that the definitions offered of "legend", "folktale" and "heroic tale" beg the question, the essential point remains that it cannot be assumed that the different genres are all alike in their implications for the historical and traditio-historical nature of the material.
19. The definition is that of R.C. Culley, "An Approach to the Problem of Oral Tradition", 118.
20. Amid the numerous discussions of this subject, see esp. R.C. Culley, "Oral Tradition and Historicity", which also has a useful bibliography.
21. For recent careful discussions, with bibliography, see esp. R.C. Culley, Studies in the Structure of Hebrew Narrative; D.M. Gunn, The Story of King David, 37-62.
22. Cf. Van Seters' criticisms of tradition-history (Abraham, 139ff.).
23. The question of what constitutes a "substantial amount" is of course a matter for debate, but the general notion is clear.

24. See the listing of alternatives in Culley, "An Approach to the Problem of Oral Tradition", 124f.; cf. Gunn, King David, 59.
25. For the evidence for writing and literacy, see A.R. Millard, "The Practice of Writing in Ancient Israel".
26. "Primitive Saga Men", 325ff.
27. Cf. Gunn, King David, 59f.
28. A. Olrik, "Epic Laws of Folk Narrative", ET of "Epische Gesetze der Volksdichtung" (1909). On the question of oral criteria, cf. also Vorländer, Entstehungszeit, 24f.
29. Cf. e.g. K. Krohn, Folklore Methodology, 108ff.; W.O. Hendricks, "Folklore and the Structural Analysis of Literary Texts", 99ff.; D.M. Gunn, "On Oral Tradition", 159; R.C. Culley, Studies, 29f.; S.M. Warner, "Primitive Saga Men", 332f.
30. Cf. above, pp. 37f.
31. "Narrative Patterns and Oral Tradition in Judges and Samuel", 311ff.; King David, 37ff. This is not dissimilar to Olrik's Law of Patterning.
32. Cf. the debate between Gunn and Van Seters in Semeia 5, 139ff.
33. As Gunn himself fully admits, King David, 59.
34. See above, p. 205, n. 141; p. 206, n. 147.
35. The relationship between 1 Kg. 19 and the Sinai tradition is likewise not to be explained in terms of conventional patterning.
36. "An Approach to the Problem of Oral Tradition", 122f.
37. The recurrent pānîm motif is, of course, quite different from a catchword.
38. See H. Gunkel, Legends, passim; H. Gressmann, Mose, passim; E. Auerbach, Mimesis, 3-23; M. Buber, Moses, 13ff.; O. Eissfeldt, Introduction, 32ff.; G. von Rad, Genesis[3], 31ff.; idem, Theology II, 410ff.; K. Koch, Growth, 148ff., 195ff.; B.O. Long, The Problem of Etiological Narrative in the Old Testament; R.M. Hals, "Legend: A Case-Study in OT Form-Critical Terminology"; O. Kaiser, Introduction, 45ff.; J.A. Wilcoxen, "Narrative"; J. Van Seters, Abraham, 125ff.; C. Westermann, The Promises to the Fathers, 1-94; idem, Genesis 12-50, 40ff.; W. McKane, Studies in the Patriarchal Narratives, passim.

It will be noted that the majority of discussions are directed towards the patriarchal narratives. This is a potential drawback in the discussion, since one must beware of prejudging the extent to which other early traditions have characteristics in common with the patriarchal stories.

39. Noth, *HPT*, 44.
40. Cf. B. Childs, "A Study of the Formula, 'Until This Day'"; B.O. Long, *Problem*, esp. 87ff.
41. Cf. above, p. 61.
42. Cf. above, p. 77.
43. Cf. above, p. 120.
44. J.G. Frazer, *Folklore*; T.H. Gaster, *Myth, Legend, and Custom in the Old Testament* (a modern Frazer); D. Irvin, *Israelite and Judaean History*, 180ff.
45. *Mose*, 199ff., esp. 203.
46. *Index*, A.132.9.
47. *Index*, D.133.4.1.
48. *Index*, S.73.1.
49. For a recent discussion of what constitutes a motif, see D. Irvin, *Mytharion*, 2ff.
50. *Index*, C.311.1.8.
51. *Index*, F.574.3.2.
52. *Theology* II, 420.
53. *Growth*, 156.
54. Cf. above, pp. 90ff.
55. For the marked catholicity and lack of religious exclusiveness in Genesis, see B. Gemser, "God in Genesis"; G. Wenham, "The Religion of the Patriarchs".

An apparent exception to this principle, the Elijah stories, is not in fact an exception. For the theology of Mosaic Yahwism plays a small role in the stories. The presentation is in terms of the solitary defender of truth against the hordes of falsehood.
56. Cf. von Rad, *Theology* I, 203ff.
57. *Theology* II, 421.
58. *Ibid.*; cf. G.W. Coats, "History and Theology in the Sea Tradition". The important implications of the different senses in which "historical" is used here cannot be discussed at this point.
59. T.L. Thompson ("History and Tradition", 58) refers to "the growing ability of historians and archaeologists to write a history of Israel's origins largely independent of biblical interpretation", and says that "In approaching the origin of Israel, one can no longer take one's starting-point from within Israel's traditions". But it is doubtful whether such an approach can in fact be sustained.
60. The most obvious difficulty, the nature and antiquity of the calf tradition, is briefly discussed in the following chapter, pp. 161ff. But see also the brief comments on 32:25-29,

below, pp. 180ff.
61. Promises to the Fathers, 71-73. Westermann's term is "theologische Erzählungen", which he considers applicable to Gen. 22:1-19, 18:17-33, 12:1-3, 15:1-6.

Notes to Chapter Five
CRITICAL ANALYSIS OF EXODUS 32-34

1. For the form-critical and traditio-historical problems concerning 34:6f.,11-26, see above, pp. 128ff, 131ff.
2. This was first suggested by Wellhausen, Die Composition des Hexateuchs, pp. 85ff., and has commanded a scholarly consensus since.
3. Pp. 84ff.
4. Cf. above, p. 27.
5. Even Rudolph who attempts to dispense with E altogether gives no serious consideration to the possibility that J could have contained both an initiation and renewal, and argues that the renewal is redactional, Ex. 34 having originally followed Ex. 19 ("Der Aufbau von Exodus 19-34"; cf. Der "Elohist", pp. 40-61).
6. See the convenient table in Zenger, Sinaitheophanie, pp. 206-231. And that is only a representative selection!
7. Exodus, p. 260.
8. Exodus, p. 607.
9. Cf. above, p. 31.
10. Contra Childs, Exodus, pp. 615f.
11. Cf. de Vaux, Early History I, p. 447.
12. So e.g. Perlitt, Bundestheologie, pp. 203ff.
13. See e.g. Simpson, Early Traditions, pp. 204ff.; Noth, Exodus, pp. 244f.
14. So Childs, Exodus, p. 559.
15. Another problem brought to the fore by the most extensive recent work on Ex. 32, that of H. Valentin (Aaron, pp. 205-303), concerns the role of Aaron. Despite the literary integrity of the references to Aaron (pp. 216-231, 266), Valentin considers Aaron's role within the tradition to be a secondary development. Space forbids any detailed discussion of Valentin's analysis. But since Valentin's traditio-historical hypothesis is a corollary of the cult legend interpretation of Ex. 32, the criticisms above of that interpretation have weighty implications for the assumptions upon which Valentin's case rests.
16. There is a list of thirteen similarities, of varying degrees

of substance, between the two accounts in M. Aberbach, L. Smolar, "Aaron, Jeroboam, and the Golden Calves".

17. There is a variation only in the introductory word: in Ex. 32:4,8, "this is" (*'ēlleh*), in 1 Kg. 12:28, "behold" (*hinnēh*).

18. Cf. Cassuto, *Exodus*, pp. 408f.; Buber, *Moses*, pp. 147f.

19. Cf. Childs, *Exodus*, pp. 559-561; de Vaux, "The Religious Schism of Jeroboam I", p. 101.

20. Cf. Noth, *HPT*, p. 143; *idem*, Exodus, p. 246; T.L. Thompson, "The Joseph and Moses Narratives", p. 162.

21. Cf. M. Newman, *The People of the Covenant*, p. 182; J.P. Hyatt, *Exodus*, p. 301; W. Zimmerli, "Das Bilderverbot in der Geschichte des Alten Israel", pp. 251ff.; A.W. Jenks, *The Elohist*, p. 51; F.M. Cross, *Canaanite Myth and Hebrew Epic*, p. 74.

22. Cf. G.W. Coats, *Rebellion in the Wilderness*, pp. 185f.

23. Above, p. 47.

24. The historical connection of the Sinai tradition with the exodus tradition is too big an issue to discuss here. Suffice it to say that von Rad's arguments for the original separateness of the themes are now widely criticized. See, for example, E.W. Nicholson, *Exodus and Sinai*, esp. p. 84; de Vaux, *Early History*, I, pp. 401ff.

25. Cf. Buber, *Moses*, p. 147; Newman, *People of the Covenant*, p. 182.

26. Cf. Buber, *ibid*. This particular argument is necessarily very tentative.

27. The evidence of Amos is ambiguous. Although he makes no specific reference to the calves, he is nevertheless strong in his denunciation of Bethel (Am. 4:4, 5:5f.).

28. Cf. A. Alt, "The Formation of the Israelite State in Palestine", pp. 224f.; J. Bright, *History of Israel*[2], pp. 219, 234, 242; J.A. Soggin, "Der offiziell geförderte Synkretismus in Israel während des 10. Jahrhunderts", pp. 179ff.

29. A minority of scholars have argued that the bull was not a free-standing object but a standard on a pole; see O. Eissfeldt, "Lade und Stierbild"; T.W. Mann, *Divine Presence*, p. 155. Such a suggestion has two advantages. First, there is good iconographic evidence for bull standards. Secondly, this would be a parallel to the serpent of Num. 21:4-9.

If this were accepted, discussion about the bull as a throne or pedestal would become redundant. The traditional understanding of the bull as a free-standing object should, however, be retained. The iconographic evidence for free-standing bulls, especially in cultic contexts, is considerably more abundant than the evidence for standards. And neither Ex. 32 nor 1 Kg. 12 gives any hint that a standard is intended.

30. This was originally suggested by H.T. Obbink, "Jahwebilder", and was further developed and popularized by Albright, From the Stone Age to Christianity, pp. 299-301.

31. Cf. J.B. Pritchard, The Ancient Near East in Pictures, p. 170, nos. 500, 501; cf. p. 163, p. 181, no. 537.

32. Exodus, p. 247.

33. Cf. L.R. Bailey, "The Golden Calf", p. 100.

34. Cf. ANEP, p. 202, no. 616.

35. Cf. H. Wolff, Hosea, p. 141.

36. Cf. above, p. 62.

37. Cf. Noth, History, p. 233; F.M. Cross, Canaanite Myth, p. 73, n. 117.

38. See e.g. Halpern, "Levitic Participation", p. 36.

39. Exodus, p. 566.

40. It is also characteristic of Elijah, Hosea, and Deuteronomy.

41. Cf. above, pp. 119ff., esp. p. 123, for the meaning of "cult legend". Ex. 32 would, in this context, be a cult legend in the same sense as Jdg. 17-18.

42. Cf. Noth, "Der Wallfahrtsweg zum Sinai (Num. 33)".

43. Old Testament Theology, I, pp. 214f.

44. Cf. J. Faur, "The Biblical Idea of Idolatry", p. 1. See also the discussion in R.P. Carroll, "The Aniconic God and the Cult of Images", pp. 51ff.

45. It is possible that Hosea's words could also be taken in the opposite way, to argue against the existence of such a commandment, the Israelites' behaviour being labelled as stupid rather than sinful. But the context of the verses does stress that thc calves are sinful and not merely foolish.

46. In addition to the statements of some such position by H. Schmid, Der sogenannte Jahwist, and J. Van Seters, Abraham in History and Tradition, there is the recent argument for a post-exilic date for J from H. Vorländer, Die Entstehungszeit des jehowistischen Geschichtswerkes.

47. So e.g. H. Gressmann, Mose, p. 240; Beyerlin, Origins, pp. 22, 112ff.

48. Cf. Görg, Zelt, p. 151. See the table in Zenger, Die Sinaitheophanie, pp. 224f.

49. T.W. Mann (Divine Presence, p. 144) cites Ex. 13:21-22, Num. 9:15-23 as parallels to Ex. 33:7ff. But these passages are

explicit summaries of what happened as Israel travelled, which could not be understood otherwise, which is not the case with Ex. 33:7ff.

50. So e.g. McNeile, Exodus, p. 212; Noth, Exodus, p. 255; Childs, Exodus, p. 590.

51. So Childs, Exodus, p. 591.

52. Cf. M. Haran, "The Nature of the "Ohel Mo[c]edh".

53. In the earliest form of the suggestion that there was an account which told of what was constructed with the ornaments and which originally followed 33:6, it was proposed that a tent, perhaps containing the ark, was the object constructed (Knobel, Exodus, pp. 321f.; cf. Dillmann and Driver ad loc.). Recently, however, commentators have usually suggested that it was just the ark that was made (e.g. Eissfeldt, "Lade und Stierbild", pp. 191f.; von Rad, OT Theology I, p. 237; Beyerlin, Origins, p. 110; de Vaux, "Ark of the Covenant", p. 141), though some have expressed reservations as to the likelihood of the whole hypothesis (e.g. Noth, Exodus, p. 254; Clements, God and Temple, p. 36; Zenger, Sinaitheophanie, p. 89; Childs, Exodus, p. 585; Fritz, Tempel und Zelt, pp. 101f.).

54. Cf. Haran, "'Ohel Mo[c]edh", pp. 53ff.; Fritz, Tempel und Zelt, p. 102.

55. Cf. D. Jobling, The Sense of Biblical Narrative, pp. 50-52. The validity of this point is independent of Jobling's overall approach and analysis which is not always persuasive.

56. The location of the tent envisaged by Num. 11-12 cannot, of course, be conclusively resolved by those texts alone, and so it is right to appeal to other passages. The question is whether Ex. 33:7-11 is the passage to appeal to. Although it is customary to exclude any perspective characteristic of P from Num. 11-12, it is quite possible that the notion of a shrine in the midst of the camp belonged to pre-P traditions and so may be appropriate to Num. 11-12 even when taken in isolation from the P material. At least it is appropriate to try out the perspective heuristically in one's reading of Num. 11-12.

57. It is, of course, possible that there could be religious reasons for locating a sanctuary outside a camp, analogous to the situation of sanctuaries outside cities. The possible significance of position requires further study.

58. The proposal to regard the tent of 33:7-11 as a temporary sanctuary is not new. See e.g. Keil & Delitzsch and Cassuto ad loc. But the argument has not previously considered the question of method. The present discussion is concerned not

with harmony for its own sake but with the grounds upon which one's assessment should be based.

59. The phrase mḥwṣ lmḥnh makes clear that a location outside the perimeter of the camp is envisaged, unlike the language of Num. 11-12 where no similar phrase is used.

60. See above, p. 91.

61. See e.g. Holzinger, Exodus, p. 116; Beer, Exodus, p. 163; Noth, Exodus, p. 267; Beyerlin, Origins, p. 3.

62. See Noth, ibid.; de Vaux, Early History I, p. 394; cf. also Eissfeldt, Hexateuch-Synopse, pp. 56f.

63. So Cross, Canaanite Myth, p. 314.

64. Cf. Cross, Canaanite Myth, pp. 314, 322.

65. On P's use of ᶜdh, cf. Driver, Exodus, p. 88.

66. As argued by Noth and de Vaux (n. 62).

67. Cf. e.g. Gressmann, Mose, pp. 246ff.; Noth, Exodus, p. 267; K. Jaroš, "Des Mose 'strahlende Haut'"; L.R. Bailey, "Horns of Moses", pp. 419f. For a significant dissentient voice, see F. Dumermuth, "Moses strahlendes Gesicht"; cf. also E.G. Suhr, "The Horned Moses".

68. Cf. above, p. 213, n. 23.

69. There are exceptions, one of the most notable being the hypothesis of Eissfeldt of a short original version of the Sinai covenant which included this pericope. Eissfeldt's reconstruction is conveniently outlined, with bibliography, in de Vaux, Early History I, p. 400. The reconstruction is, however, somewhat arbitrary and has won little acceptance.

70. The argument that the theme of travel and guidance is out of place in the Sinai tradition (so e.g. Noth, HPT, pp. 144, 204f.) raises the question of how broadly or narrowly one should define the themes proper to Sinai. It is important not to adopt a narrow definition which begs the question.

71. Early History I, p. 399.

72. "Intercession", pp. 168, 181; cf. Terrien, Elusive Presence, p. 138.

73. Cf. Childs, Exodus, pp. 559, 567.

74. There is a textual problem in that 32:9 is omitted by the LXX. Since the verse is present in the alternative rendering of the story in Deut. 9:13, it may be suggested that the verse is a secondary addition into its Exodus context as part of a harmonization with (or under the influence of) Deuteronomy.

There are, however, several considerations in favour of the MT. First, the "stiff-necked people" motif is an important connective link within Ex. 32-34, and the significance it is given in 34:9 presupposes earlier usage of the phrase. In addition to 33:3,5, its use in ch. 32, in the initial context of Israel's sin, is particularly appropriate. Secondly, the way in which the phrase functions in 32:9 as a ground for Yahweh's judgment is congruous with its usages in 33:3,5. Thirdly, 32:7-14 is a carefully redacted unit in which v. 9 fits smoothly (even though its omission is not disruptive) and which conveys an understanding of Yahweh's mercy similar to that conveyed by 34:9. Fourthly, when the "stiff-necked people" phrase carries a deep significance in Ex. 32-34 and no special significance at all in Deut. 9-10 which is a loose recasting of earlier tradition, its originality to the context in which it is of significance is likely. Fifthly, there is no other MSS evidence in support of 32:9 as an interpolation.

Admittedly this leaves the LXX omission unexplained. But that is less of a difficulty than the supposition of 32:9 as a late interpolation.

75. The fact that the kî clause is attached to the words of Moses and so differs from Gen. 8:21 where the kî clause is attached to the words of Yahweh supports the contention that it was added to an already-existing element in the tradition.

76. So G.W. Coats, Rebellion, p. 69.

77. See e.g. H. Holzinger, Exodus, p. 108.

78. Bundestheologie, pp. 156ff.

79. Der sogenannte Jahwist, pp. 83ff.

80. Exodus and Sinai, pp. 61ff.; idem, "The Decalogue as the direct address of God", pp. 422ff.

81. Deut. 4:37 uses pānîm in a way reminiscent of Ex. 33:14 but in fact more abstract in connotation. Such a usage of pānîm is also without other parallel in Deuteronomy. Deuteronomy characteristically expressed Yahweh's presence in terms of his "name".

82. Cf. C. Brekelmans, "Die sogenannten deuteronomistischen Elemente in Genesis bis Numeri. Ein Beitrag zur Vorgeschichte des Deuteronomiums"; idem, "Eléments deutéronomiques dans le Pentateuque"; W. Zimmerli, "Erwägungen zum 'Bund'; die Aussagen über die Jahwe-bryt in Ex. 19-34"; J. Halbe, Privilegrecht, pp. 256ff.

83. Apart from the sole adjectival usage of qāšeh with ᶜōrep in Dt. 31:27, occurrences of the verb qšh with ᶜrp are equally divided between dt. and non-dt. literature:

Dt. lit.: Dt. 10:16, 2 Kg. 17:14, Jer. 7:26, 17:23, 19:15.

Non-Dt. lit.: Prov. 29:1, Neh. 9:16,17, 2 Chron. 30:8, 36:13.

There are examples of stubbornness being depicted by the use of either qšh or ^{c}rp in conjunction with other words, but they are not relevant to the present point.

84. Cf. above, p. 27.

85. A tenth century redaction of Ex. 32-34 faces no obvious difficulty. If both the historical content and the literary presentation of 1 Kg. 12:26ff. is most likely subsequent to Ex. 32, and not vice versa, there is no element in Ex. 32-34, except perhaps 32:25-29, which need be taken to show knowledge of an historical situation later than the tenth century. Indeed, much of the content of Ex. 32-34, especially the concern for a movable shrine, fits naturally into the earliest period of Israel's history.

Notes to Epilogue

1. Enough has already been said on the general methodological issues, and they need not be recapitulated here.

2. If the dissociation of Ex. 32-34 from a deuteronomic redactor is correct, and yet these chapters are the most apparently deuteronomic section in Gen.-Num., this suggests the need for a re-examination of the nature and extent of deuteronomic redaction or Bearbeitung elsewhere in the Tetrateuch.

3. See e.g. J. Bright, Covenant and Promise, passim; D.N. Freedman, "Divine Commitment and Human Obligation"; T. Raitt, Theology of Exile, pp. 21f.; S. Terrien, Elusive Presence, pp. 23f.; W. Brueggemann, "Trajectories in OT Literature". J.D. Levenson ("The Davidic Covenant and its Modern Interpreters") cautiously argues against asserting any single or definitive relationship between the covenants but does not deny the distinctiveness of the indefeasibility of the Davidic covenant.

4. The conditional nature of the Mosaic covenant is frequently based upon an appeal to Ex. 19:5 with its conditional "if". But although the grammatical form of 19:5 is conditional, that need not determine its meaning. In fact it is doubtful whether 19:5 is truly conditional in sense (cf. D. Patrick, "The Covenant Code Source", p. 149). In the typical conditionals of Deut. 28 the protasis states a condition and the apodosis the result of meeting the condition - "And if you obey the voice of

Yahweh your God ... Yahweh your God will set you on high ...". In Ex. 19:5, however, the relationship between obeying God's voice and being his possession is not that between an action and a subsequent result. The protasis is a definition of the requirements of the position or vocation designated by the titles of the apodosis; it explains what being God's people means. To break the requirements of the protasis (obeying God's voice and keeping his covenant) would not mean subsequently ceasing to be God's people. Rather the act of unfaithfulness itself would be a denial of their position as God's people. But such a denial of their status need not entail the abrogation of that status.

5. Theology of Exile, esp. pp. 106ff.

LIST OF ABBREVIATIONS

ANET[3]	*Ancient Near Eastern Texts Relating to the Old Testament*, ed. J.B. Pritchard (3rd ed., Princeton, 1969).
AOAT	Alter Orient und Altes Testament
ASTI	Annual of the Swedish Theological Institute
BA	*The Biblical Archaeologist*
BASOR	*Bulletin of the American Schools of Oriental Research*
BBB	Bonner Biblische Beiträge
BDB	*A Hebrew and English Lexicon of the Old Testament*, ed. F. Brown, S.R. Driver, C.A. Briggs (Oxford, 1953 [1907]).
BJRL	*Bulletin of the John Rylands Library*
BR	*Biblical Research*
BWANT	Beiträge zur Wissenschaft vom Alten und Neuen Testament
BZAW	Beihefte zur Zeitschrift für die alttestamentliche Wissenschaft
CBQ	*Catholic Biblical Quarterly*
CBQMS	Catholic Biblical Quarterly Monograph Series
ET	English Translation
Exp.T.	*Expository Times*
FRLANT	Forschungen zur Religion und Literatur des Alten und Neuen Testaments
GK	*Gesenius' Hebrew Grammar as edited and enlarged by the late E. Kautzsch*, ed. A.E. Cowley (2nd ed., Oxford, 1910).
HAT	Handbuch zum Alten Testament
HPT	M. Noth, *A History of Pentateuchal Traditions*, ET (Englewood Cliffs, N.J., 1972)
HTR	*Harvard Theological Review*
HUCA	*Hebrew Union College Annual*
ICC	The International Critical Commentary (Edinburgh)
IDB	*The Interpreter's Dictionary of the Bible*, ed. G.A. Buttrick, et al. (New York, Nashville, 1962)
IDB Suppl.	*The Interpreter's Dictionary of the Bible, Supplementary Volume*, ed. K. Crim, et al. (Nashville, 1976)

Abbreviations

IEJ	Israel Exploration Journal
JB	The Jerusalem Bible (London, 1966)
JBL	Journal of Biblical Literature
JJS	Journal of Jewish Studies
JQR	Jewish Quarterly Review
JSOT	Journal for the Study of the Old Testament
JSOT Suppl.	Journal for the Study of the Old Testament, Supplement Series
JSS	Journal of Semitic Studies
JTS	Journal of Theological Studies
LXX	Septuagint
MT	Masoretic Text
NEB	New English Bible (Oxford & Cambridge, 1970)
NIV	New International Version (London, 1979)
NT	New Testament
OBO	Orbus Biblicus et Orientalis
OT	Old Testament
OTS	Oudtestamentische Studiën
PEQ	Palestine Exploration Quarterly
RHPB	Revue d'Histoire et de Philosophie Religieuses
RSV	Revised Standard Version (London, 1952)
SANT	Studien zum Alten und Neuen Testament
SBL	Society of Biblical Literature
SJT	Scottish Journal of Theology
ST	Studia Theologica
TDNT	Theological Dictionary of the New Testament (Grand Rapids, 1964-74). ET from Theologisches Wörterbuch zum Neuen Testament, ed. G. Kittel (Vols. I-V), G. Friedrich (Vols. V-IX) (Stuttgart, 1933-73)
TDOT	Theological Dictionary of the Old Testament, I-III (Grand Rapids, 1974, 1977, 1978). ET from Theologisches Wörterbuch zum Alten Testament, ed. G.J. Botterweck, H. Ringgren (Stuttgart, 1970-75).
Th.LZ.	Theologische Literaturzeitung
Tynd.B.	Tyndale Bulletin
TZ	Theologische Zeitschrift
VT	Vetus Testamentum
VT Suppl.	Supplements to Vetus Testamentum
WMANT	Wissenschaftliche Monographien zum Alten und Neuen Testament
ZAW	Zeitschrift für die alttestamentliche Wissenschaft

BIBLIOGRAPHY

Aberbach, M., & Smolar, L.
"Aaron, Jeroboam, and the Golden Calves", JBL 86 (1967), pp. 129-140.
"The Golden Calf Episode in Postbiblical Literature", HUCA 39 (1968), pp. 91-116.

Ackerman, J.S.
"The Literary Context of the Moses Birth Story (Exodus 1-2)", in K.R.R. Gros Louis et al. (ed.), Literary Interpretations of Biblical Narratives (Nashville, 1974), pp. 74-119.

Albright, W.F.
From the Stone Age to Christianity (New York, 1957).

Alonso Schökel, L.
The Inspired Word (London, 1967). ET from La Palabra Inspirada (Barcelona, 1966).
"Hermeneutical Problems of a Literary Study of the Bible", VT Suppl. 28 (1974), pp. 1-15.

Alt, A.
"The Formation of the Israelite State in Palestine", in his Essays on Old Testament History and Religion (Oxford, 1966), pp. 171-237. Originally published in German in 1930 and later in his Kleine Schriften II (Munich, 1953), pp. 1-65.
"The Origins of Israelite Law", in his Essays on Old Testament History and Religion (Oxford, 1966), pp. 79-132. Originally published in German in 1934 and later in his Kleine Schriften I (Munich, 1953), pp. 278-332.

Andersen, F.I.
"A Lexicographical Note on Exodus 32:18", VT 16 (1966), pp. 108-112.

Anderson, B.W.
"From Analysis to Synthesis: The Interpretation of Genesis 1-11", JBL 97 (1978), pp. 23-29.

Auerbach, E.
Mimesis (Princeton, 1953).

Auld, A.G.
"Keeping up with Recent Studies: VI. The Pentateuch", Exp.T. 91 (1980), pp. 297-302.

Baentsch, B.
Das Bundesbuch Ex. XX.22-XXIII.33 (Halle, 1892).

Exodus, Leviticus, Numeri (Göttingen, 1903).
Bailey, L.R.
"The Golden Calf", HUCA 42 (1971), pp. 97-115.
"Horns of Moses", IDB Suppl., pp. 419-420.
Barbour, I.
Myths, Models and Paradigms (London, 1974).
Bar-Efrat, S.
"Some Observations on the Analysis of Structure in Biblical Narratives", VT 30 (1980), pp. 154-173.
Barr, J.
"Theophany and Anthropomorphism in the Old Testament", VT Suppl. 7 (1959), pp. 31-38.
The Semantics of Biblical Language (Oxford, 1961).
"Covenant", in Hastings' Dictionary of the Bible (2nd ed.: Edinburgh, 1963), pp. 183-185.
The Bible in the Modern World (London, 1973).
"Reading the Bible as Literature", BJRL 56 (1973), pp. 10-33.
"Story and History in Biblical Theology", Journal of Religion 56 (1976), pp. 1-17. Reprinted in his Explorations in Theology 7 (London, 1980), pp. 1-17.
"Historical Reading and the Theological Interpretation of Scripture", in his Explorations in Theology 7 (London, 1980), pp. 30-51.
"Childs' Introduction to the Old Testament as Scripture", JSOT 16 (1980), pp. 12-23.
Barth, H. & Steck, O.H.
Exegese des Alten Testaments: Leitfaden der Methodik (Neukirchen-Vluyn, 1978).
Barton, J.
Review of D.A. Knight (ed.), Tradition and Theology in the Old Testament, JTS 30 (1979), pp. 240-243.
Beer, G.
Exodus, HAT 3 (Tubingen, 1939).
Beitzel, B.J.
"Exodus 3:14 and the Divine Name: A Case of Biblical Paronomasia", Trinity Journal I (NS) (1980), pp. 5-20.
Bernhardt, K.H.
"bārā", TDOT II, pp. 245-248.
Beyerlin, W.
Origins and History of the Oldest Sinaitic Traditions (Oxford, 1965), ET from Herkunft und Geschichte der ältesten Sinaitraditionen (Tubingen, 1961).
Booij, T.

"Hagar's Words in Gen. 16:13b", VT 30 (1980), pp. 1-7.
Brekelmans, C.
"Die sogenannten deuteronomistischen Elemente in Genesis bis Numeri. Ein Beitrag zur Vorgeschichte des Deuteronomiums", VT Suppl. 15 (1966), pp. 90-96.
"Eléments deutéronomiques dans le Pentateuque", Recherches Bibliques 8 (1967), pp. 77-91.
Bright, J.
Early Israel in Recent History Writing (London, 1956).
A History of Israel (2nd ed.: London, 1972).
"The Apodictic Prohibition: Some Observations", JBL 92 (1973), pp. 185-204.
Covenant and Promise (London, 1977).
Brodie, L.T.
"Again the Golden Calf: Shades of Hosea", Exp.T. 91 (1979), pp. 19-20.
Brown, J.P.
"The Sacrificial Cult and its Critique in Greek and Hebrew (I)", JSS 24 (1979), pp. 159-173.
Brueggemann, W.
"Presence of God, Cultic", IDB Suppl., pp. 680-683.
"Trajectories in Old Testament Literature and the Sociology of Ancient Israel", JBL 98 (1979), pp. 161-185.
Buber, M.
Moses (Oxford & London, 1946).
Buss, M.J.
"The Idea of Sitz im Leben - History and Critique", ZAW 90 (1978), pp. 157-170.
Caird, G.B.
The Language and Imagery of the Bible (London, 1980).
Calvin, J.
Commentaries on the Four Last Books of Moses Arranged in the Form of a Harmony, III, ET (Edinburgh, 1854).
Campbell, A.F.
"The Yahwist Revisited", Australian Biblical Review 27 (1979), pp. 2-14.
Carpenter, J.E. & Harford-Battersby, G.
The Hexateuch, 2 vols. (London, New York & Bombay, 1900).
Carpenter, J.E.
The Composition of the Hexateuch (London, New York & Bombay, 1902).
Carroll, R.P.
"The Aniconic God and the Cult of Images", ST 31 (1977), pp.

51-64.
"Childs and Canon", Irish Biblical Studies 2 (1980), pp. 211-236.
"Canonical Criticism: A Recent Trend in Biblical Studies?", Exp.T. 92 (1980/81), pp. 73-78.
Cassuto, U.
A Commentary on the Book of Genesis II (Jerusalem, 1964). ET from the Hebrew (Jerusalem, 1949).
A Commentary on the Book of Exodus (Jerusalem, 1967). ET from the Hebrew (Jerusalem, 1951).
Cazelles, H.
"Alliance du Sinai, Alliance de l'Horeb et Renouvellement de l'Alliance", in H. Donner, et al. (ed.), Beiträge zur Alttestamentlichen Theologie, W. Zimmerli Festschrift (Göttingen, 1977), pp. 69-79.
A la Recherche de Moïse (Paris, 1979).
Childs, B.S.
"A Study of the Formula 'Until this Day'", JBL 82 (1963), pp. 279-292.
Biblical Theology in Crisis (Philadelphia, 1970).
Exodus (London, 1974).
"The Sensus Literalis of Scripture: An Ancient and Modern Problem", in H. Donner et al. (ed.), Beiträge zur Alttestamentlichen Theologie, W. Zimmerli Festschrift (Göttingen, 1977), pp. 80-93.
"The Exegetical Significance of Canon for the Study of the Old Testament", VT Suppl. 29 (1978), pp. 66-80.
Introduction to the Old Testament as Scripture (London, 1979).
"On Reading the Elijah Narratives", Interpretation 34 (1980), pp. 128-137.
"Response to Reviewers of Introduction to the Old Testament as Scripture", JSOT 16 (1980), pp. 52-60. Childs is responding to several important reviews of his Introduction also contained in the same number of JSOT.
Clark, W.M.
"The Flood and the Structure of the Pre-patriarchal History", ZAW 83 (1971), pp. 184-211.
"Law" in J.H. Hayes (ed.), Old Testament Form Criticism (San Antonio, 1974), pp. 99-139.
Clements, R.E.
God and Temple (Oxford, 1965).
Exodus (Cambridge, 1972).

Old Testament Theology (London, 1978).
"Pentateuchal Problems", in G.W. Anderson (ed.), Tradition and Interpretation (Oxford, 1979), pp. 96-124.

Clines, D.J.A.
The Theme of the Pentateuch, JSOT Suppl. 10 (Sheffield, 1978).
"Introduction to the Pentateuch", in G.C.D. Howley et al. (ed.), A Bible Commentary for Today (London & Glasgow, 1979), pp. 97-103.
"Story and Poem: The Old Testament as Literature and as Scripture", Interpretation 34 (1980), pp. 115-127.

Coats, G.W.
Rebellion in the Wilderness (Nashville, 1968).
"Moses Versus Amalek: Aetiology and Legend in Exodus 17:8-16", VT Suppl. 28 (1974), pp. 29-41.
"History and Theology in the Sea Tradition", Studia Theologica 29 (1975), pp. 53-62.
From Canaan to Egypt, CBQMS 4 (Washington, 1976).
"The King's Loyal Opposition: Obedience and Authority in Exodus 32-34", in G.W. Coats, B.O. Long (ed.), Canon and Authority (Philadelphia, 1977), pp. 91-109.

Cody, A.
A History of Old Testament Priesthood, Analecta Biblica 35 (Rome, 1969).

Coggins, R.J.
"History and Story in Old Testament Study", JSOT 11 (1979), pp. 36-46.

Cole, A.
Exodus (London, 1973).

Collins, J.J.
"The 'Historical Character' of the Old Testament in Recent Biblical Theology", CBQ 41 (1979), pp. 185-204.

Conroy, C.
"Hebrew Epic: Historical Notes and Critical Reflections", Biblica 61 (1980), pp. 1-30.

Craigie, P.C.
"Deuteronomy and Ugaritic Studies", Tynd. B. 28 (1977), pp. 155-169.

Cross, F.M.
Canaanite Myth and Hebrew Epic (Cambridge, Mass., 1973).

Crossan, J.D.
"Perspectives and Methods in Contemporary Biblical Criticism", BR 22 (1977), pp. 39-49.

"Waking the Bible: Biblical Hermeneutic and Literary Imagination", *Interpretation* 32 (1978), pp. 269-285.
Culley, R.C.
"An Approach to the Problem of Oral Tradition", *VT* 13 (1963), pp. 113-125.
"Oral Tradition and Historicity", in D.B. Redford, J.W. Wevers (ed.), *Studies on the Ancient Palestinian World* (Toronto, 1972), pp. 102-116.
"Oral Tradition and the OT: Some Recent Discussion", *Semeia* 5 (1976), pp. 1-33.
Studies in the Structure of Hebrew Narrative (Philadelphia, 1976).
D'Angelo, M.R.
Moses in the Letter to the Hebrews, SBL Dissertations 42 (Missoula, 1979).
Davies, G.I.
The Way of the Wilderness (Cambridge, 1979).
Davies, G.H.
Exodus (London, 1967).
Dentan, R.C.
"The Literary Affinities of Ex. 34:6f.", *VT* 13 (1963), pp. 34-51.
Dietrich, M., Loretz, O., & Sanmartin, J.
Die Keilalphabetischen Texte aus Ugarit I, AOAT 24 (Neukirchen-Vluyn, 1976).
Dillmann, A.
Exodus und Leviticus (Leipzig, 1880).
Donner, H.
"'Hier sind deine Götter, Israel!'" in H. Gese, H.-P. Ruger (ed.), *Wort und Geschichte*, K. Elliger Festschrift; AOAT 18 (Neukirchen, 1973), pp. 45-50.
Die literarische Gestalt des alttestamentlichen Josephgeschichte (Heidelberg, 1976).
Driver, S.R.
Deuteronomy, ICC (3rd ed.: Edinburgh, 1902).
The Book of Exodus (Cambridge, 1911).
Notes on the Hebrew Text of the Books of Samuel (2nd ed.: Oxford, 1913).
Dumermuth, F.
"Zur deuteronomischen Kulttheologie und ihren Voraussetzungen", *ZAW* 70 (1958), pp. 59-98.
"Moses strahlendes Gesicht", *TZ* 17 (1961), pp. 241-248.
"Josua in Ex. 33:7-11", *TZ* 19 (1963), pp. 161-168.

Eakins, J.K.
"Moses", Review and Expositor 74 (1977), pp. 461-471.
Edelmann, R.
"To ᶜannôt Exodus 32:18", VT 16 (1966), p. 355.
Ehrlich, A.B.
Randglossen zur hebraïschen Bibel I (Leipzig, 1908).
Eichrodt, W.
Theology of the Old Testament, 2 vols. (London, 1961, 1967). ET from Theologie des Alten Testaments (Gottingen, 1959, 1964).
"Covenant and Law", Interpretation 20 (1966), pp. 302-321.
Eissfeldt, O.
Hexateuch-Synopse (Leipzig, 1922).
"Lade und Stierbild", ZAW 58 (1940), pp. 190-215. Reprinted in his Kleine Schriften II (Tübingen, 1963), pp. 282-305.
The Old Testament: An Introduction (Oxford, 1965). ET from Einleitung in das Alte Testament (3rd ed.: Tübingen, 1956).
"Israels Führer in der Zeit vom Auszug aus Ägypten bis zur Landnahme", in Studia Biblica et Semitica, T.C. Vriezen Festschrift (Wageningen, 1966), pp. 62-70.
"Die Komposition der Sinai-Erzählung Ex. 19-34", Kleine Schriften IV (Tübingen, 1968), pp. 231-237.
Ellis, P.F.
The Yahwist: The Bible's First Theologian (London, 1969).
Elton, G.R.
The Practice of History (Glasgow, 1969).
Faur, J.
"The Biblical Idea of Idolatry", JQR 69 (1978), pp. 1-15.
Fensham, F.C.
"The Burning of the Golden Calf and Ugarit", IEJ 16 (1966), pp. 191-193.
Frazer, J.G.
Folklore in the Old Testament, 3 vols. (London, 1918/19).
Freedman, D.N.
"The Name of the God of Moses", JBL 79 (1960), pp. 151-156.
"Divine Commitment and Human Obligation", Interpretation 18 (1964), pp. 419-431.
Frei, H.W.
The Eclipse of Biblical Narrative (New Haven & London, 1974).
Friedrich, G.
"Salpinx", TDNT VII, pp. 71-88.
Fritz, V.

Tempel und Zelt, WMANT 47 (Neukirchen, 1977).
Frye, N.
"Literary Criticism", in J. Thorpe (ed.), The Aims and Methods of Scholarship in Modern Languages and Literature (New York, 1963), pp. 57-69.
Gardner, H.
The Business of Criticism (Oxford, 1959).
Gaster, T.H.
Myth, Legend, and Custom in the Old Testament (New York & London, 1969).
Gemser, B.
"God in Genesis", OTS 12 (1958), pp. 1-21.
Gerstenberger, E.
Wesen und Herkunft des 'Apodiktischen Rechts', WMANT 20 (Neukirchen, 1965).
"Covenant and Commandment", JBL 84 (1965), pp. 38-51.
Gese, H.
"Bemerkungen zur Sinaitradition", ZAW 79 (1967), pp. 137-154.
"Tradition and Biblical Theology", in D.A. Knight (ed.), Tradition and Theology in the Old Testament (Philadelphia, 1977), pp. 301-326.
Geyer, J.B.
"The Joseph and Moses Narratives: Folk-Tale and History", JSOT 15 (1980), pp. 51-56.
Gibson, J.C.L.
Canaanite Myths and Legends (Edinburgh, 1978).
Glueck, N.
The Other Side of the Jordan (Cambridge, Mass., 1970).
Goldingay, J.
"'That You May Know That Yahweh is God': A Study in the Relationship between Theology and Historical Truth in the Old Testament", Tynd. B. 23 (1972), pp. 58-93.
Gordon, C.H.
"Homer, Caphtor and Canaan", Anadolu Arastirmalari I (1955), pp. 139-146.
Gordon, R.P.
"Exodus", in G.C.D. Howley et al. (ed.), A Bible Commentary for Today (London & Glasgow, 1979), pp. 170-211.
Görg, M.
Das Zelt der Begegnung, BBB 27 (Bonn, 1967).
Gottwald, N.
The Tribes of Yahweh (London, 1980).

Gradwohl, R.
"Die Verbrennung des Jungstiers, Ex. 32.20", TZ 19 (1963), pp. 50-53.
Greenwood, D.
"Rhetorical Criticism and Formgeschichte: Some Methodological Considerations", JBL 89 (1970), pp. 418-426.
Gressmann, H.
Mose und seine Zeit, FRLANT 18 (Göttingen, 1913).
Gunkel, H.
The Legends of Genesis (New York, 1964).
Gunn, D.M.
"Narrative Patterns and Oral Tradition in Judges and Samuel", VT 24 (1974), pp. 286-317.
"On Oral Tradition: A Response to John Van Seters", Semeia 5 (1976), pp. 155-163.
The Story of King David: Genre and Interpretation, JSOT Suppl. 6 (Sheffield, 1978).
Gutmann, J.
"The 'Second Commandment' and the Image in Judaism", HUCA 32 (1961), pp. 161-174.
Halbe, J.
Das Privilegrecht Jahwes, Ex. 34.10-26, FRLANT 114 (Göttingen, 1975).
Halpern, B.
"Levitic Participation in the Reform Cult of Jeroboam I", JBL 95 (1976), pp. 31-42.
Hals, R.M.
"Legend: A Case Study in OT Form-Critical Terminology", CBQ 34 (1972), pp. 166-176.
Haran, M.
"The Nature of the 'Ohel Mo^{c}edh' in Pentateuchal Sources", JSS 5 (1960), pp. 50-65.
"Seething a Kid in its Mother's Milk", JJS 30 (1979), pp. 23-35.
Harrelson, W.J.
"Calf, Golden", IDB I, pp. 488-489.
Harvey, Van A.
The Historian and the Believer (London, 1967).
Hayes, J.H. (ed.)
Old Testament Form Criticism (San Antonio, 1974).
Hayes, J.H. & Miller, J.M. (ed.)
Israelite and Judaean History (London, 1977).
Hayes, J.H.
An Introduction to Old Testament Study (Nashville, 1979).

Hazard, P.
The European Mind 1680-1715 (Harmondsworth, 1964). ET from La Crise de la conscience européene (Paris, 1935).
Heinisch, P.
Das Buch Exodus (Bonn, 1934).
Hendricks, W.O.
"Folklore and the Structural Analysis of Literary Texts", Language and Style 3 (1970), pp. 83-121.
Herrmann, S.
A History of Israel in Old Testament Times (London, 1975). ET from Geschichte Israels in alttestamentlicher Zeit (Munich, 1973).
Hertz, J.H.
Exodus (The Pentateuch and Haftorahs) (London, 1930).
Hollinger, D.A.
"T.S. Kuhn's Theory of Science and Its Implications for History", American Historical Review 78 (1973), pp. 370-393.
Holzinger, H.
Exodus (Tubingen, 1900).
Honeycutt, R.L. Jr.
"Aaron, the Priesthood, and the Golden Calf", Review and Expositor 74 (1977), pp. 523-535.
Huffmon, H.B.
"The Exodus, Sinai and the Credo", CBQ 27 (1965), pp. 101-113.
Huesman, J.E.
"Exodus", in R.E. Brown et al. (ed.), Jerome Biblical Commentary (London, 1968), pp. 47-66.
Hyatt, J.P.
Exodus (London, 1971).
Irwin, D.
"The Joseph and Moses Narratives", in J.H. Hayes, J.M. Miller (ed.), Israelite and Judaean History, pp. 180-212.
Mytharion, AOAT 32 (Neukirchen, 1978).
Jaroš, K.
"Des Mose 'strahlende Haut'. Eine Notiz zu Ex. 34:29, 30, 35", ZAW 88 (1976), pp. 275-280.
Jenkins, A.K.
"A Great Name: Genesis 12:2 and the Editing of the Pentateuch", JSOT 10 (1978), pp. 41-57.
Jenks, A.W.
The Elohist and North Israelite Traditions, SBL Monographs 22 (Missoula, 1977).

Jeremias, J.
Theophanie, WMANT 10 (Neukirchen, 1965).
Jobling, D.
The Sense of Biblical Narrative, JSOT Suppl. 7 (Sheffield, 1978).
Johnson, A.R.
"Aspects of the Use of the Term Pānîm in the Old Testament", in J. Fück (ed.), Festschrift Otto Eissfeldt (Halle, 1947), pp. 155-159.
Jolles, A.
Einfache Formen (Tübingen, 1958).
Jones, H.
"The Concept of Story and Theological Discourse", SJT 29 (1976), pp. 415-433.
Kaiser, O. & Kummel, W.G.
Exegetical Method: A Student's Handbook, ET (New York, 1967).
Kaiser, O.
Introduction to the Old Testament (Oxford, 1975). ET from the German, 1970, 1973.
Kapelrud, A.S.
"Some Recent Points of View on the Time and Origin of the Decalogue", Studia Theologica 18 (1964), pp. 81-90.
Kaufman, S.
"The Structure of the Deuteronomic Law", Maarav 1 (1978/9), pp. 105-158.
Kearney, P.J.
"Creation and Liturgy: The P Redaction of Ex. 25-40", ZAW 89 (1977), pp. 375-387.
Keil, C.F. & Delitzsch, F.
Biblical Commentary on the Old Testament: Vol. II, The Pentateuch, ET (Edinburgh, 1864).
Kessler, M.
"An Introduction to Rhetorical Criticism of the Bible: Prolegomena", Semitics 7 (1980), pp. 1-27.
Key, A.F.
"Traces of Worship of the Moon-God Sîn among the Early Israelites", JBL 84 (1965), pp. 20-26.
Kirk, G.S.
Myth: Its Meanings and Function in Ancient and Other Cultures (Cambridge, 1970).
Kitchen, K.A.
"Ancient Orient, 'Deuteronomism', and the Old Testament",

in J.B. Payne (ed.), New Perspectives on the Old Testament (Texas, 1970), pp. 1-24.

Kline, M.G.

"The Two Tables of the Covenant", Westminster Theological Journal 22 (1960), pp. 133-146.

Knierim, R.

"The Old Testament Form Criticism Reconsidered", Interpretation 27 (1973), pp. 435-468.

Knight, D.A.

Rediscovering the Traditions of Israel, SBL Dissertations 9 (Missoula, 1973).

"The Understanding of 'Sitz im Leben' in Form Criticism", SBL 1974 Seminar Papers I, pp. 105-125.

Knight, D.A. (ed.)

Tradition and Theology in the Old Testament (Philadelphia, 1977).

Knight, G.A.F.

Theology as Narration (Edinburgh, 1976).

Knobel, A.

Die Bücher Exodus und Leviticus (Leipzig, 1857).

Koch, K.

The Growth of the Biblical Tradition (London, 1969). ET from Was ist Formgeschichte? (Neukirchen, 1967).

"'ōhel", TDOT I, pp. 118-130.

"derekh", TDOT III, pp. 270-293.

Koenig, J.

"La Localisation du Sinaï et les Traditions des Scribes", RHPR 43 (1963), pp. 2-31.

Kosmala, H.

"The So-Called Ritual Decalogue", ASTI 1 (1962), pp. 31-61.

Kraus, H.-J.

Worship in Israel (Oxford, 1966). ET from the German (Munich, 1962).

Krohn, K.

Folklore Methodology, ET (Austin & London, 1971).

Kuhn, T.S.

The Structure of Scientific Revolutions (2nd ed.: Chicago, 1970).

Labuschagne, C.J.

"The Emphasizing Particle gam and its Connotations", in Studia Biblica et Semitica, T.C. Vriezen Festschrift (Wageningen, 1966), pp. 193-203.

Lakatos, I. & Musgrave, A. (ed.)

Criticism and the Growth of Knowledge (Cambridge, 1970).
Laurentin, A.
"W^{ec}attah - Kai nun. Formule caractéristique des textes juridiques et liturgiques (à propos de Jean 17:5)", Biblica 45 (1964), pp. 168-197.
Lehming, S.
"Versuch zu Ex. 32", VT 10 (1960), pp. 16-50.
Leibowitz, N.
Studies in Shemot, ET (Jerusalem, 1976).
Lemaire, A.
Inscriptions Hebraïques I (Paris, 1977).
Levenson, J.D.
"The Davidic Covenant and its Modern Interpreters", CBQ 41 (1979), pp. 205-219.
Lewy, I.
"The Story of the Golden Calf Reanalyzed", VT 9 (1959), pp. 318-322.
Licht, J.
Storytelling in the Bible (Jerusalem, 1978).
Lindblom, J.
"Theophanies in Holy Places in Hebrew Religion", HUCA 32 (1961), pp. 91-106.
Loewenstamm, S.E.
"The Making and Destruction of the Golden Calf", Biblica 48 (1967), pp. 481-490.
"The Making and Destruction of the Golden Calf - a Rejoinder", Biblica 56 (1975), pp. 330-343.
Long, B.O.
The Problem of Etiological Narrative in the Old Testament, BZAW 108 (Berlin, 1968).
"Recent Field Studies in Oral Literature and the Question of Sitz im Leben", Semeia 5 (1976), pp. 35-49.
"Recent Field Studies in Oral Literature and their Bearing on OT Criticism", VT 26 (1976), pp. 187-198.
Loza, J.
"Exode 32 et la redaction JE", VT 23 (1973), pp. 31-55.
Lundbom, J.R.
"God's Use of the Idem per Idem to Terminate Debate", HTR 71 (1978), pp. 193-201.
MacKenzie, R.A.F.
"The Divine Soliloquies in Genesis", CBQ 17 (1955), pp. 277-286.

Mann, T.W.

<u>Divine Presence and Guidance in Israelite Traditions</u> (Baltimore & London, 1977).

McCarthy, D.J.

<u>Old Testament Covenant: A Survey of Current Opinions</u> (Oxford, 1972).

<u>Treaty and Covenant</u>, Analecta Biblica 21A (2nd ed.: Rome, 1978).

"Exodus 3:14: History, Philology and Theology", <u>CBQ</u> 40 (1978), pp. 311-322.

McConville, J.G.

"God's 'Name' and God's 'Glory'", <u>Tynd. B</u>. 30 (1979), pp. 149-163.

McCurley, F.R.

<u>Genesis, Exodus, Leviticus, Numbers</u>, Proclamation Commentaries (Philadelphia, 1979).

McEvenue, S.E.

<u>The Narrative Style of the Priestly Writer</u>, Analecta Biblica 50 (Rome, 1971).

McKane, W.

Review of R. Rendtorff, <u>Das überlieferungsgeschichtliche Problem des Pentateuch</u>, <u>VT</u> 28 (1978), pp. 371-382.

<u>Studies in the Patriarchal Narratives</u> (Edinburgh, 1979).

McKnight, E.V.

<u>Meaning in Texts</u> (Philadelphia, 1978).

McNeile, A.H.

<u>The Book of Exodus</u> (London, 1908).

Mendenhall, G.E.

"Covenant Forms in Israelite Tradition", <u>BA</u> 17 (1954), pp. 50-76.

Mettinger, T.N.D.

<u>King and Messiah: The Civil and Sacral Legitimation of the Israelite Kings</u>, Coniectanea Biblica, OT Series 8 (Lund, 1976).

Michaelis, W.

"<u>hodos</u>", <u>TDNT</u> V, pp. 42ff.

Millard, A.R.

"The Practice of Writing in Ancient Israel", <u>BA</u> 35 (1972), pp. 98-111.

Morgenstern, J.

"The Oldest Document of the Hexateuch", <u>HUCA</u> 4 (1927), pp. 1-138.

Mowinckel, S.

<u>Le Décalogue</u> (Paris, 1927).

<u>The Psalms in Israel's Worship</u>, I (Oxford, 1962). ET from

Offersang og Sangoffer (Oslo, 1951).

Muilenburg, J.

"The Linguistic and Rhetorical Usages of the Particle *KÎ* in the Old Testament", *HUCA* 32 (1961), pp. 135-160.

"The Intercession of the Covenant Mediator, Exodus 33: la, 12-17", in P.R. Ackroyd, B. Lindars (ed.), *Words and Meanings: Essays ... to D. Winton Thomas* (Cambridge, 1968), pp. 159-181.

"Form Criticism and Beyond", *JBL* 88 (1969), pp. 1-18.

Navone, J.

Towards a Theology of Story (Slough, 1977).

Newman, M.L.

The People of the Covenant (Nashville, 1962).

Nicholson, E.W.

Exodus and Sinai in History and Tradition (Oxford, 1973).

"The Decalogue as the Direct Address of God", *VT* 27 (1977), pp. 422-433.

Niles, D.P.

The Name of God in Israel's Worship: The Theological Importance of the Name Yahweh (Michigan, 1979).

Norin, S.I.L.

Er Spaltete Das Meer, Coniectanea Biblica, OT Series 9 (Lund, 1977).

North, C.R.

"Pentateuchal Criticism", in H.H. Rowley (ed.), *The Old Testament and Modern Study* (Oxford, 1951), pp. 48-83.

"The Essence of Idolatry", in J. Hempel, L. Rost (ed.), *Von Ugarit nach Qumran*, O. Eissfeldt Festschrift, BZAW 77 (Berlin, 1961), pp. 151-160.

Noth, M.

"The Laws in the Pentateuch: Their Assumptions and Meaning", in his *The Laws in the Pentateuch and Other Studies* (Edinburgh & London, 1966), pp. 1-107. ET from "Die Gesetze im Pentateuch (Ihre Voraussetzungen und ihr Sinn)" (Halle, 1940).

"Der Wallfahrtsweg zum Sinai (Num. 33)", *Palästinajahrbuch* 36 (1940), pp. 5-28.

A History of Pentateuchal Traditions (Englewood Cliffs, New Jersey, 1972). ET from *Überlieferungsgeschichte des Pentateuch* (Stuttgart, 1948).

"God, King, and Nation in the Old Testament", in his *The Laws in the Pentateuch and Other Studies* (Edinburgh & London, 1966). ET from "Gott, König, Volk im Alten

Testament", Zeitschrift für Theologie und Kirche 47 (1950), pp. 157-191.
The History of Israel (2nd ed., London, 1960). ET from Die Geschichte Israels (Gottingen, 1956).
"Zur Anfertigung des 'Goldenen Kalbes'", VT 9 (1959), pp. 419-422.
Exodus (London, 1962). ET from Das zweite Buch Mose, Exodus (Göttingen, 1959).

Obbink, H.T.
"Jahwebilder", ZAW 47 (1929), pp. 264-271.

Olrik, A.
"Epic Laws of Folk Narrative", in A. Dundes (ed.), The Study of Folklore (New Jersey, 1965), pp. 129-141. ET from "Epische Gesetze der Volksdichtung", Zeitschrift für Deutsches Altertum 51 (1909), pp. 1-12.

Otto, E.
Das Mazzotfest in Gilgal, BWANT 107 (Stuttgart, 1975).

Patrick, D.
"The Covenant Code Source", VT 27 (1977), pp. 145-157.

Perdue, L.G.
"The Making and Destruction of the Golden Calf - a Reply", Biblica 54 (1973), pp. 237-246.

Perlitt, L.
Bundestheologie im Alten Testament, WMANT 36 (Neukirchen, 1969).

Petersen, D.L.
"The Yahwist on the Flood", VT 26 (1976), pp. 438-446.

Piper, J.
"Prolegomena to Understanding Romans 9:14-15: An Interpretation of Exodus 33:19", Journal of the Evangelical Theological Society 22 (1979), pp. 203-216.

Polzin, R.
"Martin Noth's A History of Pentateuchal Traditions", BASOR 221 (1976), pp. 113-120.

Poythress, V.
"Analyzing a Biblical Text: Some Important Linguistic Distinctions", SJT 32 (1979), pp. 113-137.

Preuss, H.D.
"... ich will mit dir sein!", ZAW 80 (1968), pp. 139-173.

Pritchard, J.B.
The Ancient Near East in Pictures (Princeton, 1954).

von Rad, G.
"Doxa", TDNT II, pp. 238-242.

"The Form-Critical Problem of the Hexateuch" in The Problem of the Hexateuch and Other Essays (Edinburgh & London, 1966), pp. 1-78. ET from Das formgeschichtliche Problem des Hexateuchs, BWANT 78 (Stuttgart, 1938).

Studies in Deuteronomy (London, 1953). ET from Deuteronomium-Studien (Göttingen, 1948).

"'Righteousness' and 'Life' in the Cultic Language of the Psalms", ET, in The Problem of the Hexateuch, pp. 243-266. Reprinted from Festschrift für Alfred Bertholet (Tübingen, 1950), pp. 418-437.

Old Testament Theology, 2 vols. (London, 1962, 1965). ET from Theologie des Alten Testaments (Munich, 1957, 1960).

Moses (London, 1960).

Genesis (3rd ed.: London, 1972). ET from Das erste Buch Mose, Genesis (9th ed., Göttingen, 1972).

"Offene Fragen im Umkreis einer Theologie des Alten Testaments", ThLZ. 88 (1963), pp. 402ff. ET in his Old Testament Theology II (London, 1975), pp. 410-429.

Raitt, T.

A Theology of Exile (Philadelphia, 1977).

Rendtorff, R.

"Genesis 8:21 und die Urgeschichte des Jahwisten", Kerygma und Dogma 7 (1961), pp. 69-78.

"Der 'Jahwist' als Theologe? Zum Dilemma der Pentateuchkritik", VT Suppl. 28 (1975), pp. 158-166. ET in JSOT 3 (1977), pp. 2-10. JSOT 3 also contains several responses to Rendtorff's work by other scholars.

Das überlieferungsgeschichtliche Problem des Pentateuch, BZAW 147 (Berlin, 1977).

Reventlow, H.G.

"Basic Problems in Old Testament Theology", JSOT 11 (1979), pp. 2-22.

Richter, W.

Exegese als Literaturwissenschaft (Göttingen, 1971).

Ricoeur, P.

"The Narrative Function", Semeia 13 (1978), pp. 177-202.

Ringgren, H.

"'āch", TDOT I, pp. 188-193.

Robertson, D.

"The Bible as Literature", IDB Suppl., pp. 547-551.

Rogerson, J.W.

"The Changing Context of Old Testament Studies", in Seventy-Fifth Anniversary Papers 1979 (Manchester:

University of Manchester, Faculty of Theology, 1980), pp. 55-76.

Rowley, H.H.

The Biblical Doctrine of Election (London, 1950).

"Moses and the Decalogue", BJRL 34 (1951), pp. 81-118. Reprinted in his Men of God (London & Edinburgh, 1963), pp. 1-36.

Rudolph, W.

"Der Aufbau von Exodus 19-34", in P. Volz et al. (ed.), Werden und Wesen des Alten Testaments (Berlin, 1936), pp. 41-48.

Der 'Elohist' von Exodus bis Josua (Berlin, 1938).

Ryken, L.

"Literary Criticism of the Bible: Some Fallacies", in K.R.R. Gros Louis et al. (ed.), Literary Interpretations of Biblical Narratives (Nashville, 1974), pp. 24-40.

Sakenfeld, K.D.

The Meaning of Hesed in the Hebrew Bible: A New Enquiry (Missoula, 1978).

Sanders, J.A.

Torah and Canon (Philadelphia, 1972).

Sasson, J.M.

"Bovine Symbolism in the Exodus Narrative", VT 18 (1968), pp. 380-387.

"The Worship of the Golden Calf", in H.A. Hoffner (ed.), Orient and Occident, AOAT 22, C.H. Gordon Festschrift (Neukirchen-Vluyn, 1973), pp. 151-159.

Sawyer, J.F.A.

From Moses to Patmos (London, 1977).

Scharbert, J.

"Formgeschichte und Exegese von Ex. 34.6f.", Biblica 38 (1957), pp. 130-150.

Schmid, H.H.

Der sogenannte Jahwist (Zürich, 1976).

Schmid, H.

Mose: Überlieferung und Geschichte, BZAW 110 (Berlin, 1968).

Simon, U.

Story and Faith (London, 1975).

Simpson, C.A.

The Early Traditions of Israel (Oxford, 1948).

Soggin, J.A.

"Der offiziel gefördete Synkretismus in Israel während des

10. Jahrhunderts", ZAW 78 (1966), pp. 179-204.
"Ancient Israelite Poetry and Ancient 'Codes' of Law, and the Sources 'J' and 'E' of the Pentateuch", VT Suppl. 28 (1974), pp. 85-195.
Speiser, E.A.
"'People' and 'Nation' of Israel", JBL 79 (1960), pp. 157-163.
Genesis (New York, 1964).
Stalker, D.M.G.
"Exodus" in M. Black, H.H. Rowley (ed.), Peake's Commentary on the Bible (revised ed.: London, 1962), pp. 208-240.
Stamm, J.J.
Erlösen und Vergeben im Alten Testament (Bern, 1940).
Stamm, J.J. & Andrew, M.E.
The Ten Commandments in Recent Research (London, 1967).
Stanton, G.N.
"Interpreting the New Testament Today", Inaugural Lecture, King's College, London (London, 1979).
Steck, O.H.
"Genesis 12:1-3 und die Urgeschichte des Jahwisten", in H.W. Wolff (ed.), Probleme biblischer Theologie, G. von Rad Festschrift (Munich, 1971), pp. 525-554.
Stuhlmacher, P.
Historical Criticism and Theological Interpretation of Scripture (Philadelphia, 1977), ET from "Historische Kritik und theologische Schriftauslegung", in his Schriftauslegung auf dem Wege zur biblischen Theologie (Göttingen, 1975).
Suhr, E.G.
"The Horned Moses", Folklore 74 (1963), pp. 387-395.
Talmon, S.
"The 'Comparative Method' in Biblical Interpretation - Principles and Problems", VT Suppl. 29 (1978), pp. 320-356.
Terrien, S.
The Elusive Presence (San Francisco, 1978).
Thiselton, A.C.
"Truth", in C. Brown (ed.), New International Dictionary of New Testament Theology (Exeter, 1978), pp. 894-902.
The Two Horizons (Exeter, 1980).
Thompson, R.J.
Moses and the Law in a Century of Criticism since Graf, VT Suppl. 19 (Leiden, 1970).
Thompson, S.
Motif-Index of Folk Literature, 6 vols. (Bloomington, 1955).
The Folktale (Berkeley, 1977).
Thompson, T.L.

The Historicity of the Patriarchal Narratives, BZAW 133 (Berlin & New York, 1974).

"The Joseph and Moses Narratives", in J.H. Hayes, J.M. Miller (ed.), Israelite and Judaean History, pp. 149-180, 210-212.

"History and Tradition: A Response to J.B. Geyer", JSOT 15 (1980), pp. 57-61.

Tolkien, J.R.R.

"On Fairy-Stories", Essays Presented to Charles Williams (Oxford, 1947). Reprinted in Tree and Leaf (London, 1964), pp. 11-70.

Tsevat, M.

"Common Sense and Hypothesis in Old Testament Study", VT Suppl. 28 (1974), pp. 217-230.

Utley, F.L.

"Folk Literature: An Operational Definition", Journal of American Folklore 74 (1961), pp. 193-206. Reprinted in A. Dundes (ed.), The Study of Folklore (New Jersey, 1965), pp. 7-24.

Valentin, H.

Aaron, OBO 18 (Göttingen, 1978).

Van Seters, J.

Abraham in History and Tradition (New Haven & London, 1975).

"Oral Patterns or Literary Conventions in Biblical Narrative", Semeia 5 (1976), pp. 139-154.

Vaux, R. de

"The Religious Schism of Jeroboam I", Biblica et Orientalia, Mélanges Vosté (Rome, 1943), pp. 77-91. Reprinted in his The Bible and the Ancient Near East (London, 1972), pp. 97-110.

"Ark of the Covenant and Tent of Reunion", A la Rencontre de Dieu, Mémorial A. Gelin (Le Puy, 1961), pp. 55-70. Reprinted in The Bible and the Ancient Near East, pp. 136-151.

Studies in Old Testament Sacrifice (Cardiff, 1964).

"Method in the Study of Early Hebrew History", in J.P. Hyatt (ed.), The Bible in Modern Scholarship (London, 1966), pp. 15-29.

"Is it Possible to Write a 'Theology of the Old Testament'?", Mélanges Chenu (Paris, 1967), pp. 439-449. Reprinted in The Bible and The Ancient Near East, pp. 49-62.

The Early History of Israel, I (London, 1978). ET from Histoire Ancienne d'Israël I (Paris, 1971).

Vawter, B.
On Genesis: A New Reading (London, 1977).
Vorländer, H.
Die Entstehungszeit des jehowistischen Geschichtswerkes (Frankfurt am Main, Bern, Las Vegas, 1978).
Vriezen, T.C.
"Einige Notizen zur Übersetzung des Bindeworts KI", in J. Hempel, L. Rost (ed.), Von Ugarit nach Qumran, O. Eissfeldt Festschrift, BZAW 77 (Berlin, 1961), pp. 266-273.
Wagner, N.E.
"Abraham and David?", in D.B. Redford, J.W. Wevers (ed.), Studies on the Ancient Palestinian World (Toronto, 1972), pp. 117-140.
Waldman, N.M.
"God's Ways - A Comparative Note", JQR 70 (1979), pp. 67-72.
Walker, N.
"Concerning Exod. 34:6", JBL 79 (1960), p. 277.
Warner, S.M.
"Primitive Saga Men", VT 29 (1979), pp. 325-335.
Weinfeld, M.
"berith", TDOT II, pp. 253-279.
Weiser, A.
Introduction to the Old Testament (London, 1961). ET from Einleitung in das Alte Testament (4th ed.: Göttingen, 1957).
Weiss, M.
"Einiges über die Bauformen des Erzählens in der Bibel", VT 13 (1963), pp. 456-475.
Wellek, R. & Warren, A.
Theory of Literature (Harmondsworth, 1956).
Wellhausen, J.
Die Composition des Hexateuchs und der historischen Bücher des Alten Testaments (2nd ed.: Berlin, 1889).
Wenham, G.J.
"The Coherence of the Flood Narrative", VT 28 (1978), pp. 336-348.
"The Religion of the Patriarchs", in A. Millard, D. Wiseman (ed.), Essays on the Patriarchal Narratives (Leicester, 1980), pp. 157-188.
Westermann, C.
Genesis 1-11 (Neukirchen, 1974).
The Promises to the Fathers (Philadelphia, 1980). ET from Die Verheissungen an die Väter (Göttingen, 1976).

Genesis 12-50 (Neukirchen, 1977-).
White, H.C.
"The Initiation Legend of Ishmael", ZAW 87 (1975), pp. 267-306.
Whybray, R.N.
"^{c}annot in Exodus 32:18", VT 17 (1967), p. 122.
"The Joseph Story and Pentateuchal Criticism", VT 18 (1968), pp. 522-528.
Widengren, G.
"What Do We Know About Moses?", in J.I. Durham, J.R. Porter (ed.), Proclamation and Presence, G.H. Davies Festschrift (London, 1970), pp. 21-47.
Wijngaards, J.
"hwṣy' and h^{c}lh, A Twofold Approach to the Exodus", VT 15 (1965), pp. 91-102.
Wilcoxen, J.A.
"Narrative", in J.H. Hayes (ed.), Old Testament Form Criticism, pp. 57-98.
Wilms, F.-E.
Das jahwistische Bundesbuch in Exodus 34, SANT 32 (Munich, 1973).
Wimsatt, W.K.
"The Intentional Fallacy", in his The Verbal Icon (Kentucky, 1964), pp. 3-18.
Wink, W.
The Bible in Human Transformation (Philadelphia, 1973).
Wolff, H.W.
"The Kerygma of the Yahwist", Interpretation 20 (1966), pp. 131-158. ET from "Das Kerygma des Jahwisten", Evangelische Theologie 24 (1964), pp. 73-97.
Hosea (Philadelphia, 1974). ET from Dodekapropheton I. Hosea (2nd ed.: Neukirchen, 1965).
Wright, G.E.
"Exodus, Book of", IDB II, pp. 188-197.
"Cult and History", Interpretation 16 (1962), pp. 3-20.
Zenger, E.
Die Sinaitheophanie. Untersuchungen zum jahwistischen und elohistischen Geschichtswerk (Würzburg, 1971).
Zimmerli, W.
"Charis", TDNT IX, pp. 376-387.
"Das zweite Gebot", in Festschrift für Alfred Bertholet (Tübingen, 1950), pp. 550-563. Reprinted in his Gottes Offenbarung (Munich, 1963), pp. 234-248.

"Ich bin Jahwe", _Geschichte und Altes Testament_, A. Alt Festschrift (Tübingen, 1953), pp. 179-209. Reprinted in his _Gottes Offenbarung_ (Munich, 1963), pp. 11-40.

"Erwagungen zum 'Bund'; die Aussagen über die Jahwe-_berith_ in Ex. 19-34", in H.J. Stoebe (ed.), _Wort, Gebot, Glaube_, W. Eichrodt Festschrift (Zurich, 1970), pp. 171-190.

"Das Bilderverbot in der Geschichte des Alten Israel", in K.H. Bernhardt (ed.), _Schalom, Studien zu Glaube und Geschichte Israels_, A. Jepsen Festschrift (Berlin, 1971). Reprinted in his _Studien zur alttestamentlichen Theologie und Prophetie_ (Munich, 1974), pp. 247-260.

Old Testament Theology in Outline (Edinburgh, 1978). ET from _Grundriss der alttestamentlichen Theologie_ (Stuttgart, 1975).

"The History of Israelite Religion", in G.W. Anderson (ed.), _Tradition and Interpretation_ (Oxford, 1979), pp. 351-384.

INDEX OF AUTHORS

Index of Authors

INDEX OF BIBLICAL REFERENCES